3 10

Trafficking
in Sheep

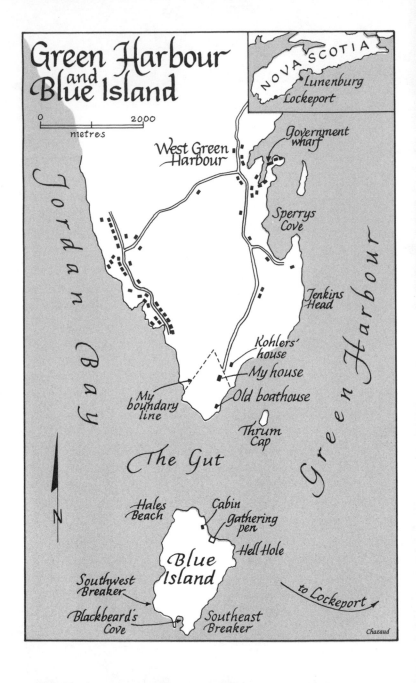

Trafficking in Sheep

A Memoir—
from Off Broadway, New York,
to Blue Island, Nova Scotia

Anne Barclay Priest

THE COUNTRYMAN PRESS
WOODSTOCK, VERMONT

Portions of this book have previously appeared in adapted form in
sheep! magazine (Countryside Publications, Ltd.)

Library of Congress Cataloging-in-Publication Data
has been applied for.

ISBN-13 978-0-88150-636-5
ISBN-10 0-88150-636-2

Book design and composition by Faith Hague Book Design
Cover design by Honi Werner
Front cover photo of author by Eric Hayes
Frontispiece map by Jacques Chazaud

Published by The Countryman Press, P.O. Box 748,
Woodstock, Vermont 05091

Distributed by W. W. Norton & Company, Inc., 500 Fifth Avenue,
New York, NY 10110

Printed in the United States of America

10 9 8 7 6 5 4 3 2 1

*This book is dedicated to the memory of
Brian Nettleton with thanks for his generosity,
knowledge and good humor.
He was a great friend.*

*I also dedicate this book to the memory of my dear friends,
Phemie and Rodney Kohler.
I couldn't have invented better neighbors.*

*I also want to honor the memory of
my beloved Border Collie, Nell.
There will never be another like her.*

～ *Acknowledgments* ～

I wish to thank Betty Levin, especially, for years of wise advice and guidance and for her generosity. We had fun when she came to Nova Scotia to help me gather my sheep, but it was still a gift and I am very thankful.

I also want to thank Barbara Leavell Smith, since she was the first to read an early version of the book and gave me many excellent comments and suggestions. I also want to thank freelance editor, Elisa Petrini, for hours of discussions on changes to be made, and Philip Rich, who also helped shape the book. Philip, ever patient and scrupulous, entitled one of his final emails to me, "Trafficking in Commas." I thank Gloria Smith, Marguerite Murray and Kathleen Tudor, all of whom made useful suggestions.

And finally, I want to thank Kermit Hummel, who had the vision to publish this book and all the staff at The Countryman Press, who have been so helpful and patient.

⟁ Prologue ⟁

Tess, my Border Collie, was holding a small group of sheep while I read them the Twenty-third Psalm, tears streaming down my face.

"The Lord is my Shepherd. I shall not want. He maketh me to lie down in green pastures: he leadeth me beside the still waters. He restoreth my soul . . ."

I finished reading the psalm, closed the Bible, said a prayer of thanks and a prayer for peace and, still crying, called the dog off and left the pasture. The sheep scattered into the field. If a neighbor had happened by the gate at that moment, he would have shaken his head and thought, "Reading aloud to her sheep. I knew it. She's totally off her rocker."

It was just before Christmas of 1988 and I wasn't off my rocker. I was holding my own little funeral service for a great friend, Brian Nettleton. It was the most fitting tribute I could think of. When I had heard of his death that morning—a stupid automobile accident—I looked out the window of my farm in Greenville, New York. I live on top of the Shawangunk Ridge, which forms part of the Appalachian Range that stretches from Maine to Georgia. From my farm I could see my rolling fields going down to the valley below and mountains in the distance. Because of Brian I now owned and managed by myself two sheep farms in two different countries. Thirteen years earlier, my life had been totally changed by the one act of buying sheep from him to put on an island in Nova

[7]

Scotia. Had I bought sheep from anyone else, they would have taken the money, brushing their hands together in dismissal, and that would have been that. My sheep would have died off eventually, if not sooner, and I would have said to myself, "Well, that didn't work," and gone on about my life. Instead . . .

∼ One ∼

I went up to Nova Scotia during the summer of 1971 to look at a piece of land that my friends, Ruth and Bob Cram, had told my ex-husband about. He wasn't interested in it and passed the information on to me. The Crams had emigrated to Canada some years earlier and lived in Black Rocks (now called Stonehurst), a small fishing village near Lunenburg on the south shore of Nova Scotia.

At that time I was living in Lincoln, Massachusetts, a suburb of Boston. A divorced mother of two boys, Jonathan and Nat, aged thirteen and twelve, I worked as an actress in a small professional theater in Cambridge, but had the summers free to spend with my kids. I was fed up with the stifling crowds on Cape Cod, where my sons and I had spent many summers. Our cottage was in Wellfleet, on one of the lovely kettle ponds. It was quiet and peaceful as long as we stayed at home, but the crowds were such that it was impossible to find a parking space at the beach or even at the supermarket. At the little yacht club that we belonged to, I had to reserve a tennis court two days in advance.

In July, I invited two brothers from next door in Wellfleet, David and Meredith Jones, to keep my sons company, rented a tent trailer to pull behind our car, and took off with the four boys. We made a beeline for Nova Scotia and the Crams, who put me in touch with a real estate dealer. She showed me a few properties nearby, none of which made my heart sing. I've bought several pieces of property over the years, during which I discovered that my heart was a dead-on indicator of whether I should buy the place or not. If my heart sang, it was the right piece to buy. And it never failed me. The few times that I bought properties where my heart stayed silent, the places turned out to be duds.

The piece that the Crams had told us about was well to the west of Lunenburg and I made arrangements to meet the real estate lady there in a week because the boys and I wanted to tour the province first. We drove around Cape Breton Island, a wild and mountainous place, staying in trailer camps here and there. One day we were driving around the Cabot Trail, which skirts the island. The road is built halfway up the mountains and we looked down on little fishing villages along the way. I have never been to the fjords in Norway, but I imagine they look much the same, steep mountains slamming right down to the sea. Spectacular.

At Chéticamp, the boys spied a wharf and asked me to take us down there so they could fish. I found a road that led us down the mountain and we walked out to the end of the wharf. Our arrival happened by luck to coincide with the changing of the tides and the boys pulled in fish after fish. Meredith got so excited he let go of his fishing rod when he cast out. The other three vied to see who would be the one to hook it back on his line. Tired and happy, we relished the dinner of mackerel that I cooked over our little Coleman stove.

Continuing our journey, we ended up a few days later on the Bay of Fundy at a camping site that offered a day camp complete with swimming pool and trampoline. The boys were sick of driving and begged to be allowed to stay behind while I drove the two and a half hours south to look at the property

I had come to Nova Scotia to see on the southwest (Atlantic) shore. After reassuring myself that the program was well run and the pool well guarded, I took off.

I met the real estate agent in Lockeport and we drove in tandem to West Green Harbour, ten miles away. She stopped short of the property at the house of a neighbor, Rodney Kohler. Rodney's family had once owned the property that was now for sale. His father had built the house there and Rodney had grown up on the place. After his mother's death it had been sold to some Americans. In 1968 the house burned to the ground and the owners decided they couldn't bear to return, so the land was up for sale. All that was left of the house was an empty cellar-hole. There were fifty acres of pasture, woods and marsh, mostly marsh.

Rodney came with us to show us the land. We went through a gate and drove past a small cottage on a half-acre that belonged to Rodney's sister-in-law. Lila Kohler, his brother's widow, didn't live there, but she didn't want to part with her cottage. Beyond Lila's cottage, the land opened up to reveal a point of land. An eight-acre field sloped gently down to the ocean both in front of us and to our left. Wild roses and raspberry bushes abounded in the field to my left; a large pasture lay straight ahead.

Rodney had mowed a path through the bushes that led to a small fish house where he kept his nets. His lobster traps were piled on wooden poles on either side of the path. Next to the fish house stood a large boathouse where he kept his dory. Both buildings were made of wood with golden lichen growing over the sides. The ocean splashed against rocks all along the shore; seagulls, looking for tasty morsels, swooped and screeched overhead.

The agent wanted to see the edge of the property and walked off with Rodney, but I was content to stay where I was and enjoy it alone. A half-mile offshore lay a beautiful island that looked blue in the mist. The ocean to the south and east and the swamp to the north and west would assure my privacy. As the mist became fog and rolled in across the end of the point, Rodney and the agent were swallowed up in it, her yellow dress and straw hat the last things to fade.

My heart sang at last. "Gloria, gloria in excelsis Deo." I fell in love. I fell in love with the point, with Rodney, with Nova Scotia—all of it, even the fog. I couldn't believe my luck. It had everything I wanted—privacy and peace in a spectacularly beautiful place. I was to discover that the island—Blue Island— would be even more beautiful.

Rodney and the agent emerged from the fog and I signed the papers on the spot, giving her a check as deposit. I asked Rodney if I could bring the children back to spend the night on the point and he said yes, so I took off again for the long round trip to get them.

About halfway there, in the town of Milton, I passed what looked to be a very old house. The windows were shimmering in the sun, the way old glass does. The grass was knee high, which told me there was no one living there. Perhaps it was for sale. Perhaps I could buy it and move it onto the point. The idea of moving an old house was fresh in my mind, since the Crams had moved theirs. Nostalgic for the old house in Wilton, Connecticut, that I had loved so as a child, I welcomed the idea of finding and moving one.

I parked the car and inquired about the house at the next door neighbor's. She told me that the owner was in a nursing home and, since she was *non compos mentis*, nothing could be done with the house until she died. We exchanged phone numbers and I continued on my way.

Late in the afternoon, the children and I arrived back at the point, still in heavy fog. All day long I had been driving in sunshine while the fog stayed rooted to the shore. We walked along the rocky beach to the east with the waters of Green Harbour to our left. At the end of the point we saw a long, crescent beach that extended about two hundred and fifty yards and ended at a huge rocky promontory. Beyond it, enshrouded in fog, was Jordan Bay.

The beach is made up of smooth, round rocks that get slammed into the shore by storm after storm each winter to a height of about twenty feet. The rocks at the edges are sharp-edged because they don't get the full force of the sea. My favorite sound is the noise the rocks make as a gentle tide rolls over them on its way in, "Gudda, gudda, gudda" and out again, "Gudda, gudda, gudda." It is a sound that I evoke in the winter when I am far away from the ocean.

Behind this sea wall is a marsh full of wild cranberries. The marsh extends northeast for about three miles, all the way to the main road. A line drawn up the middle of the marsh divides the properties of the people living on Jordan Bay from those living on the Green Harbour side. Besides cranberries, the marsh holds small bunches of trees here and there and wildflowers such as small orchids, pitcher plants, blue flag, and bluehead lilies with their shiny-blue, strange-looking berries. To the east, Green Harbour extends northeast past the sheltered harbor where the fishermen keep their boats.

We walked back to our tent and ate our supper. Rodney turned up and invited the boys to go out fishing with him in the morning. Jonathan and Nat were thrilled, but the Joneses pointed out that their mother was expecting us to leave the next day and they didn't want to disappoint her. Realizing they were a bit homesick, I could see they were adamant and gave in.

We left early in the morning to catch the ferry, stopping at the Kohlers' to say goodbye. They were both out, but their daughter-in-law was there. She told me Rodney was worried that I wouldn't allow him to keep his boat down at the point or to fish from there. I assured her he would always be welcome and she was much relieved. In fact, the question had never even crossed my mind.

I went home, already looking forward to the following summer when I would have more time to explore the area and enjoy an ocean wilder that I had known at the Cape. My only regret was that I hadn't bought the place earlier, when my sons were younger so that they would have fallen in love with it too, as small children. As it was, they had many friends in Wellfleet whom they didn't want to leave—a nice bunch of kids who loved to sail, play tennis and spend time together on the beach. So for the first few years I stayed in Nova Scotia only briefly in the summer so we could be together in Wellfleet.

～ *Two* ～

One way or another, I had to have a house on my property, either by building one or by moving an old one. The Crams had paid only $500 for the house that they moved. Mindful of the many miles between Milton and my property, I spent many days, during the summer of 1972, driving down every dirt road that led to the water within an hour of my place, hoping to find one closer to me than the old house in Milton. At the end of one such road, I came to a lovely old house belonging to Mr. and Mrs. Howard Walden.

In response to my knock on their door, Mrs. Walden came out and we sat there on the steps, companionably chatting in the sun about this and that. She produced the Halifax paper, which she had been reading, and asked me what I thought of a paragraph on the inside pages describing a break-in at the

Democratic Headquarters in the Watergate Hotel. What could this mean? We discussed it, but there was so little to go on, we didn't get very far. Since I was to be in the Massachusetts delegation to the Democratic Convention in Miami later on in the summer, I was keenly interested.

Her daughter, Elizabeth Hyde, came out and introduced herself. We talked for a while and she said she was getting ready to go out to McNutt's Island, where she had a house, and had to leave to load her boat with supplies. She invited me to come out anytime I wanted to. I didn't take her up on that until three years later, when we found out how much we had in common and became good friends.

Continuing my search, I looked at barns, I looked at houses. I found nothing. Eventually, I heard that the owner of the house in Milton had died, so I got in touch with her son, who lived in Ontario. He was anxious to unload the house but didn't want to sell it separately from the land. He wanted to be done with it. I couldn't cope with owning any more property and reluctantly let it go. He sold it to a local person.

As I have said, the reason I was so compelled to find an old house goes back to my childhood in Wilton, Connecticut. Our house there was built in the eighteenth century, a lovely building with wide floorboards, low ceilings and a stone fireplace so big that I could stand in it upright. There was a huge barn where a dairy farmer kept the hay that he mowed from our fields, a cottage for the hired man and his wife, and an outdoor sleeping porch—a square building separate from the house with no windows, only screens, where my older brother and sister and I slept on hot nights. I adored the place.

My mother saw to it that we had animals to take care of: chickens and ducks, ponies to ride—later horses when we grew older. We even had goats for a while, until keeping them inside the fence became a losing battle and we gave them back to our neighbors, the Breeds. I spent many happy hours with Mrs. Breed, helping her with the goats, which she milked, and churning butter from her cow's milk. I can still smell her cool cellar where she stored the vegetables she canned from her garden. My love of animals got its start in those early days in Wilton. But despite all the animals we had, I never knew any sheep.

My mother worked hard to make our garden beautiful. My father had a small carpentry shop with lathes and work-benches. He was a perfectionist, being a surgeon, and he loved to make small pieces of furniture with fancy legs turned on his lathe. One summer in a ceremony that my mother recorded on her movie camera—another one of her pleasures—he presented me with a bedside table that he had made. It graces the place next to my bed in Nova Scotia, aged now to a lovely nut-brown color.

My mother also loved to paint. Her oil painting of our dear old house in Wilton hangs on the wall over the tiny fireplace in that same bedroom. After I was married, I bought it from her for a nickel, the only painting she ever sold.

In my memory I see New York in brown, white and gray, but Wilton in warm colors. Leaving Wilton in the autumn to go back to the city for school was torture and I lived for the day when we would return.

It wasn't until well after I had bought my place in Nova Scotia that I made the connection. Since there was no house on the property, I was able to rent Lila Kohler's cottage for the few weeks I was there. She lived in Lockeport, about ten miles away, where she worked as a live-in housekeeper for an old lady. She rarely came out to West Green Harbour, but she didn't want to sell her house because it held all her furniture.

The cottage had no plumbing and no refrigerator. The second summer I brought up a refrigerator, which I would eventually move into my house, but for the first summer I had to buy large blocks of ice, which I kept in a Thermos picnic cooler for my food. I drew water from a well and kept the buckets in a little shed attached to the house. We used the out-house, located behind the house across the lawn.

Lila's house had three bedrooms, so the boys and I each had our own space, plus a long narrow living room and a good-sized kitchen. Upstairs there was a loft with tiny win-dows at each end. In good weather I would brush my teeth outdoors in the field with seagulls wheeling and screeching overhead and the sound of waves pounding on the shore. As my teenage boys would have said, "Not too shabby."

One day, while I was brushing away, I realized that I had found my "Wilton" in Nova Scotia. I was home again.

The following summer when I got back to Nova Scotia, I called the local buyer of the Milton property, Brian Man-thorne, on a hunch. I explained that I had been interested in the house just before he bought it and by any chance would he be interested in selling me the house to be removed from the property.

"Well, sure," he said. "I bought the place just for the lot."

I tore up to Milton to look at it again. It was just as I re-membered, a typical Cape Cod house with two square rooms on either side of the center chimney and two smaller rooms at the back. The stone fireplace in the living room was as big as the one I remembered from my childhood in Wilton. Upstairs were three tiny bedrooms. There was no plumbing, so I didn't have to worry about pipes breaking during the move. The only elec-tricity was a braided cord that came through a hole in the wall and sagged its way to a single bulb in one of the main rooms.

There was a lot to do before I could make a commitment.

The Crams put me in touch with their house mover. But I also needed to line up a carpenter in the West Green Harbour area to go to Milton to get the house ready to move and then to put it back together in situ. I went back and started calling and interviewing carpenters. I got hold of the house mover and he gave me a price. At last, I called Mr. Manthorne and told him I was ready to buy his house.

"Oh, I'm sorry. I sold it to a young man from Cherry Hill a few days ago."

Stunned, I asked him whether he knew if the buyer had a house mover lined up. He didn't know. I was getting ready to go back to Cape Cod and gave him my number there to call in case the sale fell through.

When I got back to Wellfleet, there was a message for me from Nova Scotia. I called the number and was told that the buyer had backed out, unable to find a mover. Hah! Remembering what the Crams had paid for their house, I offered him $500 Canadian.

"The other fella was going to pay me seven hundred fifty," he said resentfully.

"Okay, eight hundred then." Months later he confessed that he would have set fire to the house had I not been interested in buying it.

I sent off the check and called Millage Cameron, the carpenter I had chosen, to ask him to go up to Milton as soon as possible to start taking off the roof, numbering the three dormer windows and the roof beams as he took them all down, and doing whatever else he had to do to prepare the house for moving.

With the roof off, there would be no need to worry about taking down electric wires that crossed the road, since the single-story house would go under them all easily. This saved a great deal of money because the utility companies charge a huge amount to take wires down. With a forty-three-mile trip, there were bound to be dozens, if not hundreds, of wires crossing the roads. I also called the mover and got him on schedule. He called me some weeks later to tell me that he had had to remove the fireplaces and chimney because the stones had crystallized and wouldn't survive the trip. Their collapse could destroy the house. Disappointed, I had no choice but to agree.

I asked him to call me well before the move because I wanted to be there and witness its arrival. In December the phone rang.

"We got your house up on the truck and it's sitting outside Liverpool. We'll get it down to your place tomorrer."

It was Percy Wentzel, the house mover, calling me from Nova Scotia. I had met Percy the summer before. I had always visualized a "Percy" as an effete Englishman, tall and willowy, perhaps with a serious overbite. Not this Percy. I can't speak to the state of his dental occlusion, but willowy he wasn't. He looked rather like the drawing a very young child might do of a fat man. Two circles, one small, one large, on top of one another with nothing in between. No neck. He was about five feet four inches tall and spoke with such a strong accent I needed an interpreter to understand him. He was, however, a prince among house movers.

"*What?*" I expostulated. "Why couldn't you have let me know sooner? I wanted to be there when it arrived on my farm. Well, I'll have to see what I can do."

Nat and I caught a flight to Yarmouth from Boston, rented a car, and by twelve-thirty the next day were at the corner of the main road where it branches off to West Green Harbour and on down to my farm. What to do? I longed to see the house come careering down the road, but perhaps it had already gone by.

Old Mr. Sperry, who lived in the house on the corner, was cutting wood outside his house. I decided to ask him what might seem to be an insane question, but I couldn't think of another way to ask it.

"Have you seen my house go by?"

"Yep. Went down about a half hour ago." He went back to his wood pile without a shred of surprise in his voice.

We drove down the two and a half miles to the very end of the road and, indeed, there was a long-bed truck with my house on it swinging madly from side to side as it made its way across the bumpy field to turn around. It looked like a boat riding the waves at anchor in a huge storm. The truck reached the cellar hole that had been dug out for the purpose and filled with gravel so that the truck could drive in and out the other end. There, too, was the entire neighborhood. Fishermen, their wives and children, were all out on a cold December day to see the show. One by one they looked at me with polite incredulity. Then, shaking their heads slightly, they looked back at the house.

I, too, looked at my house. Indeed, it was the most God-awful looking thing I'd ever seen. One hinge on the front door had given way and the door hung there like a crooked smile. Many of the shingles had fallen off and, of course, the whole top floor had been removed for the moving. It looked like a two-hundred-year-old badly beaten-up trailer with shingles (some). My neighbors' heads were still shaking in disbelief. I couldn't explain, but thought: "Just wait, you'll see. It will be beautiful someday."

Since I was an American, it was assumed that I was a multi-millionaire (aren't we all?) and therefore I must have paid many thousands for this wreck of a house and many more thousands to have it brought down here. In fact, in addition to the $800 I paid for the house, it cost $6,000 to have it moved.

While putting it all back together—plus having plumbing, electricity, a kitchen and one and a half bathrooms installed and new shingles and lots of new sheetrock applied—ended up costing a bit more than triple that, I still feel it was a bargain for a six-room, two-hundred-year-old house.

As workmen got busy setting jacks under the house, I overheard Percy telling one of my neighbors that he had driven down the highway at thirty miles per hour. Too wide for the truck bed, the house stuck out about eight feet on each side. Much of the road is only two lanes and I shuddered to think what it would have been like to follow it mile after mile. After winding up the jacks to clear the truck bed, the men and the truck drove away. One by one the neighbors left. The show was over.

Nat and I went inside. One window had fallen out and there was one crack in the plaster. Otherwise the house had made its long trip unscathed.

We spent some time with the mason who would build the foundation walls under the house when the weather permitted and some more time with another mason who would rebuild the chimney and fireplaces. Then Nat and I returned to Massachusetts, fully confident that work would start soon and I could move in sometime the following summer. No work could be done until the foundations were in and the house lowered down onto them.

About a month later I called the mason. "Have you built the foundations yet?" I inquired.

"Naw, too cold. Weather has to be at least forty-five degrees for the mortar to set."

So I started watching the weather reports and calling him. Weeks went by. Still too cold.

One day the weather report called for ten days of warm,

sunny weather for the entire Northeast. I called the mason and told him.

"Can't do it now. My mother's in the hospital with a broken leg."

"But I'm so worried about it."

"Oh, don't worry," he said kindly, "it's a clean break and she'll be fine."

I screamed to myself, "Not your mother, you idiot, my *house!*" but then gave up and left him to do it whenever the hell he wanted to.

It got done in May. By that time all the ceilings were cracked and had to be removed, even thought the carpenters had valiantly tried to cover the whole top of the house with plastic to keep out the rain. It was a serious loss, as the original plaster was made with goat hairs running through it to give it strength and thus had historic value. (I have visions of naked goats running around who had provided masons of that era with hair.)

The house, which had been sitting on jacks all this time, could now be lowered and the carpenter, plumber, electrician and chimney mason could all do their jobs. Because the carpenters took on six or more contracts at once and ran from one to the other, all this work took three years to accomplish. Luckily, I was able to rent Lila's house meanwhile.

⸺ Three ⸺

Now that my house was more or less under way, I turned my attention to Blue Island. A half mile offshore to the southwest, it was right smack in the middle of my view.

In response to my inquiries, I was told rather breezily,

"Oh, it belongs to the Crown." Well, it didn't belong to the Crown (the government) at all. It had been accorded by land grant in the 1780s to two men, Samuel Marshall and William Hale, so they could start a brickworks.* In the nineteenth century it was settled by local families, who lived out there to be nearer the fishing grounds. In those days they rowed dories to their nets every single day, and then on to Lockeport, several miles away, to sell the fish. Being on Blue Island saved them hours of rowing.

There were seven households on the island. They kept barnyard animals and raised their own food. It was a rough life. They had no power or phones and the children had to go to school via the dories every day. Often, heavy seas would prevent their going for weeks at a time. A cruel phrase grew from that: "As ignorant as a Blue Islander."

There is a story that once, during a fierce storm, a woman and her husband and their baby were on their way to the mainland when their boat capsized. The woman, who was carrying the baby, was saved because her voluminous skirt was filled by the wind and she was blown safely across the water to the shore. Her husband drowned.

My elderly neighbor, Rodney Kohler, told me that many years ago, he spied some people on the shore of the island waving a red cloth. He figured there was an emergency. The ocean was frozen that year, an extremely rare event, and the islanders couldn't get off for supplies. He organized a rescue party. Six men pushed a dory out onto the frozen ocean and ran alongside it all the way to the island, prepared at any moment to jump into the boat should the ice break under them.

---

* Marion Robertson, *King's Bounty: A History of Early Shelburne, Nova Scotia* (Halifax: Nova Scotia Museum, 1983), 13.

Sure enough, the people were close to starving. They were brought ashore temporarily, their lives saved.

Little by little, probably with the advent of outboard motors, families moved off the island. They even floated their houses off, on boards nailed across two dories like a catamaran. By the 1920s all the families were gone, having settled in villages on the mainland. Even so, Rodney told me, in late summer the front of the island would often be full of people picking blueberries, many years after the residents had moved off.

Eventually the island, bereft of people to keep the fields clear, grew up to black alders and huge brambles. The blueberry bushes were overwhelmed. Of the 138 acres, only the outside rim was negotiable on foot. Spruce woods occupied about two-thirds of the land. It was impenetrable.

One day, Rodney took me around the island in his dory so I could get a closer look. The only safe place to land is on the northern end, facing the mainland. The east side is made up of huge rock cliffs, some broken by little gulches, each one named by the fishermen. One of these, "Hell Hole," is a split in the rock, sixty feet high, V-shaped, about twenty feet across at the entrance. In a storm the waves rocket fifty feet into the air above the rock sides as they hit the end.

Farther along is a "porpoise hole" that, at mid-tide when the wind is right, spews out water with a bellowing roar, water that has been trapped with air behind it in a cave below. When I take children around the island, I tell them there is a sea monster in the cave. We wait quietly as a large wave fills the cave, then there is a deep roar and a huge spray of water explodes onto the rocks. It's quite scary.

The rock face nearest to the path of the water is covered with small clumps of seaweed, fed by the regular explosion of spume. At the southern end of the island, an enormous

U-shaped cove about the size of a football field, called "Black-beard's Cove," dominates. At the inside end of the cove, a wall of round rocks twenty feet high attests to the fury of the winter storms that bash in there and roil the rocks around until all their rough edges are gone, smoothed out as they rub against each other. The west side of the island is lower, the rock formations like ledges that slope down to the sea. And everywhere in the sea, rocks, rocks and more rocks, guarding the island.

I started hearing rumors that the island was for sale and then, in 1973, I learned that a developer was trying to buy it. I panicked, imagining horrid little houses dotting the northern end, noisy water-skiers plying the waters, and *worse*. I didn't know what "worse" was, but I was sure there was bound to be something.

It was pure paranoia on my part. There was no summer resort anywhere near there, very few foreigners, virtually no summer people at all. But it struck a nerve. I went into Shelburne, the nearest big town, eighteen miles away, to see the real estate agent who also happened to be my lawyer.

"What's up with Blue Island, Jim?"

"Well, a developer has taken out an option to buy it. It's his second option. The first one ran out three months ago and this one runs out tomorrow. He doesn't seem to be able to raise the capital to buy it."

"What's the story? I thought the island belonged to the Crown."

"It hasn't belonged to the Crown since the eighteenth century. Two of the descendants of the families that lived there sold it to a developer a couple of years ago. He then turned around and put it on the market. When the other folks heard about it, they rose up in a rage. It didn't belong just to those two men. There were other families involved. So the whole thing went to court for a 'Quieting of Titles Act.' Hearings were held and anyone who had a claim came to the hearings and offered what proof they had. Finally, the judge ordered the hearings closed and everyone had to sign off, even the Crown. That was the Quieting of Titles. He then ordered that the island be sold with 65 percent of the proceeds to go to the developer, who, after all, had thought he'd bought the whole island, and 35 percent to go to the rest of the owners. A committee has been formed to decide who has a rightful claim and who doesn't. Meanwhile it can be sold."

"Same developer buying it?"

"No. Another one from Yarmouth. An American."

"You say the option runs out tomorrow."

"Yup."

"I'll be back tomorrow!"

Dazzled by the exquisite timing, I saw an opportunity to secure my view. By another coincidence, I had the money available. My mother had sold her house in Connecticut and divided the proceeds among me and my siblings. My share would more than cover the cost of the island. I went back to his office the next day, signed a contract and put down a deposit. Along with the island and the deed, I was given a huge aerial photograph of the island, forty-eight by twenty-four inches. I also got a copy of the Quieting of Titles Act.

Shortly afterward, I went home to Massachusetts. Going through customs in Maine, I couldn't resist unrolling the photograph in response to the question "Did you buy anything in Canada?"

I had left my sons on their own in Wellfleet for the couple of weeks I had been away. When I got there, I spread the photo on the dining room table.

The boys went around and around the table with Nat mumbling "You're mad, Mom, you've gone quite mad!"

I took it he was pleased.

The following summer, the boys came up to Nova Scotia with me. The three of us hitched a ride with Rodney, since he was going out in his dory to check his fish nets, and walked around the island. We followed a path along the outer edge of the island that the fishermen had made when they came out looking for lobster traps that had floated ashore. We saw dozens of nests made by Great Blue Herons on the tops of tall spruce trees in a thick wood. Herons are so big that they can step from treetop to treetop. Their babies can't, however, and they can be quite comical as they stumble about on the branches, their wings getting in the way. I love to watch herons fly overhead because they cross their feet as they fly.

We had to be careful where we walked because herring gulls nest on the ground, making a shallow bowl in the grass. It was July and the nests each had three eggs in them. The parents buzzed us aggressively when we got too close.

We passed Hell Hole and looked down its straight sides to the bottom, sixty feet below, to gentle waves pulling and pushing rocks as they went in and out. The ground above the schism was strewn with rocks of all sizes, thrown up there in wild storms. We got to Blackbeard's Cove. The right side of the cove is a ledge that slopes so evenly down to the sea that the edge is a perfectly straight line. The left side is made up of craggy cliffs and a rocky, uneven shore. Two shoals with waves breaking over them stand guard at each side of the entrance.

We explored the west side of the island and found a deep narrow gulch where the waves swished in and out and hit the end with a splash, sort of a miniature Hell Hole. Then on the north side, as we rounded the end of the island to bring us back to our landing place, we had to skirt an enormous swamp. Again, the waves had thrown rocks up on the shore to form a steady breakwater for a thousand feet or so, ending in a pile of craggy boulders. We picked our way across the rocks, glad to be back at the beginning again. Nat sat down and declared, "This is the most beautiful place I've ever seen."

～ *Four* ～

Our neighbors in the village, almost all of them fishermen, earned their livelihoods from the sea with fish, abundant then, and a six-month lobster season. There were about a hundred households in the village. The houses were modest, the yards well kept. Many had an outbuilding with two hundred or more lobster traps piled up outside it off-season. Summer is the time for repairing them. Most of the houses face the road, away from the sea.

The women mostly stayed home to care for the children, kept neat houses and cooked wonderful meals, but rarely ventured out onto the water. The myth was that women brought bad luck in a boat. Some women worked in the fish plant where the local fish was processed for export, some as teachers, others as health care workers.

I was told that in the old days, cows wandered about freely in the town. In the evening, young boys from each family would go to fetch the cows home for milking. The cows would be turned loose again the following morning after milking. People fenced in their houses and gardens to keep the cows out.

I have found the people to be helpful and kind. Their sense of humor is much like the one found in Maine: understated. My American friends Jim and Marguerite Murray bought their place on Jordan Bay in the early 1970s. There was a small house and a good bit of shoreline, but the land leading to the bay was impenetrable at the time of their purchase. They wanted to look at the property from the rocky beach and so drove down to the pole landing about a quarter of a mile away. A fisherman, Earl Scott, was mending his nets in a field nearby.

The Murrays wanted to be careful not to trespass or to be seen as arrogant Americans, so they asked Earl if he thought it would be all right if they walked down the rocks to their new property.

Earl looked thoughtful for a moment and then said, "Well, I don't think it'll hurt 'em any."

I bought some firewood from Burnley Smith once and made out the check to Bernlie Smith. "Well, yes," he said, looking at the check, "I guess you could spell it that way."

Rodney and Phemie Kohler, born shortly after the turn of the century, had both grown up in West Green Harbour. Except for some work that took them away, they had lived there all their lives. Rodney was a little boy when his father built their house on the point, right where mine is now. At the age of five, he was looking down into the cellar hole, lost his balance and fell in on his head. He was unhurt, but we all teased him that his stubbornness may have been due to the fall.

Rodney's father fished for a living. The fishing season runs all year, but the lobster season in the south shore runs only from the end of November to the end of May. In January and February most lobstermen take their traps out of the water for those months rather than risk losing them to the winter storms. During those months, then, Rodney's father, Frank Kohler, cut wood every day. He would hitch up a pair of oxen at about four in the morning, drive them many miles into the woods, cut wood all day, come home and be in bed by seven-thirty. The same for the next day. And the next.

The Kohlers went into Shelburne only for salt and barrel

staves. They grew, raised and caught most of what they ate and bought whatever else they needed in Lockeport. It took Frank Kohler eighteen hours for the round trip to Shelburne by ox-drawn cart and the same amount of time to row there in a dory with another man.

One summer day Frank Kohler and a neighbor set off for the long row to Shelburne in a two-man dory, did their errands and turned right around to head for home at about midnight. By that time, the fog had rolled in for a peasouper. They had rowed straight and true to the end of Shelburne Harbour, turned left and rowed the five nautical miles for many more hours. Finally, they heard the splash of waves on some rocks.

Mr. Kohler said to his neighbor, "I bet that's Sou'west Rock" (a very large rock just off Blue Island).

"Well, put me down there and I'll tell ya," said his friend.

They edged over to the rock and the neighbor clambered out. "Yep, it's Sou'west Rock, all right. We're almost home. We'll head northeast and be there in no time."

All this at night in a dense fog.

Rodney had to quit school in the seventh grade to help with the lobstering and fishing. He once told me with great pride that his three sons had all finished school and that all three had left the province. We were standing at the end of the point at the time. I didn't say anything, but I looked out at the glorious view and thought, "How sad. How very sad that there wasn't enough work apart from fishing to keep them here."

One time I was taking some friends out to Blue Island. We were all walking down the wide path to Rodney's landing. Rodney was with us and someone remarked on how beautiful it was. Rodney shot back, rather crossly, "I don't think it's beautiful." We laughed, but later I came to understand why he said this. In many ways, though the sea was his livelihood, it was also his enemy. Wild sudden storms claimed the lives of several of his neighbors. The last thing they wanted to do was to look at the sea when they didn't have to be on it. Still, I know he loved it, tough master though it was.

Rodney had four siblings, two brothers and two sisters. The sisters married and moved away, one brother moved to the States, but Rodney and his brother Cecil stayed in West Green Harbour to fish. Their father gave them each a small piece of land to build a house on and raise their families.

In 1951, Rodney came home from Lockeport one day and threw his keys on the table. His son, Merrill, told me about it.

"I've just seen the beginning of the end of the fishery as we know it," he said to his family. How prophetic he was. He had seen the first of the draggers. These are boats that drag heavy nets, weighted down with chains that catch everything in their path, scooping up the baby fish along with the adults in their giant nets, killing off the future. Although some of the draggers were Canadian, most were fish factories from Norway, Russia and Japan. Fish were caught, cleaned, packaged and frozen, all on the ships. Little by little the fish stocks declined until, by the early 1990s, it wasn't worthwhile going out anymore. Fishermen couldn't catch enough fish to pay for their gas.

But back then, there was enough for everyone. Men in their thirty-two-foot boats fished all summer and caught lobsters all winter. Hard work, but a good living. Now, fifty years later, the waters are silent day and night in the summer. Even the seagulls are gone, deprived of scavenging behind the returning boats. The boats are tied up to the wharf. The Canadian government, which encouraged Canadian draggers with subsidies in the first place, has imposed strict quotas. A boat can only go out once or twice a summer. Lobstering, now, is the only viable fishery.

Phemie Kohler grew up over near Jordan Bay about a mile and a half north of the Kohlers' present house. When she was a young woman, she went to Halifax to work as a nurse-maid for a rich family. She was there for some years and when she left, she told me with a happy smile, they had to hire three people to take her place. She also told me that when she and Rodney were a young married couple, Saturday nights were special. Someone would come around with a pickup and a bunch of friends would pile in the back and go off to Locke-port for the evening. Lockeport was a thriving little town in those days with grocery stores, dry goods stores, three hardware stores, a blacksmith's shop and more. All the businesses were open on Saturday nights and all the young people congregated there. In my imagination I visualized a scene from *Hello, Dolly!*

Phemie made beautiful quilts, the old-fashioned traditional Nova Scotia way, with every stitch hand-done. I bought one every year for many years until all my beds were taken care of, then one or two more as gifts. Finally, just before she died, she gave me a quilt that she had made especially for me. I took it to New York. It's a perfect way to remember her by. Each time I make my bed, I think of her—of her intelligence, her glorious sense of humor, her delicious meals and, above all, our friendship.

From time to time I would have to go to Yarmouth to pick up or drop off my kids or other visitors at one of the ferries that came there from the States. On one trip, I noticed a pile of lobster traps by the side of the road with a sign on them: FOR SALE $15. On my way home I stopped there. It would make a perfect gift for Rodney. He and Phemie did so much for me and I could never possibly repay them. Rodney had complained to me earlier how much it cost to build a trap. He figured that with the special kinds of wood, the spike for bait, and the netting at one end to keep the lobsters inside, it came to about $40. At only $15, a trap in excellent condition was surely a bargain. Delighted, I bought one and put it in my VW Rabbit. I was so excited and couldn't wait to give it to them.

I pulled up to their house on the way home. "Hurry and come outdoors," I told them. "I have a surprise for you."

They followed me out to the car. I opened the back of my car and pointed. Silence. Then Phemie started laughing so hard I thought she was going to fall down.

"Oh, my dear. Oh, *my dear*!" Then more whoops of laughter. Rodney was chuckling to himself.

"Anne, I guess you haven't seen them, but the boathouse is full of lobster traps that are almost finished. I have enough to last the rest of my life. Anyway, this is the wrong size."

I looked at the trap with new eyes and, indeed, saw that it was a good deal bigger than the ones Rodney used. They thanked me kindly, though, and invited me in for tea.

Occasionally, Rodney took me out fishing in his dory. After heading the dory out to the waters alongside Blue Island, he would stop the motor and we would drop our lines over the side. One day I heard a very loud "whoosh." When the sound came again, I asked Rodney what it was.

"Whale," he said nonchalantly.

I looked behind me just in time to see the back of a whale as it dove for herring.

Another time I caught a really big cod. When we had hauled the dory up to the top of the landing, I told Rodney I was going to get my camera to photograph my fish. I ran to the house, a distance of about a hundred and fifty yards. By the time I got back, he had not only cleaned the fish, but filleted it. I took a picture, anyway, of him holding a fillet in each hand, smiling broadly. It's a much funnier picture than it would have been if he'd left it whole.

Once each summer, he and I had a major fight. Usually it was about some transgression that Rodney felt I had made against his traditional rights of residency: "You Americans think that you can come in here and . . ." Or we fought over something that I felt strongly about that Rodney had done down on my place, such as hacking away at some perfectly good beams that were part of my collapsed boathouse so he could get at some anchors that were trapped underneath, or the time his grandson, Ken, was shooting at some seagulls right next to my house while I was out on the island. Each time we fought, I would end up in tears—Rodney was very tough and never gave an inch. I would go running in to Phemie, sobbing, "Rodney yelled at me."

Always, Phemie would comfort me with the words, "Don't let it bother you, dear. Rodney used to yell at the boys all the time and they cried too. He doesn't mean to hurt you, it's just his way. He really loves you."

On the day that I was out on the island and spotted Ken shooting seagulls right next to my house, I was really angry. Once ashore, I went to the Kohlers' house and confronted Rodney. I pointed out that shooting seagulls was illegal, shooting next to a house was illegal and I didn't approve of shooting seagulls anyway. He started giving me the "Oh you Americans think you can come in and tell us what we can do and what we can't do" routine when Phemie came into the kitchen and said, "Shut up, Rodney, you don't know what you're talking about." To my surprise, Rodney burst out laughing. Apparently, his bluster wasn't as rooted in anger as it sounded.

They introduced me to pickled herring, which I loved. I

loved them so much that Rodney offered to pack up some herring in salt for me to take back to New York and to teach me how to pickle them. We were down at the point and he was getting some herring ready to pickle. They had been salted for some time. He showed me how to skin the fish first, then how to cut it up before putting it in fresh water to leach out the salt. There was no fresh water there, so I assumed he would throw the fish away.

"It would be a shame to waste this herring," I said, looking at the pieces of fish.

"It would," he said, and popped a piece in his mouth. He handed me a piece and I popped it in mine.

"Mm, good," I said. "*Very* salty, but still delicious."

We ate the whole fish. Later that afternoon, I went down the road to their house. As I was sitting down with Phemie in her living room, she said, "I hear you was down to the point, eating raw fish with Rodney."

"Yes, it was delicious," I said in all innocence.

"Well, you can just forget about running in here if Rodney yells at you. You're on your own from now on."

I laughed. She didn't. She meant it. The idea of eating raw fish was that repugnant to her.

They were wonderful people. They treated me like family and I loved them like family. About three evenings a week I'd go down to their house for "cards." Often other neighbors would show up. I can still hear Rodney's knuckles hitting the table hard, as he threw down a discard. They were playing whist and I can still see Rodney's happy smile as he gathered in his winning hands.

Late one foggy August evening, I left the Kohlers to walk home. The wild roses by the side of the road were in full bloom, the wild raspberries ripe. The fog smelled of roses and raspberries. I believe strongly that we create our own heaven or hell here on earth. This was my idea of heaven.

◠ Five ◠

It was clear that I would need a boat. By chance there was an ad in the local newspaper, *The Coast Guard*, for a dory not far from my place. I bought it.

A dory is a narrow boat with both ends equally pointed. Quite often they were put aboard large vessels that fished out in the open ocean, where they lay on the deck, upside down, until a group of men needed a small boat to reach something closer to the shore. They are excellent boats, very solid and virtually uncapsizable. The usual one is about seventeen feet long with two thwarts (seats), although they come in longer lengths too.

Rodney had cut off one of the sharp ends of his dory, which he had replaced by a small stern to accommodate an outboard. I would have to have mine similarly transformed.

By another piece of good luck, there was an ad for a British Seagull engine for sale. Most outboards' shafts are too short for a dory—they wouldn't even reach the water—but the British Seagull outboard has a very long shaft, and with only four and a half horsepower, it's just the ticket for a dory. I painted mine green and called it *The Blue Island Ferry*. Now, at last, I could go out to the island on my own.

I kept my dory down on Rodney's landing at the end of the point. The landing consisted of poles, eight or ten feet long, placed horizontally at about two-foot intervals. They were nailed to posts that were literally hammered into the rocks with huge wooden mallets. The points of the posts would poke down into the interstices between the rocks, helped along by much wiggling on the part of the men wielding the mallets. They were down at least three feet and were solid as the rocks that held them.

At the top of the landing was a capstan with a long rope attached that could be pulled all the way down to the water—at low tide, a distance of about forty feet. To pull a boat up the slope, we attached the rope to a sturdy ring in the bow of the dory, climbed back up to the top and started to push the capstan around, each of us at the end of a long pole that stuck through the middle of it. Around and around we would go, like donkeys, until the boat was on the level at the top. Rodney greased the poles with lard to speed the way.

Once I had my own dory, Rodney became my mentor. He was insistent that I not go out when it was too dangerous and taught me what to look for—the direction and strength of the winds, the shape and height of the waves. One day I told him I intended to go out to the island (I always let him know in case I got into trouble and didn't return at a reasonable hour) and he said I mustn't go. It was a beautiful day with not a ripple on the water or a cloud in sight. I was frustrated and said, "Why, Rodney, why can't I go out today?"

He got quite cross and said, "Go ahead. Go ahead if you want to. You don't want to listen to me. Just *go ahead.*"

I didn't go, but went home and fumed for a while. Several hours later the wind came up, the waves were high and it looked like a storm in the making. I went down to the Kohlers'.

"All right, tell me. The sun was out, there was no wind and no sea. How did you know it was going to blow up?"

Rodney smiled and shrugged, but didn't say anything.

"Come on, Rodney. There had to have been *something.*"

Rodney smiled again and then sheepishly admitted, "It was the glass."

"The glass? What's that?"

"The barometer. It was way down."

I had to laugh. The devil! He clearly didn't want me to know all his secrets.

A few weeks later, Barbara Mackenzie-Wood, a friend of mine from the theater, and her then husband, Carlie Fleischmann, came from Connecticut for a visit. They had brought a tent and suggested we camp on the island. I had never done that and was delighted with the idea, especially to have company for my first night out there. The weather was perfect and we gathered all the things we would need. I had my own tent and we took some fresh mackerel that Rodney had just caught, salad and breakfast makings. We piled into my dory and went out, climbed up the hill to a clearing, built a fire and drank some Canadian beer with our delicious dinner.

The view up the harbor was extraordinary. We looked north to Jordan Bay on the left and northeast to Green Harbour on the right. My point was in the middle, with my lovely old house well back from the water, its roof on at last. In the middle of Green Harbour we could see little Thrumcap Island. It had quite a few trees, all with cormorant nests. Seagulls nested in the grass or on the rocks. East Green Harbour, which borders Green Harbour to the east, is dotted with little houses up on top of the hill by the road.

In the 1970s there was still an abundance of fish. We watched a few boats as they headed out to their fishing grounds. They carried huge wooden tubs containing coils of heavy fishing lines with hooks every few feet, baited usually with mackerel, and a colored buoy at each end of the line. Each fisherman had his own buoy colors. Once at the fishing area they would play out these lines, a process called "setting trawl," barrel by barrel until all were empty. About twelve hours later, their lines played out, they would start back, hauling in each line, removing the fish from the hooks and setting them on square plastic tubs full of ice. Later, they would gut the fish as the boat headed home, setting them back in the tubs and covering them with the ice. Scores of seagulls would follow each boat, filling their bellies with the fish waste as it was thrown over the side. The boats would be gone overnight and come back next day to unload the fish at the wharf in West Green Harbour. There, each boat's catch would be lifted out of the boat, weighed and recorded.

From there, the fish would be loaded onto a huge truck in tubs of ice and taken into the fish plant in Lockeport to be processed for export to the States or to cities in Canada. For generations, fishermen had supported their families this way, which allowed the stocks to maintain themselves and multiply in a sustainable way.

We turned in for the night when it got dark. At 5:30 AM, the seagulls woke me up, screeching and fighting over the mackerel scraps we had left behind. Half awake and not too pleased, I peeked outside the tent to see what the ruckus was all about. When we finally got up, we looked about and could see nothing. Nothing but fog. We couldn't even see the sea, let alone any land. We ate our breakfast and decided to pack up and go home. I followed my usual modus operandi, which was to row the dory out a bit in order to get the outboard well away from the bottom and the rocks. Then I started up the motor and we were on our way. We couldn't see where we were going, but I figured that if I just went straight, we'd get to the other shore pretty soon. Wrong. Barbara pointed at the water to our stern.

"Look at our wake, Anne."

I looked. It made a graceful curve behind us. We were going in circles. There was no way of telling how long we'd been doing this, nor where we were in relation to anything.

"Better stop the engine," Carlie advised. "I'll row for a while and we can listen for waves breaking on the shore." Carlie was on leave from the U.S. Navy and I respected his suggestion.

He rowed. We listened. We could hear waves breaking in every direction. Carlie kept on rowing anyway and, miracle of miracles, the island came dimly into view. We went ashore and sat on the rocky beach waiting for the fog to lift. Three lonely bodies sitting on the rocks. We had no food left, so this seemed the best plan. We tried conversation, but all of us were apprehensive and we quickly ran out of things to talk about. The fog was cold, we couldn't *see* anything and we were getting hungry. We hunched closer together. How long could the fog last? Days?

No more than an hour later we heard the put-put sound of an outboard. Rodney's boat appeared through the fog with Rodney at the helm.

"Oh, Rodney. You came to rescue us. Thank you, thank you."

"When I saw the fog this morning and you didn't show up, I figured you might be stuck out here. Now let me tell you something, Anne. Never, *ever*, go out in your boat in August without a compass."

I went right out and bought a compass and have never, *ever*, gone out without it, August or not.

I had no immediate plans for the island, but I wanted, at the very least, to open it up so that we could walk into the interior, explore the woods, and not merely be confined to the rim. I fantasized building a house out there one day, giving a lovely headland to each of the boys for them to build houses and bring their own children there, far in the future.

I couldn't afford to hire people to clear it, having shot my wad on the island itself. By luck, Jonathan was going to a private school that had a wilderness program. I offered the use of the island to the school. It more than qualified as wilderness.

A group of kids, Jonathan included, went up for a couple of weeks that October with a teacher. They set up their tents near the shore the first night and it snowed a foot! The Canadian Coast Guard, alerted by the fisherman who had taken them out there, came to check on them to make sure they were all right. They were fine.

Bless them, they hacked their way up the hill from the shore, making a wide swath, and found a field on top where they could set up their tents. They kept on going and made an excellent trail, cutting right through the middle of the island, opening it up so that I could see what was involved.

Later, in the summer, I started finding cellar holes where the houses had once been. (So far I have found five out of the seven.) Each had its own dug well, none of which I've ever been able to find, as the owners filled them with rocks before moving off so no one would get hurt.

There is also a small graveyard. Only one grave has a regular stone, David Scott's. His mother, Cordelia, was born on the island and lived there until her family moved off. David never lived on the island and died quite young, but his mother felt strongly about the place and had him buried there. The other gravestones were markers shoved in the earth, head and foot. All were buried at the base of a huge lilac bush up the hill from an orchard.

Jonathan and his classmates had made an excellent start, but there was still a lot more clearing to be done before I could enjoy what the island had to offer. Lots of people advised me to put sheep out there and, indeed, local people had kept sheep on the island for years, as is often done on the myriad islands that dot the Nova Scotia coast. I didn't know anything about sheep and wasn't sure I wanted to.

Some friends of mine in Massachusetts also joined the chorus. Then I talked to Elizabeth Hyde, whom I had met outside her parents' house in 1972 when I was looking for a house to move. She lived on McNutt's Island, not far from Blue Island, where some people had put about a hundred sheep, all doing very well, she said. So I started thinking about it.

～ Six ～

In August I went out to McNutt's Island to visit Elizabeth for the first time. Being a guest in her house meant being thrown back in time. She had no electricity and cooked on a wood stove, lighting the house with kerosene lamps. The house was always a blaze of light and the meals extraordinary.

McNutt's is a large island—about two thousand acres—situated just outside the mouth of Shelburne Harbour, west-southwest across the water from my place, about five miles away. It is relatively flat, its topography quite different from Blue Island's, and not nearly so beautiful (in my humble opinion). Elizabeth lived in a very old house, which she had lovingly restored. Outside the house there was an apple orchard on a hill going down to the water where I saw sheep grazing peacefully.

I decided to pursue an idea that my friend, Betty Levin, a near neighbor of mine in Lincoln, Massachusetts, who raises sheep, had planted in my head. Betty had told me about the Nettletons, a family in Nova Scotia, who had a few hundred sheep, some cattle, a pony and, of course, Border Collies. Brian was a veterinarian and he and his wife Martha had six children. They had emigrated to Nova Scotia from England in 1959.

When Betty was describing them, my mind must have wandered for a moment, because I thought I heard her say the Nettletons were a "darling little couple." I therefore had a vision of an elderly, white-haired couple, a bit doddery, and rather small.

I called the Nettletons from Shelburne as soon as I came ashore from McNutt's. Brian answered and I told him I was interested in talking with him about putting sheep on Blue Island, mentioned Betty, and asked if I could come up to see them. They were a good three and a half hours away in Truro.

Brian said, "Sure." He mentioned that there were no motel rooms available in Truro that week and invited me to stay with them. Truro is known as a "cow town," about sixty miles north of Halifax, near the end of the Bay of Fundy. The surrounding countryside is made up of cattle farms, rolling fields of hay or corn and large barns; in short, about as different from the rocky coast of the south shore as one can get.

"But I won't get there until 11 PM or so."

"That's okay." He gave me directions.

I felt terrible keeping this elderly couple up so late, but accepted. When I got to their house, I rang the doorbell. The door opened and I looked up and up and up until I got to Brian's face with his brown mustache and welcoming smile. He looked to be in his forties—about my age. Martha came to the door and she was even younger than he. Whether they were darling or not only time would tell, but they were neither of them the slightest bit small. It took me a while to adjust my images, but a cup of tea did the trick and we all went to bed.

Later on I confronted Betty about her description and she claimed she had been talking about the children!

What Betty also told me was what Brian and Martha represented to the sheep industry in Nova Scotia, having accomplished more than anyone has ever given them credit for. Coming from a part of Britain that was heavily populated with sheep farms, they were well aware of the value of sheep to a community. Because of its largely rough terrain, Brian and Martha saw Nova Scotia as a perfect venue for sheep farming and vowed to build up the industry. It took years of hard work, encouraging farmers to raise sheep, guiding them and helping to build up the superstructure to support them. I was to discover for myself how helpful they could be.

Next morning at breakfast, Brian described the twelve sheep he was going to sell me (I hadn't mentioned buying any) and then took a picture of two cattle out of his pocket.

"Since you say the island is too overgrown to get into, I think you should buy these two cattle. They're range cattle—half Galloway and half Black Angus—and they've always wintered outdoors. They'll open up the island for you. They're in calf and should calve sometime in the spring."

"But don't they need care while they are calving?" I asked, knowing nothing about anything.

"They'll be all right. They've lived out on the range. They will barge through the bushes and brambles."

It seemed to make sense.

Then he said the words that were to change my life:

"But I won't sell you any sheep unless you promise to manage the flock."

Everything I knew about sheep could be summed up in five letters: S H E E P. I knew how to spell the word and that was it.

"What does that entail?"

"Well, you have to shear them, vaccinate them once a year, worm them, put the ram out at the right time of the year—around Christmas for island sheep so the lambs will be born in May when the grass is already growing—and take the lambs to market."

Thinking of the island's topography with its rough trails, steep gorges, rocky beaches and impenetrable woods, I couldn't even start to imagine what it would take to do what he suggested. I had no sheepdog and, in any case, didn't know how to handle one. I was away in winter. There was no barn for the sheep, no fences, no pens. I sat, stunned into silence.

Finally, I said, in a very small voice, "But I don't know how to do any of those things."

"I'll help you."

That was the second set of magic words.

"Okay," I said. Brian was so sure, exuding authority, that I was filled with confidence and jumped headlong into a whole new world.

On the way back home, doubts crashed in. How was I going to do this? In winter, I lived in Massachusetts, a day and a half's drive from Nova Scotia. How did I know the island would support that many animals? How would we get them out there? What would happen if there was a crisis in the middle of winter? What if there really wasn't enough food for them on the island? The questions roiled in my head for three and a half hours.

I called Brian the next day and told him of my worries, especially about the capacity of the island to support that many sheep and cattle. He said he would come down to see.

A few days later he arrived with his nine-year-old son, Ian, and his Border Collie, Spot. After beaching the dory on some rocks, we walked the path that skirted the island.

Brian became ecstatic. Each new patch of grass elicited enthusiastic descriptions of when the sheep would want to graze in that particular spot. There were grassy points of land jutting out into the sea and less desirable grassy places in the woods where the sheep would graze in winter when all the rest was eaten.

By the time we had circled the island, I saw it in a whole new light. It was lush with *food*, wonderful, nourishing food that would keep my animals happy and healthy throughout the year. A large swamp near the top fed a small pond near the shore that would be their source of water. Their main food in winter would be kelp, which washes onto the rocky shore all winter long. Kelp is very rich in minerals and is the most nourishing of all the seaweeds, I believe. What I didn't know then was that it would impart a very special and delectable flavor to the meat.

I told Brian about the sheep on McNutt's Island and he wanted to go out and see them. Elizabeth had no phone, so I couldn't let her know we were coming, but we got a ride out in a fishing boat and started walking. We walked along some headlands until Brian spied some sheep in the woods. He sent Spot out to gather them. Spot disappeared. Brian whistled. No Spot.

"He didn't obey you," I said. "Shouldn't he have come back when you whistled?"

"He knows something I don't know and he's aware of that. Were I to whistle for him again, he would come, but he knows I want him to bring in sheep."

Shortly, as predicted, sheep started popping out of the woods and down the hill that lay between us and the woods with Spot on their heels. I was impressed.

When the sheep were close by, Brian lunged forward and grabbed a sheep by its hind leg. He turned it onto its rear end to look it over. By its teeth he could tell it was pretty old, yet it was fat and healthy.

"My, these sheep are in good shape. They clearly get

enough to eat on this island, so I have no doubts at all about putting sheep on Blue Island."

I was reassured and asked Brian to go ahead and ship them to me.

He called a few days later and said he had decided to add six sheep of his own and two heifers as well. This was great news for me, since it meant he would have a financial interest in the enterprise.

∽ Seven ∽

When it came time for the truck to arrive with the sheep and cattle, Rodney agreed to help move the sheep in his dory and I recruited a group of friends to help me load them into our two boats. Among the helpers was a very strong carpenter, Lloyd Cameron, Millage's son, who was working on my house with his father and brother.

The livestock truck arrived and the driver, quite drunk but affable, backed it down the path that Rodney had made to the shore. We took the sheep off the truck one at a time, leading them to the shore, tying their feet together before lifting them into the dories. We could fit five sheep at a time into each dory. Once out at the island, we would untie their legs and turn them loose.

We had made a couple of trips when one of the sheep whose feet were poorly tied got away before she could be lifted into the boat. She dashed into the ocean, a foreleg and a hind leg still tied to each other. It was a fatal situation. Sheep don't swim particularly well in any case because of their heavy fleece and thin legs, but whenever she tried to swim, her rear leg would pull her front leg back and her head would go under.

I shoved my boat in the water and grabbed hold of her, shouting to the men on shore to take her from me. By this time she had swallowed a lot of water and was coughing badly. Meanwhile, another sheep had gotten free and was dashing down the shore away from everything. We got the wet sheep back to the house and tied her to a tree.

It was time to tackle the cattle. The drunken truck driver opened the back of the truck, got hold of a heifer, and *left the gate open*. The other three cattle leapt off the truck in slow motion and disappeared into my field. No fences, no gates. They were free.

"Let's at least get this heifer out to the island."

I recruited Lloyd as oarsman and we tied the heifer's head to the outside of the stern of my boat. This was the method in the old days for taking oxen out to the island, but what I didn't know was that they put the head of the ox over the back end, inside the boat, and tied it to the stern. My heifer decided she was going to die and, because of the slack in the rope, she was able to flip over on her side.

Lloyd tried valiantly to row, but he was dragging a large deadweight sideways in the water and couldn't manage it. We turned back and brought the heifer ashore. Instantly lively, she dashed up the rocks to join her colleagues in the field.

I had sixteen sheep safely on the island. That was something. But I also had a sick sheep tied to a tree, another sheep wandering around on the rocks, bleating her head off, and four cows loose in my field.

The men helped me get the sick sheep into the barn and then everyone left. I figured the loose sheep might come looking for company and go into the barn herself, which, in fact, she did during the night.

The sick sheep died the next day. She had swallowed a great deal of water that probably got into her lungs. The man who had tied her feet together the day before commented, "Well, I guess I'd better relearn my knots." This made me pretty upset, but with volunteers there isn't much you can do.

Moments after I found her dead, two men came to call. One of them was Karl Erdmann, a neighbor and friend. Karl and his wife Erika had moved to West Green Harbour around the time that I did. He was an engineer and had decided to take early retirement. They had emigrated to Canada after escaping from East Germany just before the Berlin Wall was erected. The other man was a friend of Karl's, a local dentist whom Karl thought of as a potential suitor for me.

Karl had come by a little earlier to tell me to get myself ready for this gentleman caller. He was considerably more excited than I was. After finding the sheep dead, I had no stomach for romance and kept my work clothes on. The two men kindly helped me bury her in the swamp. End of romance, but mission accomplished. The following day, Rodney helped me get the errant ewe into my boat and I took her out to the island.

I had to get the cattle into the barn somehow. But I had no feed to attract them and I didn't know what on earth to do. I was worried they would wander down the road and cause an accident, or even worse, eat Rodney's garden, a quarter mile down the road. Rodney was proud of his garden and had a fierce temper.

I went to see Rodney and Phemie.

"How on earth am I going to get those cattle back into my barn?" I asked them. "Do you know anyone who could help me?"

"Well, dear," Rodney said, "the Fredericks keep cows in East Jordan. They're the only people around here who do and they might help you out."

East Jordan is only about five miles away and I drove

around to their farm, arriving just as their son was coming in with a load of oats.

I introduced myself and told him my problem with all the anguish that I felt.

"Just let me feed these oats to my cattle and I'll be right down."

When I got home after doing a few errands in Shelburne, I found to my amazement that the Fredericks were at my place and had already gotten three of the cattle into the barn. The fourth wasn't so easy. Old Mr. Fredericks had her by a rope and was trying to lead her to the barn. She bolted, but he held on. He fell down somewhere along the line, but didn't let go. She went around my well, dragging poor Mr. Fredericks, flat on his stomach, still hanging on to the rope, bless his heart. She kept going around the well until the rope was all used up. It's lucky she didn't have the imagination to unwind off the well at that point.

Luckier still, Mr. Fredericks was all right, mad as a hornet, but all right. With the help of his sons, he got the cow into the barn and tied her up. Then he came out of the barn, brushing his hands together in dismissal.

"Your friend in Truro sure saw you coming," he said. "You'd better call him to come get that damn cow. She almost killed me."

I was horrified, thinking what could have happened. I thanked him profusely and his sons too and they left. I was overwhelmed to think that they had come to my place without any thought of compensation, never having seen me before, but out of a tradition of good-neighborliness typical of Nova Scotians.

I didn't have a phone yet (it took me three years to get one and even then it was a party line with thirteen people on it), so I went up to Rodney and Phemie's to call Brian.

I was close to tears by then. "You've got to come get those cattle. One of the cows is a monster. She almost killed a man. I'll never get her to the island. She's dangerous. She's horrible. Please come take her away."

Brian was infuriatingly calm. "Well, yes, I could hire a truck at great expense and exchange her for another one. But the other choice would be for me to come down with a crew of people and we will get her on the island for you."

Reluctantly, I agreed.

"Since you have carpenters there at your house, see if you can get them to make some kind of a barge to float them over on."

That made sense, since swimming them over had not been a notable success.

A few days later Brian called me on the Kohlers' phone.

"I'm coming down this weekend with a crew to get the cattle out to the island. Okay?"

"Yes. Wonderful."

"Look Anne. One of the men I'm bringing is an alcoholic and has just gone on the wagon, so don't offer us any alcohol to drink."

A few days later, after dinner, Brian arrived with a young, very Teutonic German vet named Horst, who had recently arrived in Canada, and another man named Ralph, who had lost a hand and had a large hook at the end of his arm. Which one was the alcoholic? I didn't know and offered them tea.

After a bit, Brian whispered to me, "How about a drink?"

I whispered back, "I thought I wasn't supposed to because of the alcoholic recently on the wagon."

"Oh" said Brian in a normal voice. "He didn't come."

Early next morning Brian went into the barn to look over the situation. It had no roof, since I had just moved the building from about eleven miles away, but there were four walls and stanchions to contain the cattle.

"Let's take the calm cow and one of the heifers first."

The men led the two animals down to the shore. My carpenter, Millage Cameron, and his sons had built a square platform with two stanchions at one end to hold the cattle. I thought it was a fine vessel and had painted "Millage's Folly" on the side of it.

The cattle were loaded on with no trouble. Rodney was waiting with his dory and I joined him with mine. We each tied a line to a corner of the barge and proceeded to drag the platform across the half-mile gap.

It didn't work well at all. The platform, being square, went sideways. Glide gently through the waves it did not. It took forever to get there. Luckily there wasn't much of a sea or we never would have made it. When we got back to shore Rodney suggested calling his nephew Tud Scott, who had a big fishing boat, for the next trip.

The men went into the barn to get the "monster." She came out like a bull. Brian was holding onto a rope on one side of her, and Horst on the other. Brian told Ralph to hold onto the tail. If the cow went one way, Ralph was to pull the tail the other way to set it straight and vice versa. Poor Horst, who had no gloves on, lost most of the skin on his hands.

At one point, Ralph got his hook caught in Brian's net undershirt. The hook was solid and Brian wondered why Ralph was pushing him. (He said later that the shirt only held because it was an excellent Scandinavian one.) So the cow was pulling Horst and Brian, and Brian was pulling Ralph, who couldn't get free of Brian's shirt and was running as fast as he could to stay on his feet. They finally managed to get the cow back into the barn, where Brian administered a tranquilizer shot.

They waited a few minutes for the medication to work and then tried again. Again she snorted and dragged them around, this time without Ralph's hook in Brian's shirt. Again a trip to the barn and another shot. Three shots were needed before they could start moving her down to the shore.

By this time quite a crowd had gathered: Phemie and Rodney, some American neighbors, other Nova Scotia neighbors that I didn't even know. Surprising how word gets around when you think you're alone on a remote point of land.

The cow led them a merry chase right down to the rocky beach where she passed out cold, several feet below the ramp going to the barge. Brian asked Rodney if he had a block and tackle. Rodney said he didn't. The truth was he didn't want any part of these shenanigans. So the men heaved and heaved in an attempt to roll her back *up* the steep, rocky beach to the bottom of the ramp. I kept reminding them that the cow was pregnant.

Finally, without a word, Rodney went into his fish-house and appeared with a perfectly good block and tackle. No one mentioned his earlier denial. They used it to haul her up the ramp and into the barge, Brian belting out the English version of the Volga Boatman's Song "Yo-o heave ho! Yo-o heave ho!" all the way.

Tud was patiently waiting offshore in his fishing boat. We loaded the last heifer easily, ran a line from the barge to Tud's boat, climbed aboard and took off for the island. Once there, Tud got us right to the shore. The cow was still unconscious.

"I've always heard," said Brian, "that if you sprinkle water in a sleeping cow's ear, it will wake her up."

I learned much later how many things Brian invented as he went along, but he was very persuasive. He was a vet and a farmer, after all. He scooped up a handful of water and dumped it in the cow's ear. She shot to her feet, wide awake, as he had predicted, and started towards the wrong edge of the barge. We didn't want her swimming back to the mainland, but Brian got her turned around and she jumped off the barge, raced up the shore into the bushes and started eating.

"There, you see? She's fine," said Brian, grinning broadly.

Phemie told me later that when she got home the phone was ringing. It was her sister, Lottie.

"I've been calling you all day, Phemie? Where you been?" Lottie asked.

"Oh," said Phemie, "I've been to a rodeo!" She rolled the word off her tongue in the telling and laughed in delight. She'd gotten quite pink from the sun.

So ended my first week of farming.

I went out to the island from time to time to wander around and enjoy it. When I went out alone, I always asked Rodney if it was safe to go. One day I told him I was going out.

He claimed later that he said, "You better get out there early and leave the island by 11 AM. An easterly storm is coming up." What I *heard* was, "You better be sure to go out today because an easterly storm is coming in *tomorrow.*" Quite a difference!

I had overnight guests who didn't leave until 11 AM and that is when I went out. I had left a pot of honey and some peanut butter in the lean-to for emergencies, but I also took a picnic lunch. I didn't plan to spend the night and had no spare clothes. I pulled the dory up beyond where the tide was when I landed and went about my business, checking on the sheep, seeing where they were hanging out and assessing where I would need to do more clearing.

The storm came up so quickly I had no warning. I ran

back to the landing, piled everything in the dory and rowed out to where I could start the outboard. I couldn't make it. The wind was so strong it pushed me back onto the rocks before I could get the outboard started. I tried several times and finally had to give up. I rowed back to the shore and pulled the dory up as far as I could, realizing that I would be there for some time. For some odd reason, I decided to take the outboard off and lug it up to the lean-to. Perhaps I felt it wouldn't stay elevated and might get smashed into the rocks. It was heavy.

I took refuge in the lean-to and assessed my food situation. Not good. I didn't see how I could possibly stretch out the food I had for a possible three-day storm. By this time my blue jeans were wet up to my knees from pulling the outboard out of the boat. I was cold. Every once in a while I ran down to check the boat and to pull it further up on the rocks as the tide came in higher and higher. Unfortunately, the lean-to faced eastward, so although I could get out of the rain, the wind whipped right in.

I was feeling extremely sorry for myself when I heard the unmistakable sound of a motor, a big motor, not Rodney's outboard. I went running down to the shore and could see the fishing boat coming towards the shore. It was Tud Scott. I waved and jumped up and down. Did he see me? Soon it became clear that he was coming right to me. I ran back to the lean-to and grabbed my outboard and ran down to the shore. It didn't seem so heavy now. I placed it inside my dory and stood there ready. I wanted to be sure to be ready, ready, ready, so he wouldn't change his mind.

Tud came within shouting distance of the shore and called out something I couldn't hear. I shoved my dory into the water and grabbed the oars. The waves and the wind grabbed the boat and pulled me back to the rocks just as they had before, but this time a massive motivation overtook me and I felt a strength I hadn't found earlier. I made it to Tud's boat. He was laughing! He grabbed the dory's painter (the rope at the bow end) and helped me into his boat. He was a big bear of a man in his forties, but looked younger, and as kind a person as they come. He tied my line to the stern of his boat and we steamed back to the mainland.

As we passed my landing he asked me if I wanted him to let me off there with my dory. I was exhausted and shook my head. He said he'd tie my dory to his boat at the Government Wharf and I could get it tomorrow. We went into the harbor and secured our boats.

As we started out in his truck, he asked me if I'd like to come home for a cup of hot tea. I thanked him warmly and said no, I wanted to go home. I knew that his wife wasn't home and I didn't want any gossip. (I saw Charlotte the very next day and she said, "We-e-ell, I heard Tud was out to see you at Blue Island yesterday." Her face was so merry I had nothing to worry about, but I assured her that he saved my life.)

When we passed Rodney and Phemie's house, Rodney was outdoors dressed in a suit and tie. Tud stopped the truck and I thanked Rodney warmly for calling Tud. "I was worried when you didn't come in and I didn't want to go to the Masons until I was sure you were all right." He waited until the next day to give me hell.

When I got home, I built a fire in the fireplace in my bedroom and brought my supper upstairs to bed with a large glass of sherry. Safe at home, I stuck my tongue out at the island and let loose a big Bronx cheer.

A week or two later, Carroll Scott, one of the local fisherman, came down to my point and I found him standing on the lawn, looking out to sea.

"What are you looking for, Carroll?"

"JR's late coming in and I'm just looking to see if I can spot his boat out there."

A moment of silence.

"By the way, Anne, you shouldn't be keeping critters out on the island. Sheep are okay. Lots of people keep sheep on islands, but not critters." He shook his head in disapproval. I assumed he was referring to my cattle.

"Oh?" said I.

It was quite plain that Carroll had come especially to transmit a strong message to me and that JR's tardiness had nothing whatever to do with his appearance. In fact no one had ever come down to my shore looking for a tardy fisherman, nor ever did again.

I had no intention of taking the cattle off the island and, indeed, later on in the summer Carroll himself teased me that he was going out to help himself to some nice beef. But his rebuke was disquieting all the same. I had no doubt that I was the subject of many a dinner-table conversation because of all the things I was doing, but I didn't want to go against the grain of the whole community. Later, as I got to know Carroll better, I realized that he pretty much disapproved of everyone and that I wasn't unique in that respect.

～ *Eight* ～

In September, shortly before it was time for me to go back home, my friend and neighbor Betty Levin from Lincoln, Massachusetts, came to visit because she wanted to go to the annual sheep fair in Truro. She arrived on the boat with her wonderful Border Collie, Tyne, not having brought a car because she was planning to go back with me. I met them in Yarmouth and we went up to the sheep fair the next day.

Brian and Martha had organized the annual Sheep Fair in Truro some years earlier. It was a wonderful weekend-long event. It started off with a bang on Friday night with a supper, a speaker and a dance. Saturday, while there was an auction of rams, ewes and lambs going on in one barn, a craft fair that Martha had organized was in another barn. She had found out what women in many disparate communities were doing in the way of sheep-related crafts and brought them together in an organization. Booths were set up and the women sold their products there. Saturday night found us enjoying a barbecue outdoors.

Sunday was devoted to a sheepdog trial. This would take place in a large field. Three sheep were released at the top of the field while a handler and dog waited for them at the other end. The handler then gave the dog a command to go one way or the other. The dog would run way out around the sheep and bring them through a set of gates in the middle of the field to the handler, drive them around behind the handler and away through another set of gates about fifty yards away. From there the dog would drive the sheep to a third set of gates across the field, then back to the handler, who would have opened the gate to a holding pen. The dog would drive the sheep into the pen. The handler cannot move at all until the dog brings the sheep near the pen, but has to direct the dog with whistles, sometimes by voice, sometimes by shouting and screaming. A judge would deduct points for each section of the course where the sheep had not gone in a straight line from one part to another. The trials are great fun to watch and daunting to run. The intelligence of the Border Collie is legendary and the relationship of shepherd and dog is extraordinary.

Betty entered the sheepdog trial on Sunday with Tyne, who did very well. It was a hot day and there was a large puddle on the course. Tyne got the sheep going nicely toward one of the gates, then took a little detour herself and dunked herself in the puddle to cool off, much to Betty's amusement and the crowd's as well. I was impressed with how relaxed she was. I was such a novice that I would have been much too tense to laugh in the middle of a competition.

Brian won the trial with Spot. To entertain the crowd, the winner and the second place finisher had to compete with ducks after the trial was over. Each was given five ducks to work. They started at a separate given place in the field and each had to get his ducks into a separate pen, both contestants working at the same time. Whoever got the ducks penned first would win.

The second place finisher's ducks decided early on that they didn't want to be separated from their friends and waddled over to join Brian's ducks, despite the dog's efforts to bring them back. So now, Brian had ten ducks to pen. Brian was a ham. All the while clowning for the audience and telling funny stories, he was whistling commands to Spot quietly through his teeth. Spot took it all seriously, was crouched down in the Border Collie stance and working very well. The only giveaway was a large drool coming out of his mouth as he contemplated the fat rear ends of ten ducks. He penned the ducks, intact, with no trouble. The crowd loved it all.

Betty saw a beautiful, black Border Leicester ewe lamb that she wanted very badly and decided to bid on it at the auction. Betty raises Border Leicesters and she recognized this one as being from a very special line. Sheep from this breed have lovely wool, excellent for knitting garments, quite unlike the Scottish Blackface that I had on the island with their hairy, itchy wool. On the other hand, Border Leicesters require more feed and care and would never survive on an island as mine did. Betty won the bid on the lamb and then had to figure out how to get her back to Lincoln. She fretted about shipping it, worrying that the trucker would take days getting there, which would create a stressful situation for the sheep. I listened for a moment and said, "Why don't we take the sheep down in my VW Rabbit?"

"Oh, would you?" Betty leapt at the chance.

"Sure, why not? I'm not taking much back with me, so I'll have plenty of room."

We loaded the sheep into the back of the Rabbit, with Tyne fully focused on her to keep her in her place. It was wonderful. She fit exactly in the baggage space behind the back seat, although when she was standing up, I couldn't see out the rear window. As we drove back to my place I spotted a bale of hay that must have fallen off someone's truck. I stopped and picked up it up. This would feed the lamb very nicely on our long trip to the U.S.

Back at the house, we tied the lamb to a tree and she munched happily on the lawn for a couple of days until we were ready to go back to the States. Betty named the lamb Anne and she grew up to be a very beautiful sheep.

I think of Betty as the conscience of the sheep and Border Collie world. She has very high standards for both species and won't tolerate anyone who exploits them. Many times I've worked dogs with her on her farm where she whispered so quietly to her dogs that I could hardly hear her. Then we'd go into the house where she yelled bloody murder at her husband and children! She is always ready to help, no matter how tired she is. Many's the time I have called her and always have I learned something new from her advice.

Yet it was her husband, Alvin, who pointed out that the writer of the Twenty-third Psalm knew about sheep. Sheep won't drink water that is moving, such as a stream or river. "He leadeth me beside the *still* waters . . ."

～ Nine ～

We all met at my place five days before Christmas, the appointed time for putting a ram on the island. This was my first ram, which would lead inexorably to my first lambs and I was excited. I drove up from Massachusetts with Jonathan and Nat and Stephanie, a friend of Jonathan's from college. Brian came down from Truro, bringing his daughters, Fiona and Sarah, and Guy, a friend of his son Gordon. (Gordon had been grounded for some misdeed, but the friend came anyway.) They also brought a handsome Scottish Blackface ram with magnificent horns curved like a circular staircase. Brian put him in the barn, where his long black and white fleece blew like hair in the draft. He looked tough and fit. As Martha said to me earlier on the phone, "He's the one to go out to the island. You couldn't kill him if you tried."

More exciting than all of this was the fact that I was going to be in my own house, at long last. The carpenters, the electrician and Karl had all finished their work. The house was tight and ready to move into. The refrigerator had been moved from Lila's house into my kitchen before leaving in August.

The actual kitchen of the old house had been literally a little shack attached to the entrance room on the back side and I had left it behind in Milton. What had been the parlor in the Milton version would make a perfect kitchen. It measures twelve feet by fourteen feet. I spend a lot of time in my kitchen. The sun pours into that room. There are three windows, all with terrific views. Two of them look out on my sheep pasture with the ocean and Blue Island beyond. The other, over the sink, looks out over little Thrumcap Island in Green Harbour. Most important of all, I'm not a "parlor person," preferring a more informal lifestyle. What was the former owners' dining room became my living room with its huge fireplace; the long room along the back, my study; and the small bedroom in the corner became a full bathroom.

I redesigned the upstairs to have two big bedrooms. The carpenters built a new steep staircase from the front hall, going up the side of the chimney. The staircase branches off to each of the bedrooms, thus avoiding the necessity of a hallway behind them. I had them put a lavatory in between at the back, accessible to both bedrooms.

We didn't have any furniture yet, as I was planning to bring up a U-Haul in the spring with furniture from my mother's house in Connecticut. Later, I added pieces I bought at local auctions, which were gold mines in those days. For our Christmas, I borrowed chairs and a table from Lila's house and we slept on the floor in sleeping bags.

With the temperature at six degrees Fahrenheit indoors and out, our first task was to light some fires. (The pipes had been drained.) There was an oil cookstove in the kitchen and the huge fireplace in the living room. We cut up some firewood and I proceeded to light a fire. I was sadly short of paper to start it with and was doing my best to get the fire going with a tiny bit of tinder. The fire was sputtering along when I left the room for a minute. I came back to find that Brian had torn my efforts apart and was building a new one. I was furious.

"What are you doing to my fire?"

"It wasn't doing very well."

"It was just about to get going and now you've wasted what little paper I had."

"Nonsense. It would have gone out in a second."

I fumed and stormed into the kitchen. I complained loudly to Fiona and Sarah, who declared their father to be a sexist pig. This looked to be a big row over nothing, but feelings were high. Brian changed the mood abruptly by suggesting that he and I go up the road to see Phemie and Rodney. This we did, our spat forgotten, and had a cup of tea and homemade cake with my dear neighbors. As we walked back, it was dark already and we could see huge sparks spewing from the chimney.

"I guess they got the fire going all right!"

They had built what amounted to a bonfire in my fireplace, using up every stick of firewood. I didn't say a word about that, though. It was cozy and warm and they had made their point about women building decent fires.

During that week, Brian confided to me that someday he would like to write a book with all the funny stories and adventures he'd had as a veterinarian. James Herriot's books about his veterinary practice, taking care of sheep and cattle for Yorkshire farmers, had recently been published in the United States. I suppose Brian thought he could write a Canadian equivalent. He never did, and anyway I have no idea whether he had the necessary writing skills, which Herriot certainly had in abundance. He told me later that he had worked as an apprentice for James Herriot, whose real name was Alf Wight. Brian and Martha had arrived in the "bed-sitter"—a studio apartment in the clinic—shortly after their marriage and after Brian's graduation from veterinary school in Scotland. By the time he told me this, I had read some of Herriot's books, which now acquired a new dimension.

The weather was terrible for three days, with a strong wind, heavy seas and rain. It was too rough to go out to the island. Brian and I went to see Tud Scott and his wife, Charlotte, to ask Tud if he would take the ram—and us—out to the island as soon as the weather was fit. They gave us delicious cakes and tea and Tud agreed to take us out. But finally the Nettletons couldn't stay any longer. Christmas was around the corner and they had to get home. So it was going to be up to us.

The day before Christmas, the wind abated at last, the sun came out and it seemed a perfect day to transport our ram. I called Tud from Rodney and Phemie's house.

"Tud. At last. We can go out to the island today. When would it be convenient for you to go?"

"Oh, I can't go today," said Tud, "I have to do my Christmas shopping."

I couldn't believe it. Why hadn't he done his Christmas shopping during the past week when it was too rough to do anything else? I thought of the days we'd been waiting, the great distances we had come and other futile things that you can't say when someone is doing you a favor, but *Christmas shopping!* I managed to stay quiet.

"Could you take us out after you've done your Christmas shopping?"

"No. It'll take all day, 'cause then I got to wrap my presents. But I'll take you tomorrow if it's fit."

"Tomorrow? But that's Christmas."

"I don't mind. I'll take you tomorrow if I'm not doing anything.

"Well, okay. If you're sure it's all right."

"Ye-e-es, finest kind." Only he pronounced it "foinest koind."

I turned from the phone and told Rodney what Tud had said. Rodney roared with laughter.

"What he means is he'll take you tomorrow if he's sober."

"At ten o'clock in the morning?"

"You see, Anne, everyone around here is related to everyone else and they all spend Christmas morning going from one house to another. By the end of Christmas *Day*, we-e-ll" He roared with laughter some more.

I went back to the house. That evening we enjoyed our own Christmas Eve traditions. Even though the children were no longer children, we still hung our stockings in front of the fireplace. There was no fire in it because we had burned all the firewood when the Nettletons were there. Jonathan, Nat and Stephanie slept in the warmth of the kitchen with the oil stove roaring all night. But I slept upstairs, just because I had waited such a long time for the house to be habitable. I had no furniture, so it meant sleeping on the floor in a sleeping bag, but it was *my bedroom*, dammit, and that was where I wanted to be.

When everyone downstairs was asleep, I crept down to the living room and filled the stockings. It was excruciatingly cold, my fingers were frozen, but it was a tradition that was important to me, crazy or not.

Christmas morning was zero degrees Fahrenheit, but sunny and calm. The kids and I opened our presents and prepared to go out to the island.

I walked down the road and called Tud. "How about it?"

"The harbor is frozen solid. I can't get my boat out of there."

My heart sank. "What'll we do?"

"Wait 'til it melts, I guess."

I walked back to the house in a funk. The weather was calm, at last. If we waited until the harbor ice melted, who knew what the weather would be like then? We had already been forced to wait for a week because of bad weather and it could turn rough again quickly.

My sons took a different tack.

"The harbor may be frozen because it's shallow and sheltered, but the ocean isn't frozen. Why don't we take the ram out in your dory?"

Why not, indeed? We went down to the landing. It was covered over with huge boulders, some weighing as much as four hundred pounds, heaved in there by the stormy sea. We set to work rolling the rocks off the poles so we could get my dory down to the water.

The boys got the ram and walked him down the path to the shore, each holding him by a horn, one on each side. We loaded the bow with a bale of hay, our picnic lunch and a bucket of feed in case I saw the cattle. I wanted to get close enough to them to see what condition they were in.

The boys lifted the ram into the boat and laid him down. Even though they had tied his feet together, he heaved about violently.

Jonathan took charge.

"Nat and I will row. Stephanie, you get in the stern and Mom, you have to lie on top of the ram to keep him from getting to his feet."

I obeyed. It was nice and warm on top of the ram. I kept my hand over his horn, which was perilously close to Jonathan's family jewels. The ram didn't stir except when one of the boys would say, "Oh look, there's a seal." I would pop my head up to see over the side and the ram would heave about.

"Lie down, Mom."

I obeyed.

We got out to the island in good time, lifted the ram out

of the boat and watched him disappear into the swamp at top speed. Moments later he was back and raced up a path to the inside of the island.

"He sure smells the females, but he doesn't know where they are."

The cattle were nearby and I went to get a look at them. My pockets were full of concentrated dairy feed, which they smelled. They ate eagerly from my hands, and the fierce one, who had almost killed my neighbor in August, nuzzled my face. Their coats were thick and they looked great.

We walked up the path to the center of the island and I was happy to see that the grass and clover I had planted had grown and that much had been eaten. We went on to Hell Hole and, to my delight, saw sheep on the way. After we had eaten our lunch, the boys rowed us back to the mainland. We stowed the dory for the winter in Rodney's boathouse and went back to the house. Next day, we packed up and drove back to Massachusetts, feeling pretty good, having just accomplished our first farming task with no outside help.

But I never saw that ram again, dead or alive. He must have burned himself up breeding all those ewes.

Later on, David Hamilton, an actor friend with whom I was working that year, asked me who took care of my sheep on the island in winter.

"The Lord is my shepherd," I replied.

"Oh," he said, "how nice. Good help is so hard to find nowadays."

～ *Ten* ～

Sometime during the spring of 1976, I was in Massachusetts when I got a call from Millage, the carpenter. Some fishermen had seen one of my cows in death throes on the shore. They had called a vet from Bridgewater, about seventy miles away. The local people didn't know Brian, who was much further away. The vet came down to West Green Harbour and Millage got them both a ride out to the island.

There was an old folks' tale about a hole in the heather somewhere on the island. Millage felt called upon to tell the vet about it. There was talk about calling in the SPCA and Millage was worried. Not nearly so worried as I was, but there was nothing I could do until I got up to Nova Scotia in July.

As soon as I arrived, I went to see the vet, who shall remain nameless. He was very stern and disapproving.

"What's this about a 'hole in the heather'? It sounds like a serious danger to livestock."

"I have no idea what it is. I think it's a rumor myself. No one I've talked to knows where it is and I've talked to people who used to live there. Quite frankly, I think it was one of those threats that parents use to control their children and then eventually come to believe in themselves. Either it doesn't exist or it's so far in the woods that the animals wouldn't be drawn to it. It's sure to be very small. In any case, there is no heather on the island."

"Well, how about 'Hell Hole'?"

"Hell Hole certainly exists. It's an enormous split in the rock that forms two sixty-foot cliffs. It's huge. The animals would be sure to know about it by now. It's called 'Hell Hole' because the water surges up it into the air like a giant geyser during storms."

"Well, Mrs. Priest, you have no business keeping that many animals on such a small island."

The guy clearly had no idea what he was talking about and I struggled to stay polite.

"I don't think that a hundred and thirty-eight acres is too small for eighteen sheep and four cattle."

Abashed, he said, "But Mr. Cameron told me it was only five acres."

"But you went out to the island. You saw it for yourself."

"Yes, but I only saw that small area where the dead cow was lying."

I struggled to keep silent.

"Goodbye, Mrs. Priest."

I wanted Brian to come down to see the dead cow. He drove down from Truro with his dog, Spot, and we went out and he examined the cow.

"From the look of the piles of dung nearby, I would say she was lying here for several days," he said. He cut her open and pulled out the dead calf. They had been dead long enough that there was no smell. "Just as I thought. The calf was coming out backwards. What a shame."

I was really upset. "I haven't seen the other cow, either."

"Have you seen the heifers?"

"Yes."

"How do they look?"

"Their coats are shiny. They've grown and they look good to me."

"I'm afraid we have to assume that the other cow has died too."

I felt terrible. They must have suffered horribly. It wasn't supposed to happen. I still feel terrible about it to this day.

Many years later Brian admitted he'd made a mistake putting pregnant cows out on an island. They had never lived on an island before and needed time to learn how to survive the winter. Their impact on the island was dramatic, however. Some areas that had been impenetrable now looked like a park. We walked around the island, seeing little groups of sheep here and there. We found the heifers and Brian was astounded at how well they looked.

Spot went off the path at one point. We followed him and found a dead sheep whose leg had been trapped under a fallen tree.

"She must have slipped down the bank, caught her leg and not been able to get up. It was one of mine," he said. Having just lost two cows, I didn't mind his losing a sheep one bit.

We had work to do. We had to build a holding pen for the sheep and possibly the heifers too. Later in the summer, Brian would be coming down again with a crew to shear, worm and vaccinate the sheep. I couldn't wait to see how many lambs we had. I had ordered ear tags from a sheep supply company because Brian explained that it was important to put tags on all the sheep for good record-keeping. Over the years, this has proved to be invaluable. At first, I used aluminum tags, and later changed to plastic ones. With ear tags, I record which lambs belong to each ewe and can gauge their productivity. I keep track of health problems, lambing problems, who has twins and triplets and how well the lambs grow. Years later, I created a program on my computer where I can see all the progeny of any given ewe and who her parents were with all the ear tag numbers. The plastic tags I use come in different colors. I use a different color each year so I can tell the age of a ewe at a glance. I don't name most of my sheep, but refer to them by their ear tag numbers.

We had no materials to build a pen, so Brian suggested we build one out of black alder bushes. The alders were a curse anyway, as no animals would eat them and they prevented grass from growing. There was a lean-to still standing, left over from a lobsterman who liked to camp out there for part of the lobster season. We cut a lot of alders and Brian taught me how to weave them tightly into a fence, starting at each edge of the lean-to. We ended up with an oval pen about fifteen feet across. It was remarkably good, very dense, about three feet high. Sheep respond well to visual barriers and this passed every test. Brian said he would bring a gate or two when he returned.

We went back to my house and I cooked dinner. Dinner over, Brian moved over to the settee and I stayed at the table. We talked for a while. Pretty soon Buttons, my calico cat, went over to Brian and put her front paws up on his knees, looking up adoringly at him. Next thing I knew, she was on his lap. I was amazed. She had never even approached anyone but my family since I'd gotten her twelve years earlier and I said so. Brian smiled and said he had a way with animals. He stroked her and I started telling him a long story. I got quite lost in the telling of the story for a while and then looked over at Brian. He and the cat were both sound asleep.

Brian had brought down two pure white, little Saanen goat kids when he came to see the dead cow. He hadn't asked me if I wanted goats, but thought I should have them. They would help clear the island, since goats will eat bushes that sheep won't touch.

"Let's call the one with the pretty face Catherine, after Rodney and Phemie's granddaughter," he suggested. "And we'll call the one with the prickly head, Anne."

Luckily I thought that was funny, so Anne, the horned one, and Catherine they became. They were adorable. I kept them around the house for a month before taking them out to the island, tying them with a long rope to a concrete block so they could graze easily on my lawn.

I wanted the goats to get to know me before they went out on their own, so I handled them a lot and fed them from my hand. Sometimes they roamed free, though. On one of those days Rodney came down to his fish-house as usual. My mother and Jonathan were both down for a visit and we watched the scene from the kitchen window. Rodney always walked as though he had heavy rubber boots on, kicking his feet out to the side as he went, which gave him a rolling gait. He walked that way even when he was dressed up to go to town in street shoes. The two little goats trotted daintily along the path behind Rodney, unbeknownst to him. They followed him into the fish-house. Moments later two little white goats flew through the air into the bushes, unhurt.

My mother was over eighty-five that summer, yet she insisted on going out to the island for a picnic. Jonathan helped her into my dory, we shoved it down the poles to the water and sped out. Mom clambered over the side onto the shore and really enjoyed being there. She loved the sea and had spent many happy summers sailing as a child. I think she was entranced with my owning an island. She wanted to taste every bit of the Nova Scotia farm, if possible. She was a game one.

A few days after my mother left, I took the goat kids out to the island where they were to spend the winter. I spent some time improving the alder pen and planned to start clearing alders and bushes to encourage grass to grow.

One day I was working in the holding pen, when I saw that my boat had drifted away from the shore. Luckily there was no wind to speak of, so the dory was moving pretty slowly. I started running down to the water the moment I saw it, shedding clothes as I went. I had on heavy hiking boots and had to sit down to take them off. Then came the big decision. Should I leave my underwear on or take everything off? I didn't want to have wet underwear on for the afternoon, but if a fishing boat came around the corner while I was rowing back, would they think I had on a bathing suit if I kept on my underwear? Since there would be no question should I have nothing on, I chose to keep the underwear.

I swam out to the boat as fast as I could. About halfway out, when it was clear to me that I would make it, I started laughing and almost choked. Dories are amazing boats, almost uncapsizable. I grabbed hold of the gunwale and pulled myself aboard. The boat didn't even come close to shipping water. Luckily, too, I had left the oars inside. I rowed ashore, trying to look nonchalant, and made it without being discovered.

Brian came down in early August with his dogs and a couple of his kids. The pen was built, but we had to pile up a wall of rocks to stop—or at least slow down—the sheep as they came roaring down the beach in order to get them into the pen. The barrier made, we went out to gather the sheep with Spot. Brian told me that Scottish Blackface sheep, as a breed, are not good "flockers," which means that they might be in small groups, even in ones and twos, so we had to search the whole island for them. Still, it was quite easy then, not only because Brian was experienced and Spot a first-class dog, but because the sheep, having spent their first five years on a farm, were accustomed to being herded, weren't afraid of people and were therefore pretty calm during the gather. The challenge was to keep them from going into the woods, where they would scatter out of reach of the dog, by flanking them constantly towards the outside rocks. There were lots of lambs. Brian figured, not counting the few sheep that hadn't bred, that we had 150 percent lamb crop, which is to say half of them had twins. That was exciting, and was a very good percentage for a first lambing on an island. In fact, it's a decent percentage on a regular farm.

Next day we went out to McNutt's Island and repeated the process. The sheep on McNutt's were owned by two people. One was Harry Van Buskirk, the lighthouse keeper.

This was convenient, as he provided transportation out to the island. The majority of the sheep were owned by Walter Perry, who lived in Yarmouth and owned hundreds of sheep on several islands. He would never say how many.

Brian was negotiating with Walter to buy his sheep. He was entranced with the idea of sheep on islands. It was closer to the Scottish way of raising highland sheep than anything else in North America, low-maintenance and very appealing to him.

Brian and Martha's eldest daughter, Fiona, and I stayed behind in the large pen. Fiona was to set up the electric shears while the others gathered the sheep. On Blue Island, they hadn't bothered to lug out a generator for the electric shears but used hand shears for the few sheep out there. Hand shears look like gigantic scissors and are sometimes sold as grass shears. They are kept razor sharp and are amazingly effective— in the right hands. But there were close to one hundred sheep on McNutt's and hand shears would be too slow. Fiona had to find a tree to hang the electric motor from. A segmented shaft hanging from the motor twirls extremely fast and drives the shears.

"Okay, Anne. I've done the setup and there's no one in sight. Would you like to have a shearing lesson?"

"Oh, yes. I'd love to learn so I can do my own sheep someday."

Shearing looks to be extremely difficult to those who know nothing about it. How to start—and where? How to keep the sheep from running away? How to keep from cutting them? All questions bound to paralyze a beginner.

There were a couple of sheep in the pen already and Fiona turned one up on its rear. This involved grabbing its head and turning the head sharply against its body while pushing down on its rear end. As the sheep lost its balance and fell, Fiona righted it into a sitting position. Sheep give up easily once they are resting comfortably on their rear ends; they stop fighting and relax.

"I'm going to teach you the moves without the shears running. That way you won't have to worry about cutting the sheep or damaging the wool and you can learn what to do with your hands and feet."

She spent close to an hour demonstrating the different moves and, most importantly, the footwork, getting me to do each part once she had showed me how. A good shearer can shear a sheep in less than two minutes. In the twenty years I sheared sheep, I never did it in less than ten, usually closer to fifteen. Not only did I get tired, but so did the sheep, who like as not tried to get up somewhere along the line, making me more tired, more cross, and the sheep more irritated as well. It pays to be good. Fiona went on to win competitions, but that day on McNutt's she was just a teenage kid, helping out a friend in a brilliant way.

In early September, I went up to the annual Sheep Fair in Truro. The speaker for Friday's dinner that year was Madame Jehanne Benoit, a very interesting woman from Quebec, who was famous for her fine sheep farm and its attached shop where she and her husband sold lamb and other sheep products. She had written an excellent lamb cookbook. My tattered copy is testament to how much I use it.

After dinner, the dancing started. It was a good crowd and we all had a good time. Sometime during the evening Brian lost one of his shoes. After everyone had helped clean up the place, Brian asked me to help him find his shoe. We looked in every corner of the room, to no avail.

"Well, let's look outdoors," said Brian, who was feeling no pain.

"Did you go outdoors during the evening?"

"Might have. Don't remember."

So we poked about in the grass all around the building and in the parking lot. No shoe. Everyone had left by that time, but there was a trailer parked near the building with lights on inside.

"Look," said Brian, "there's people in there. Let's go ask them if they've seen my shoe."

We knocked on the door.

"Come in!"

Seated at a table, all in a row facing the door, were two couples. One of the women was busy buttering toast. Beside her rose a very large pile of cinnamon toast, whose aroma was tantalizing.

"Have you seen my shoe?" asked Brian.

"No, but won't you come in and have some tea and toast?"

That's how we met the New Zealanders, Pam and Kent Wright and Anne and Philip Woodward. They have remained close friends of the Nettletons to this day.

We sat and ate our fill, enjoying the Kiwis' company. Philip said he was going to enter the shearing competition next day. Brian said he was, too, and vowed to beat Philip.

Brian never did find his shoe.

Next morning he was up at dawn, practicing his shearing technique and trying to improve his speed as well.

The only shearing I had ever seen was earlier that summer on the islands. Watching Philip Woodward that day was a wholly different experience. His movements were fluid. There were no pauses. One motion led smoothly to the next. He pushed the shears through the wool like a speedboat in water with the wool falling aside like waves. His feet, his body and the sheep all moved together as if choreographed by a great dancer. He finished in a minute and a half. Brian didn't stand a chance.

In December, it was once again time to put a ram on my island. Jonathan was away working during Christmas and I was in a play with performances right up to Christmas Eve. Nat and a friend of his, Ben Weissberg, drove all the way to Nova Scotia in Nat's VW minibus and met me at the airport in Truro. We went up to the Nettletons for Christmas dinner and spent the night there. Early next day we loaded two rams into the back of the VW bus and drove down to West Green Harbour. One of the rams was for Van Buskirk, the lighthouse keeper on McNutt Island, who came to get it shortly, and one was for me.

This time the weather held, although it was very windy. Clayton Burke, a lobster fisherman, agreed to take us out. We threw a couple of bales of hay from the wharf into his boat. I leaned over to decide where we should put the ram when I felt a heavy shove from behind and flew into the air. Rammed by the ram! I landed in the boat, sprawled out on the hay bales, about seven feet below, unhurt. The ram followed me down, luckily not on top of me. The problem of loading had been solved—unplanned, ungraceful and with no injuries other than to my dignity.

A short way out of the harbor, Clayton steered his boat into a small inlet called Sperry's Cove. He pulled quite close to the shore, where I saw his father, Royce Burke, standing. Royce pushed his yellow dory out to us with a great shove and Clayton caught it handily.

"We'll need the dory to land on the island in this wind," Clayton explained.

Once at the island, we transferred the ram to the dory, climbed in ourselves and landed on the beach. The ram took off. Nat wanted to show his friend, Ben, the island and I had some things I wanted to check on, so we agreed to meet at Hell Hole for a picnic.

We all got to Hell Hole at the appointed time.

"Did you see any sheep, Nat?"

"Yes, I saw the ram we brought out and he was chasing a sheep."

"Sounds promising," I said. Just then the ram appeared, hot on the heels of a sheep.

"There he is now," said Nat.

"Yes, but that sheep he's chasing is a ram lamb."

"Oh, wouldn't it be a bitch if he was gay!"

We both thought of the hundreds of miles Nat and Ben had driven and the expense of my plane ticket.

Well, he wasn't gay, as the goodly number of lambs the following spring were to testify to, only trying to destroy the competition.

Studies have been made, however, to ascertain whether any rams are, in fact, gay. The researchers found that about 11 percent of rams are gay, roughly the same percentage as in humans. Perhaps the radical right would like to bring them in for religious counseling.

～ *Eleven* ～

In the years since I'd put sheep out on the island, I had tried various ways of clearing land to enlarge their grazing areas.

I had heard that there was a rugby team in Truro that was raising money to go to England for a competition by clearing land for farmers. They went out to the island in the spring of

1977 before I got there. They did a fine job, clearing twenty-two acres in two days.

I went out to the island as soon as I could get my boat in the water and climbed up into the fields where the soccer team had cleared. It was impressive. Walking around the island, past Blackbeard's Cove, and over to the west side of the island, I came across Catherine and Anne, my two goats, sunning themselves on the huge ledges that sloped gently to the sea. They looked wonderful and had grown amazingly well. I called to them to tell them how beautiful they were and they came over to me. I turned to continue on my journey and they followed me into the woods where the path went. After a few minutes I heard the high bleat that they make. I turned around and they had stopped. They wanted to go back to the rock, but they clearly wanted me to say goodbye. I did so and waved and they turned and went back to their places in the sun.

Elizabeth Hyde, my new friend on McNutt Island, had two teenage kids, Joanna and Howard, who were looking for occasional work. Their half-sister, Thea, was visiting and the four of us went out to the island with my Lab dog, Socks, two tents, rakes and cutting tools. The three of us females crowded into my tent and Howard took Socks into his tent. The soccer team had let all the bushes lie where they had fallen so we spent days piling all the debris into long windrows so that the grass would grow and the sheep could get around. The kids were terrific workers. We could see the ocean from everywhere on the hill because of the clearing and it was spectacular.

In August, Brian organized a shearing workshop in Cape Breton, near his other farm there, and I decided to go. Sheep have to be shorn annually for their own health, whether the wool has any value or not. Scottish Blackface wool is very coarse, even hairy. I often describe it as "the itchy part of Harris Tweed." But the fleeces from Blue Island were so full of twigs, sand and other debris that they were usually worthless and had to be thrown out.

There are dozens of breeds of sheep with varying characteristics of wool. It can go from coarse to medium to soft; from a long staple to medium to short; from straight to crimpy. Each one has its own use. In Britain, the Scottish Blackface wool is highly prized for use as carpet wool as well as Harris Tweed. Fleeces from other breeds are used for blankets, sweaters and suits, even lace, all depending on their particular qualities. Lanolin, a by-product, is extracted in the washing stage.

Socks and I drove up to Cape Breton, which, in fact, is a huge island connected by a causeway at the Strait of Canso. Its landscape is wilder than the South Shore, where I live. There are fjords where the mountains drop right down to the sea, coal mines, and steel mills seriously threatened by the economy, farms and villages—evergreens everywhere.

The countryside, soils and general look of the province are completely different in all the various sections of Nova Scotia. The area near the Bay of Fundy has a gentler climate than the rest. It's called the Valley and is the sector where most of the fruit and vegetables are grown. The soil around the Truro area is red. The terrain is open and grows excellent grass. Most of the dairy farms are there. The soil near the Northumberland Strait is red also and, sheltered by Prince Edward Island, has a moderate climate.

The Nettletons' farm is in Arichat, a fishing village on Isle Madame, which lies close to Cape Breton's south coast. The participants in the workshop were a diverse group. My roommate was a South African woman who now lives in Prince Edward Island. The young son of Monsieur and Madame

Benoit was in the group. Then there was Yoshi, a young Japanese student, Jim from Prince Edward Island, and even a few Nova Scotians! I was the only American.

We were all equally green. Some of us learned a lot quicker than others, which is probably the case in any class. I found the coordination of footwork and the different holds on various parts of the sheep—all while shearing—very difficult to coordinate, despite my lesson with Fiona the year before. It's important to keep the head of the shears so close to the sheep's body that you can see the pink skin showing through the fuzz that's left behind. It's also important to do each stroke only once. If you have to go back and clean up an area that didn't get close to the skin, that's called a "second cut." The wool from that cut is too short to be of any use. People who spin with spinning wheels hate second cuts because every last bit of fluff must be removed or it will create "pills" in the yarn—those little balls of wool that appear on a sweater here and there.

Even the left hand has a job. The shearer grabs the wool with the left hand to tighten the skin so the shears won't nick the sheep. When you're shearing the right side of the neck, your left knee is holding up the sheep on its left side. The sheep is draped with its neck across your left hip, your left arm is holding the sheep's head to one side and you're shearing with your right hand holding the shears, up the neck and directly across the jugular vein. The shears are out of sight, buried under the wool, since this is the initial foray into that section. The sheep is understandably nervous and *so are you*. It's hard to remember to protect the wool when you're crossing the jugular.

While the workshop group was still intact, Brian recruited some of them to come down to the South Shore to shear my sheep and those on McNutt's Island, which he had bought from Walter Perry that spring. They were to arrive around dinnertime.

In all the times Brian came down to my farm, he was never once on time. Usually he was about four hours late, an annoying habit when one has planned a good dinner. Martha shared in that angst. She and Brian had six children in about eight years. There were many evenings, when he was out on call, that she wondered if she was going to be a widow with six small children when Brian hadn't turned up hours after he was due.

Impatiently, I kept looking out at my gate to see if they were arriving. I saw a truck parked there, but didn't think anything of it, since people come down to the gate to smoke, drink, chat or whatever at all times of day. But it stayed there, which was unusual, so I walked down to investigate. An adorable man with curly, dark brown hair and plump, very pink cheeks got out of the truck and held out his hand.

"Henry James, here. Brian invited me down. I hope it's all right."

English, too. Since I had just played a role in a play adapted from Henry James's nineteenth-century novel *The Bostonians*, it took me a moment to adjust. I invited him in. He was an English professor and he and his wife were under Brian's protective tutelage with their few sheep, as I was.

Brian arrived later with a load of people, a couple of his kids, some of the people from our shearing workshop and the young daughter of an English friend.

My house is quite small—six rooms total—and we were a jolly crowd in a mighty small space. People slept in beds, on sofas and on the floor. No one seemed to mind. Luckily, since I wasn't expecting such a crowd and hadn't enough provisions, Martha had packed a huge picnic box with loads of food. She stayed behind in Truro to take care of the Nettletons' own farm.

Next day, we gathered my sheep on Blue Island easily—they were still tame—and, with our large numbers, took care of them in good time. When we got back to the mainland, we found two more people had arrived, the shearing instructor and his daughter. That night there were twenty-one in my small house.

We went off to McNutt's Island early next morning. Van Buskirk, the lighthouse-keeper, took us out in his fishing boat. We set up the pen and went looking for sheep.

Brian's wicked sense of humor came into play. Since he now owned most of the sheep on McNutt's, he had felt obliged to give Elizabeth a fee because she owned most of the land his sheep grazed on. He had given her two ewes and a lamb to get her started with her own flock. One of the ewe's horns was broken off.

As we walked the island, Brian reached down suddenly and plucked a piece of grass from the field. "Look," he said to Elizabeth and her children, "See how this piece of grass has been grazed unevenly. One edge is bitten way down and the other is quite long. It must be that ewe with the broken horn has been grazing here. Since she has only one horn, her head would be cocked to one side."

It made all sorts of sense to me and all of us nodded in silent "ahas," very impressed.

Years later, when he and I were discussing Elizabeth, Brian brought up the subject of the crookedly eaten grass. "You know," he said, "I caught a glimmer of amusement in Joanna's eyes when I said that about the ewe with the single horn. I think her mother swallowed the whole thing, but I'm sure Joanna caught on."

I turned on him, laughing, "Oh, you rat! Elizabeth wasn't the only one who was taken in. We all believed you because you were the expert."

He pretended to be penitent and laughed happily.

There were so many lambs that Brian decided to castrate the males, so we had not only to shear, vaccinate and worm, but castrate as well. At one point I was working with Brian and Henry James. Brian had been slitting open the end of the scrotum with his sharp knife and slipping out the testicles. The lambs were small and it was quite simple to do. It was late in the day and we were all tired. All except Brian. He was never tired.

"Oh, Henry," he said. "In Australia they pop them out with their teeth, like this." And he put the cut edge of the scrotum up to his mouth and pulled out the testicles. "Why don't you try it?"

"I'm sorry, Brian, I can't. I have a loose tooth."

I roared with laughter, imagining his wife, Jenny, greeting Henry at his door and Henry's having to explain how he had lost his front tooth.

With such large crowds, some of our trips out to the island in my dory were a bit hairy, as we carried gates athwart the boat that were a lot wider than the boat itself. I realized that had a wave tipped us strongly in either direction, we could have capsized. I decided I needed a bigger boat and by chance had the money to pay for one. My mother's sister, Betsy, died that spring and I had inherited $2,000. I decided to spend it on having a boat built for myself.

Elizabeth had an excellent boat called the *Molly*, a skiff-boat, which was broad and roomy and very seaworthy. I went to see its builder, Tom Peterson. He received me into his house, which was immaculate, and I was fascinated by his hairdo. He lived alone and had clearly cut his own hair with a bowl over his head. It must have been a fairly small bowl because his hair was shaved about three inches upwards from his neck. It turned out he was retired and didn't want to build any more boats. He recommended Sherman Williams.

I went to see Sherman and saw a nice boat, half built in his shed, exactly what I wanted. I asked him to build me one just like it and he agreed, naming a price of $1,200. I told him the color I wanted. The boat would be seventeen feet long and about seven feet wide.

Sometime during our conversation his hat fell off. His hairdo was far more interesting than Tom's. Most of his head was bald but for a rim around the edge. This he had grown to a great length, which he wound around and around his head like a turban and fastened to itself with bobby pins. What was it about boatbuilders and their hair?

Although the justification for getting a bigger boat was connected to the moving of equipment and helpers across the water, the fact was that I had decided to sell the sheep. I was planning a major change in my life and career, including a move to New York City in the fall to pursue my work in the theater. The two professional theaters in Boston had closed and New York would offer wholly different work opportunities. I needed the option not to go to Nova Scotia in the summer, should I have a good part in a play. A young man, Peter Rogers, had recently moved into the neighborhood with some sheep, but didn't have enough land to expand his flock. Brian suggested I sell Peter my sheep, which I did, with the stipulation that he keep at least twenty-eight on the island and give me a butchered lamb for my freezer as a grazing fee.

I picked up my new boat the following summer and motored home using my four-and-a-half horsepower engine. We barely crept along and it was very clear I needed a more powerful one. So I bought a used twenty-horsepower outboard, which took care of the rest of the inheritance from my Aunt

Betsy very nicely. It was—and is—a wonderful boat. In over twenty years of using it, I've never had a moment of fright. I called it the *Betsy* after my aunt, who was broad in the beam and utterly reliable.

Joanna Hyde surprised me with a generous gift. She painted nameplates for the *Betsy*—one for each side of the bow and a third for the stern—that said *Betsy, Blue Island, N.S.*

The pole landing was too small to accommodate a boat of this size, so I was forced to keep it in the harbor, which is about a mile and a half back up the dirt road from my house. A large wharf where the fishermen tie their boats, three deep, is called the Government Wharf.

Even though I no longer owned sheep on Blue Island, I still felt the need to clear more and more land on the island to satisfy my desire for greater accessibility. My mother had given me a monstrous machine when she came to visit. It was the precursor of the string trimmer, but was a massive thing that was used by the utility companies to keep land open under power lines. I had to wear a heavy harness that went over my shoulders and crossed my body back and front. The machine had a chain-saw motor at the top and a sharp cutting blade at the end of a six-foot rod. It was heavy, noisy and brutal. I'm physically very strong—the women in my family, especially, are built to last. Still, that brush cutter was a challenge. The gas tank held gas for fourteen and a half minutes of running time and I counted every one. My energy lasted for thirteen. The last minute and a half was agony each time.

I spent many hours in those fields cutting away. I camped out near the shore in a grassy spot, where there was a small pond nearby for water. I noticed, however, that almost every time I set up my tent on a beautiful sunny afternoon, the fog would come in or it would be raining by the next morning. I decided I needed a cabin.

First I asked Peter Rogers—the purchaser of my Blue Island flock and a carpenter—if he would build one for me. He said he would, but wouldn't have time to do it for about a year. A *year*! I couldn't wait that long and decided to do it myself. I had learned carpentry in fourth grade in private school in New York and it never even occurred to me that I couldn't put up a cabin by myself. But having never built a building before, I had to find out how, so I asked Peter.

"It's not too hard," he said. "First you have to build the floor. You need to set out some concrete blocks at the corners, and probably one halfway down each side. Be sure they are level. Then get some heavy timbers, say eight inches by eight inches, and lay those sills across the blocks. Then you nail floor joists—two by six inches would be okay—to the sills, and nail your floor boards to the joists. And you build the sides up from there."

I decided to build a cabin measuring eight by ten feet.

A couple of years earlier, the boathouse, on the mainland down on the shore next to the fish house, had blown down in a winter storm. I had had it rebuilt and some of the old timbers were left over. I was able to scavenge enough for the sills of my cabin. Then I bought what lumber I needed for the joists and to finish the floor, and made my plans to get it all out to the island.

It took longer to move the materials out there than it did to build the cabin. First I had to load the lumber in my truck and drive it out to the Government Wharf, unload it, and reload it into my new boat. Then, once out at the island, I anchored the *Betsy* and transferred the wood in very small loads into my very small punt and rowed it to the shore. The sills, however, were much too big to put in my punt, so I tied one end of a long rope to a cement block that I put in my punt and tied the other end to the sill, which I floated along behind me, hauling it ashore once I'd landed the punt. After that, I had to lug all the materials up the rocky shore to the flat grassy place I had chosen as my building site. I could only float one sill across at a time. The floor joists were lighter and I could get one or two at a time into my punt. It took forever.

I followed Peter's directions. While I was digging a place for one of the cement blocks, I dug up the small porcelain head of a doll. The delicate face and head were intact, the painted eyes, cheeks and lips still bright. I dug right and left, looking for other parts of the doll, but no arms, legs, or body were anywhere to be found. I took it ashore and showed it to Phemie, who recognized the genre right away.

"Oh yes, I remember those dolls. Down here we couldn't afford dolls that were all porcelain and we had these dolls with porcelain heads and a soft cotton body. Of course, the body would have rotted away in all the years since there were children on the island."

Finding it made me imagine small children playing where I was now building a cabin, playing with toys that were treasured because they had so few of them.

I finished the floor and had to figure out what to do next. Peter hadn't been very clear about how one person could raise the sides of a building.

In the course of going around the neighborhood, looking at people's outbuildings, I went to see Karl Erdmann. Karl and his wife Erika had moved to West Green Harbour from Montreal around the time I bought my land. He was an engineer, retired, and had built his house himself, so I figured he was a good resource. I had seen a lot of him in the preceding two years because he had installed the plumbing in my house.

I told him what I was doing.

"Anne, come look at my shed. It's an excellent choice for someone who is building one all by themselves."

It was an unusual shed in that the sides were slanted.

"You cut two-by-fours to support the roof, join them, and nail them to the uprights to make a truss to which you will nail the sides."

I didn't understand a word of what he was saying.

"Come inside. I'll show you."

It was a neat little building. I could see what he was talking about. The whole shed was like a hip roof, nothing more. But it still looked beyond my capabilities.

"Look," said Karl. "Get the lumber and bring it here and I will cut the angles for you on my table-saw. We'll number them all and I will show you how to make plates out of plywood to attach the roof two-by-fours to each other. You will use the floor of your cabin like a huge work table to put them together."

Again, getting the materials out to the island was the most time-consuming part. It all worked out pretty well, except that Peter had put more goats out on the island and they came to the building site to drive me crazy. That was their avowed purpose. They got in between the hammer and the nails. They got their noses so close to the saw I'd have to stop. They jumped around that platform as though it were being built as a trampoline for them.

The weather held wonderfully well and, despite the goats, I got the cabin finished before the end of the summer. I bought a little wood stove and installed it. Rodney gave me a stove-pipe he didn't need anymore and I bought a little cap for the top. I had to cut a hole in my precious roof for the pipe. I built my first fire. It drew. It *worked*. I brought my cat, dog and some food out, along with my little battery radio and a sleeping bag, and spent the night. With some rocks from the beach I made a fireplace outdoors, built a fire with driftwood, and cooked my dinner. I sat in the doorway of my new cabin, eating my dinner and downing a beer, all the while listening to a Vivaldi concerto on the radio. Life was good.

I had found such peace that I resented it all the more one day when I was clearing brush in the upper field and saw a boatload of people come to the island. They couldn't avoid seeing I was there, since they passed right by my boat on its mooring, but they landed anyway. I knew who they were and I didn't want them there. Besides, I wanted privacy. Why else would one buy an island? I was very upset. What to do?

I remembered a story about Alexander Woollcott, who owned an island somewhere. He had invited the Marx brothers to come and stay. On one particular afternoon, after everyone else had gone off for the day, Harpo was lying naked in a hammock, reading, when the butler came out to him.

"Excuse me, Mr. Marx," said the butler, "but a party of strangers in canoes has landed on Mr. Woollcott's beach and I know he hates to have anyone come onto the island. What do you think I should do, sir?"

"Leave it to me," said Harpo.

He went inside, put on his big yellow curly wig and, still naked, went to the toolshed to look for one final thing. Finding it, he climbed the hill behind the beach without anyone seeing him, then came running down the hill, swinging the axe over his head and giving an Indian war cry. The picnickers left in a hurry.

I considered doing the same thing. My hair was short and curly in those days and I had a hatchet handy. Then the awful possibility that the sight of a naked woman in her fifties, five foot three and a half inches tall, would not only be *not* frightening, but hilarious, decided me against it.

I went down, fully clothed, and asked them to leave. They did.

～ *Twelve* ～

One summer, as usual, I went to work to get my boat ready as soon as I came up to Nova Scotia. The previous fall I had tried a new scheme for wintering it. Karl had suggested Sperry's cove, near to his house. It is a quiet cove with a reed and dirt edge to it. There were the remains of a pole landing that I would be able to fix up and use. Since I still didn't own a boat trailer, it looked like a good idea and indeed it was. I used it for several years. I brought the boat in at very high tide, got some men to help me pull it up above the tide line and flip it over. Then I covered it with a tarpaulin and left it there for the winter.

I had to scrape the paint off the entire bottom. Before re-painting it, I hammered cotton caulking into the cracks between the boards. I had done this with my dory under Rodney's supervision and thought I should do it to my skiff-boat. But the construction is different in the two boats. The dory is a lapstraked boat, that is, the boards overlap like clapboards in a house, while the boards on a skiff-boat are butted up against one another. But what did I know? So I went ahead, without asking anyone's advice and caulked the bottom, feeling very competent and professional. Then I painted it red down to the waterline with a green copper-based paint on the bottom to protect it. It was ready to go in the water and I was proud.

I went to see Tud Scott and asked him if he could get some guys to help me push it in the water. Someone had already lifted my outboard into the back of my VW.

"Sure," said Tud. "You go get Clayton and I'll go down to the Government Wharf and pick up Austin."

"I can pick up Austin," I remonstrated.

"Oh you wouldn't want him in your car. He smells so bad."

Clayton wasn't home, so I drove on down to Sperry's Cove by myself. A few minutes later, Tud turned up with a group of men.

"Where's Austin?" I asked.

"Oh, he smelled so bad, I didn't want him even in the *back* of my truck."

We climbed down the bank to the boat and they flipped it over. Inside, was a little snake that zigzagged all over the bottom, trying to get out. I had a brilliant science teacher in fourth grade who brought a snake to school one day for us to touch and hold. All my classmates screamed the way little girls do, but I remember being fascinated that it wasn't slimy in the least, but smooth and cool to the touch. So, without even thinking, I jumped into the boat, grabbed the snake and threw it into the bushes. There are no poisonous snakes in Nova Scotia, so I had nothing to fear.

I needed someone to bring down the outboard before the men pushed the boat into the water and asked Tud if he would get it.

"Oh I couldn't," he said. "I'm all over weak seeing you pick up that snake."

"You're kidding."

"No, really. I'm all over weak. I couldn't possibly lift up your outboard now."

I remembered then that the local people have an innate terror of snakes.

Weeks later, I was talking with Clayton Burke. The subject of snakes came up and I casually said, "I like snakes."

"Yes, I know. I *heard*."

Someone else got the outboard and the men shoved the boat into the water.

It sank in about two feet of water.

I was appalled.

"Oh, my God. Do something. This is horrible. What's going on? Why is this happening?"

The guys looked at me calmly.

"It'll take a few days for the boards to soak up."

"Soak up? What do you mean? I had planned to go out to the island today."

"You ain't goin' nowhere for a while. The boards have to soak up the water, they're so dry. You shouldn't have corked her anyways."

"I shouldn't have caulked her? Why?"

"You only want to cork a dory."

They left.

It was a week before the boards swelled up tight, but swell they did and it was tight all right.

While I was waiting for the boards to swell, I needed to find my mooring in the harbor. When I first got the *Betsy*, Tud helped me to set up a mooring for it. A couple of summers earlier, I had bought an old V8 engine for $10, attached a heavy chain to it and asked one of the men to drop it into the harbor from his boat. A wrought-iron hook was attached to the chain, and to that was tied a rope with a buoy. The buoy that marked my mooring usually disappeared during the winter. With no buoy to hold them up, the hook and chain would sink out of sight. That year I couldn't find the darn thing and asked Tud for help. He suggested we row out at low tide in my punt to look for it. He found it immediately and secured a buoy to it.

"Now we're out here, let's row around and look for some scallops," Tud suggested.

"There's scallops in this harbor?"

"There should be some out near the buoys at the entrance to the harbor."

Tud rowed us out there and, indeed, there were some scallops.

We rowed around some more and chatted. It was a lovely warm day and neither of us felt like working.

"I guess you make lots of money working in the theater in New York?" he asked.

I laughed. "I was paid ninety-nine dollars a week for the last play I did."

Tud was amazed. "Ninety-nine a week! Why do you do it?"

"Because I *love* the work," I replied.

He looked thoughtful for a moment and then said quietly, "I *hate* my work. But that's all I know to do."

"Oh, Tud." I was stunned and overwhelmed with sadness. All the romance that those of us who don't fish associate with fishing—the independence, the sea, battling the elements, the beauty of it all, day after day—came crashing down.

Despite my being an oddity, I had the silent support of the men at the wharf. They were always ready to help whenever I needed a hand, just as they helped each other. But the wonderful thing about it was that I never *ever* felt condescended to. I asked for help and got it, but no one ever made me feel that I didn't belong there. I also know that I gave considerable pleasure all around when I fell into the water, which I did about once a year. One of the fishermen, Clare Williams, particularly enjoyed it. One time, I brought the *Betsy* into the back harbor and tied her to a post. I rested one foot on her bow and the other foot on the shore. The *Betsy* moved out into the water and, losing my support, I fell in and sank to the muddy bottom with a thump. Poor Clare missed it and was so disappointed.

I kept my punt, a nine-foot orange wooden plywood thing, in that same little back harbor. There was a flat bank, edging the harbor. Except at low tide, when there was no water to speak of, I could row up to the bank, climb out of the punt, and haul her right up onto the bank. One day when I was doing this, Uriah Stewart, who lived across the harbor, shouted to me across the water.

"Well, I see you ain't got no weaker over the winter."

⌒

I hired Joanna and Howard again to clear more land for pasture. Behind the cabin there rose a hill with a big apple tree at the bottom, two more apple trees, and a huge lilac bush at the top. In between was nothing but black alders and brambles. A slight clearing revealed a cellar hole. This seemed to be a good place to clear because it had been lived in and the land probably used for pasture.

We worked like crazy. Howard attacked the biggest alders with a chain saw and I used my monster brush cutter. Joanna pulled the heavy roots out of the ground. There were lots of blackberry bushes too, eight feet tall with vicious thorns. I call them "killer brambles" because I am convinced that they take aim and attack me whenever I turn my back. Even the dead ones. Some kind of post-mortem memory! The thorns get caught in my hair, my woolen sweater, my very soul.

We piled the cut things in the old cellar hole and set fire to it. It was a tremendous job and took days and days. We kept the fire going the whole time. One of those days it poured rain and we were glad to have the cabin. We stayed in it for most of the day, reading, telling stories, singing and having a good time next to the little stove that kept us cozy and warm. We kept the food and all our supplies in the cabin where I slept. Joanna and Howard slept in a tent.

On one of the evenings, two fishermen came out to see us, attracted by the smoke, I suppose. They were completely blotto and, in fact, one of them smashed the bottle he was drinking from on the rocks as they came in. I wasn't at all pleased, but I was much too concerned about their drunken state to chide them for breaking a bottle. We inadvertently solved the problem quite nicely. The three of us met them with great enthusiasm and said, "You must come up and see the work we've done." We took them up the hill and went on and on and *on* about the clearing we were doing, going into everything in great detail, showing all the alder roots we'd dug up and how much we'd burned already and how much more we had to do and on and on some more until they were so bored they walked down the hill without a word, got in the boat and went away. Whew.

As successful as the three of us had been and as dramatic as the impact of the rugby team had been earlier, I fretted constantly about clearing additional pasture on the island. It seemed as though the alders grew back as fast as we cut them. I had heard that pigs are very efficient at rooting out bushes and conceived of an idea. Perhaps if I poked corn in and amongst the roots of a huge stand of alders I could put pigs out there and they would kill the alders as they rooted for the corn. But I was always worried about what the community would think—and might act on.

I went to see Phemie with my idea. After explaining my theory, I said, "Do you think people would criticize me if I put pigs out on Blue Island?"

"Anne. People would criticize you if you put angels out there!"

I abandoned the notion.

⁓

Peter had fenced in the fields around my house, since he kept buying more sheep and goats and didn't have enough room on his own property. It gave him about eight more acres of grazing land. I was glad to have the sheep there to keep the land cleared, so it worked well for both of us. He had bought some goats and kept them on the point along with quite a few sheep. Among the goats was a billy-goat who groaned constantly because the nanny-goats got sick of his breeding them and would lie down to foil him. It was very funny until he started standing on his hind legs in his frustration, displaying himself to anyone that happened to walk by, whether it was me or my male dog, Sox. The humor paled quickly.

One day I saw Peter taking away one of the nanny goats, who had kids and was still milking. I asked him where he was taking her.

"I've sold her to some people who have a kid that can't tolerate any kind of milk except goat's milk."

("Well, that figures," I thought.) Aloud I asked, "How old is the kid?"

"About three or four months, I guess."

"Really?" I said. "I'm amazed she will allow the kid to suck on her."

Peter laughed and said, "Well, they'll milk her first."

"Gosh," I said, "that's an awful lot of trouble to go to for a baby goat."

"It's a baby *human*," said he, roaring with laughter.

Wonderful language, English.

Later on in the summer, sick of being bitten by mosquitoes every time I relieved myself in the bushes on the island, I decided to build an outhouse. Luckily, I had an easy source for the lumber.

The kitchen in my house on the mainland had proved to be most unsatisfactory. I had given the carpenters carte blanche, always a mistake. They had planned to make the counters, drawers and cupboards out of plywood. I had no idea how ugly it would be. My house is over two hundred years old; thus it was especially insulting. I told them I wanted the cupboard doors to be beveled, thinking that would take away some of the starkness of the plywood. They made them overlap, so that whenever I opened one cupboard door, the other would swing out and bang me in the knee. The drawers were so deep in both directions and so wide I could hardly open them. There was a Formica top to the counter and that was okay, but I decided to scrap the whole darn thing and start afresh.

I went to a woodworking place that had been recommended and asked the owner if her men would build me a new kitchen using old wood. She was intrigued by the idea and agreed with enthusiasm. I went home and drew up some plans that showed exactly what I wanted. Earlier in the year I had bought an antique cupboard door in New Hampshire and also another very old piece of wood. I asked them to use the door for the cupboard under the counter and to copy it for a pair of doors for a wide wall cupboard to hang over the counter. The single piece of plain wood I wanted used as a hinged door for my garbage pail.

I also wanted the counter to be maple butcher board. She built just what I wanted, but she went one step further. She had gotten hold of an old elm that had fallen down, from which she made a kitchen counter for herself and had enough left over to make the butcher board counter for me. Her men came to install the whole thing and I was thrilled. She had used some old wood for the cupboard, which looked nicely aged. I stained it and it fit into the old house perfectly.

What to do with the old plywood counter and doors? I used them to build the seat, floor and seat covers in my outhouse on the island with the Formica counter as the seat. It seemed a fitting place to put it all and pleased my ancestral

Scottish thriftiness at the same time. Building the outhouse it-self wasn't hard. The hardest part was digging a hole deep enough in that rocky soil. The building itself was so small that I could hold up the sides as I built them. A door had floated ashore one day and I used that too. Nat turned up while I was building and helped me finish it.

Part of my deal with Peter when I sold him the sheep was that he would give me a butchered lamb each fall as a grazing fee for keeping his sheep on my island. It was duly delivered to me cut, wrapped and frozen. This raised the question of how to get it back to New York without it thawing and spoiling. Years earlier, I had bought a very small freezer—four cubic feet—that was so lightweight that I could lift it myself. The freezer just fit into the back of my VW Rabbit. I put the lamb into it, as well as some frozen vegetables from my garden and some strawberries I had picked at a U-Pick and frozen. I brought a long heavy-duty extension cord and plugged the freezer into the motel room where I spent the night on my way home.

~ Thirteen ~

Upon my return to Nova Scotia in the spring of 1982, Rodney and Phemie told me the sad news that Tud Scott had died the month before. He was still young—in his mid-forties. When I asked what he had died from, they said it was uncertain. He had had a blackout once before while working on his boat at the wharf. That time, everyone assumed it was monoxide poisoning because his engine was running—and it may have been—but it was more likely a stroke. This time he fell off the wharf, hit a rock, and then fell into the water. The autopsy revealed that he did not drown and was probably dead when he landed. Rodney and Phemie were devastated. He was Phemie's nephew, but more like a son to them.

"When I heard your footsteps on the wooden walkway," Rodney said, "I thought to myself, 'Oh, who has died now?' Someone would have brought them the news in person, not by phone." His eyes filled with tears. "I'm so glad it's you."

Tud's death was a major loss to the community, which was still in shock. He and his wife, Charlotte, were real leaders in the village and much beloved. There was a fisherman named Lance who often fished with Tud in his boat. He was a hopeless alcoholic and quite a sweet person. Phemie told me that a few years earlier, when Lance had become very ill, Charlotte cooked up meals that Tud brought over to him. Later they got Lance into a nursing home to be taken care of. They did things like this for people without being asked. Things needed to be done and they did them. Tud was a good friend and I miss him still.

Saddened, I continued on to the house and unpacked the car. I needed to get going on all the things in store for me that summer, including getting back into the sheep business.

Peter Rogers had been working as a carpenter since moving to West Green Harbour. He was tired of being poor and didn't see much future for himself in the area, so he decided to go to law school. He had written me with the news the previous fall and said I could buy the sheep back or he would take them off the island.

What a dilemma. My acting career had been going well in New York in the four years since I had sold the sheep and it was more important to me than anything else. Actually, I had managed to spend most of the summers in Nova Scotia during that period. But I hadn't *had* to and now I would be forced to spend enough time to gather all the sheep to shear, worm them and take the lambs to market. On the other hand, so much progress had been made in opening up the island in the six years they had been there that I didn't want to waste it.

I made the decision to buy back the sheep and sent Peter a check. He told me later that after he had gathered the sheep in the fall to take the lambs off for butchering, he had given a giant party to celebrate. Since he had been working five days a week, he had only had the weekends to gather sheep on the island. The weather didn't always cooperate on weekends and he had been hard put to get the work done each year. He was thrilled to be out of it. He planned to be in West Green Harbour for the summer of 1982 and offered to help me catch the sheep at shearing time, but after that he would be gone and I would be on my own.

Worse yet, the Nettletons were going to leave Canada for several years. They had had a tragic time with their sheep. The Cape Breton Development Corporation, DEVCO, had imported some sheep from Scotland and England some years earlier. They had kept them in quarantine for three years and had recently held a huge, widely publicized sale to auction them off. People came from all over North America to buy the sheep and Brian and Martha bought some too.

When some of the sheep they had bought at the auction started dying, naturally they were alarmed. Brian, being a vet and also being British, recognized the disease that was killing their sheep, pulmonary adenomatosis, a viral disease that causes tumors to develop in the lungs. It had not been present in North America before the DEVCO sale. He accused DEVCO of knowingly selling diseased sheep. DEVCO denied it. They battled it out for some time and eventually DEVCO agreed to buy some of the Nettleton flock for "research." Meanwhile, the Nettletons had to sell the rest of their sheep and cattle just to keep going, including the flock on

McNutt's Island. Dispirited and angry at an ungrateful industry they had worked so hard to build up, they decided to volunteer for overseas duty with the Canadian University Service Organization, or CUSO, similar to the Peace Corps in the United States.

They were to leave for Papua New Guinea in the fall, but meanwhile Brian was working in Yarmouth, only an hour and a half away, covering for a vet who was on vacation. He said he would come over and we could see how my sheep had fared over the winter. Since I hadn't put my boat in the water yet, we asked a fisherman to ferry us out and back. Brian brought along Chili, his little Jack Russell Terrier. Cape Island fishing boats have very low sides and Chili was running on top of one of the gunwales.

"Aren't you worried she'll fall overboard, Brian?"

"Oh, no, she'll be okay."

A few minutes later he looked around. "Where's Chili?"

We looked to our stern and there was Chili, swimming along in our wake in the freezing cold spring ocean. Brian tapped the fisherman on the shoulder and pointed behind us. Chili disappeared completely behind each wave. As soon as she saw the boat turn toward her, she started wagging her tail as she swam.

"She thinks she's won," said Brian. He reached down and plucked her from the water. She shook herself off and jumped on a fish crate.

"Well, that was fun," she seemed to be saying. "What's next?"

Walking around the island, we came across body after body of dead sheep, most of them lambs. In order to bring the number of sheep up to the required twenty-eight, Peter had put a large bunch of lambs out at the end of November. It was too late in the season. They had been born on the mainland, had never experienced eating seaweed, had gotten bred in December on the island and it was too much for them. They all died.

I was furious and complained bitterly to Peter when I saw him later, but he just shrugged it off.

"You wanted me to bring the numbers back up to twenty-eight and those lambs were all I had."

"But why did you put them out in November? There was no grass for them to eat and they couldn't learn to eat seaweed quickly enough to keep them from starving. And those that survived early winter would have died from being pregnant in such poor condition."

"Anne, I was so busy all fall, I couldn't get them out any earlier. That's just the way it is. It's one of the reasons I'm glad to be out of the business of island sheep."

I was beside myself, but there was nothing I could do about it.

⁓

Later on in the summer, I asked a whole bunch of friends to come help gather the sheep. I had made peace with Peter and he came with his dog. The alder pen that Brian and I had built back in 1976 had long since collapsed and rotted away. Peter had built a sturdy new pen out of Page wire. He put gates at both ends so that when the sheep were not being gathered, both gates would be left open and the sheep would be accustomed to walking into the pen and out the other side, making them more inclined to go into it during the gather. It was a very intelligent idea.

We caught them all . . . except the breeding ram, who escaped at the last moment. It was late in the season and we decided to take the ram lambs, slated to go to the butcher, off the island after shearing and worming the ewes. As the men were leading the sheep to the boat one by one, a very large ram lamb escaped, jumped into the water and swam away. Remembering only too well the disaster on the day I had brought the sheep out to the island in 1975, I was very anxious. But one of the men rowed out to him very quickly, another man grabbed him by a horn and they brought him back in. He was fine.

Not having a dog was going to be a serious problem. Peter had sold his sheepdog, Baumann, to Van Buskirk, the lighthouse keeper on McNutt's, and Van was generous in letting me borrow him. Baumann was very keen, very experienced, and often did the job on his own while I was still trying to remember what the commands were.

I went out to the island from time to time, as weather permitted, to try to catch the breeding ram.

On one of those occasions, Baumann and I were at the southern end of the island near Blackbeard's Cove. He had gathered a group of about five sheep, the ram among them, and we were driving them along the path, hoping to be able to get them all the way around to the pen on the north side. (It wasn't until years later, when I really knew what I was doing, that I understood what an impossible task this was.) I tripped on a rock, started to fall headlong and threw my hands out in front of me to break my fall. Baumann, being extremely sensitive to hand signals, read this as a command to walk up on the sheep more aggressively to drive them away from us. The sheep took off. So did Baumann. By the time I had scrambled to my feet, they were out of sight.

I went on, always hoping, from blind headland to blind headland, that Baumann would have them cornered on the next one. I started imagining alternative ways of catching the sheep. Perhaps I could get an airplane to spot them and drop a giant net on top of them. Or maybe I could hire a cowboy in a helicopter to lasso them from the air, since everyone knows sheep don't expect any danger from above. I got to the front of the island, nursing another lovely fantasy that Baumann had penned them all and that he and they were waiting patiently for slow old me. But, of course, not an animal was in sight when I got there. No cowboy, no giant net, no Baumann, not even a helicopter. Nothing. I walked all the way back around the island to the south end. When I got to where I had last seen sheep, I happened to glance in the woods to my left. There were five sets of black and white legs. I looked a little higher and there were the faces of five sheep, one of them the ram. I could swear they looked smug. Without Baumann I could do nothing and they knew it, which is why they didn't run off. I walked on a little ways and there was Baumann holding another group of sheep up against a large rock. Since the ram wasn't with them, I called him off. In any case, I was so exhausted there was no way I could manage to drive them around the island at that point, even had I been skilled enough.

It was becoming clear to me that sheep were not so stupid as people think they are. In the more than twenty-five years that I have kept sheep, my respect for them has grown. People often say to me, usually nodding with a knowing look, "Sheep are pretty stupid, aren't they?" Most often these are people whose last contact with sheep was Little Bo Peep.

My usual answer is to say, "Okay, it's true that no sheep has ever written a sonnet or developed an atomic bomb, but they have their own intelligence. They excel at being sheep, which means learning how to survive." For instance, they are pretty good at math. They are intelligent enough to know that if one of them is alone in a field and a wolf should come into the field, the chances are pretty good that it will be killed, but if they are one in a flock of a hundred sheep, their chances of being killed are reduced to one in a hundred. Their only defense is flight. Nature program after nature program on TV shows flocks of Thompson's gazelles or other wild antelopes fleeing a predator, the narrator explaining how smart they are to group together to avoid death.

Yet when humans cram into a crowded subway, people comment, "Ach, how like sheep." Where's the predator, I'd like to know? To get sheep to crowd into a subway car, you'd need a damn good Border Collie or two. We are so anthrocentric that we only recognize intelligence in other species if they remind us of humans, which sheep don't.

Sheep have good memories. It is a tragedy that trophy hunters often kill the wild ram with the biggest horns in the mountains. Being the biggest, he is probably also the oldest and has years of memories to tell him where alternate routes are to lead the flock to feeding grounds, should rock slides or avalanches block their usual path. Without those memories, the rest of the wild sheep can starve to death and sometimes do.

Often I will hear people complain bitterly about sheep being *so* stupid when they won't do what the humans want them to do, such as go into the barn or even into a truck that is going to the slaughterhouse. Impatience is a human trait, I guess.

No one thinks that Border Collies are stupid, but even they have their eccentricities. Baumann's was his obsession with my cat, Buttons. At first she was frightened of him, but once she realized that he was totally under my control—and he was extraordinarily obedient, even for a Border Collie— she took merciless advantage of him. I used to take him with me when I went shopping. One warm day, when we came home from town, Buttons was outdoors. The instant Baumann got out of the car, he looked around for Buttons. I told him to lie down and he did. Buttons came out from behind the boathouse and slowly sashayed toward him. He started shaking all over. She went right up to him, cocked her head toward his face—without touching him—and flicked her hips and her tail right at him. I exploded with laughter. Poor Baumann. He couldn't move because he was on a "stay."

In the kitchen he was equally obsessed with her. She always sat on a little bench that has a mattress on it at the end of the room. Baumann would position himself under the kitchen table so that he could stare at her. After a while she'd stand, stretch extravagantly, jump off the settee and slink across the floor to lie under the woodstove. Baumann would get up, hop himself around without taking his eyes off her and lie down. A little while later, she'd reverse the process and Baumann would hop himself back around again. One time, either out of frustration or because he didn't want to leave her for one second to go outdoors, he stood up and peed against the leg of the table. I yelled at him and, in his confusion, he went into the living room and peed against a blanket chest. Poor Baumann was unceremoniously thrown out the door.

In September, I went to Truro to the sheep fair, as usual. The auction was a melancholy affair. The Nettletons were selling what was left of their stock preparatory to going to Papua New Guinea. Because of the disease that had infected the sheep, they weren't allowed to sell them for export to the United States, where there was a good market for the Scottish Blackface breed. The prices were way down, as a result, and Martha was doing the selling, tears streaming down her face. A kind friend bought many of them, but their losses were still deep. Brian's friends wouldn't allow him into the sale barn, fearing that he would punch someone in the nose.

Some in the sheep industry denounced him for ruining the market by making the disease public.

"I had to make it public. I'm a veterinarian. It would be completely unethical not to."

Those same people sold their diseased animals freely all over North America.

⁓ *Fourteen* ⁓

Later that fall, I played Amanda in a local production of *The Glass Menagerie*. When I was offered the part, I had to decide whether I could bear to work in an amateur production. Canada was outside the jurisdiction of my union, so I was okay on that score, but the prospect of working with untrained, inexperienced actors was something I had to consider carefully.

I remember being in a play once, before I turned professional. The director, who was also my acting teacher, had many years of experience behind him. He taught acting at Boston University and was the resident director of the Provincetown Playhouse on Cape Cod. He drove us hard and made changes constantly, in order to get the best balance, humor, rhythm—for myriad reasons. Finally several of the actors, who were all amateurs, objected strongly. They didn't want any more changes. Ed was shocked and angry, but he recognized the limitations of the situation. A willingness to try and keep on trying to find the right choice is something one gets used to in professional theater. In my opinion, since my life is full of risk anyway, it's what makes the work really fun. I adore the rehearsal process for that very reason. You have the freedom to fail, to take risks, to fall flat on your face—or to find what you are looking for. Often, amateurs will find something that works for them and hang onto it, afraid to let it go.

There are other differences too, but this one is paramount. I realized that if I decided to accept the part, I would have to remember to be patient *all* the time. Amanda is one of the great parts for a woman. I was over fifty and probably wouldn't get another chance to play her. Lee Keating, who was directing, was a good friend and that helped. True, he had never directed before, but had played in a great many amateur productions. I trusted his integrity, felt confident I could work with him, and accepted.

The early work was very hard. The actors mumbled incoherently. I couldn't understand a word anyone was saying and no one looked at anyone else. But after a while the actors grew under Lee's patient direction and the play started to come alive. I had some ideas that I shared with him for possible choices that actors might try. Later, I heard some of these ideas come out of him, transformed into his own words in his own way. I had never directed and it felt good to be able to contribute some of my expertise to what was turning out to be a very rich experience.

Then a bombshell hit. Both my sons were in Texas. Nat was taking a trip in the southern part of the state. He called me late one afternoon to ask if I had heard from Jonathan. I hadn't. He then told me that Jonathan and his wife and five-week-old baby had been in a terrible automobile accident. He didn't know much more than that.

I was at home, working on my lines with my friend Katie, one of the production staff. We were due at rehearsal in a few minutes. I drove into Shelburne with Katie, completely numb. I got to Lee's house and called the number in Austin that Nat had given me. The friend that Jonathan and his family had been staying with answered the phone. I asked after Jonathan. She said he was badly hurt, but okay, and his wife Haleya too. I asked about the baby, Abram.

"Oh, he was killed," she said.

I held myself together until I could get Lee's attention. He was talking to his son and a friend of his son's. He came into the room and I asked him to hold me tight. Only then could I tell him about the accident. Only then did I dare let myself go into the depths of my grief. I had never seen this little baby, never held him, but he was my flesh and blood and I felt his death just as acutely as I would have had I known him. Knowing how much Jonathan loved him made it unbearably painful. Lee went to the rehearsal hall to tell them what had happened and to call off the rehearsal. His young son kept me company until his return. There was no question of my going home to an empty house, so I stayed there overnight.

Rehearsals were put into abeyance so that I could go down to Texas to be with my sons and daughter-in-law. Being there with them helped begin to close the rawest, most painful wounds and I went back to Nova Scotia after a few days, able to continue with the play.

Since then I have had several friends who have suffered losses as painful as mine and all have said the same thing: some friends are supportive and give what help they can, while others seem unable to deal with the situation at all and simply ignore it. It happened that way with me. I was hurt at the time and appreciated those who could give me hugs and love all the more, but I later understood those who couldn't. I think the loss was more than they could even bear to imagine.

Soon after that, the play opened to wonderful reviews and great audiences. It was deeply satisfying to me, both artistically and personally. I was very glad to have decided to do it.

Since we only performed on weekends, I had ample time during the week to renew my efforts to catch the errant ram. I enlisted some of the cast and crew of the play. Lee came, also Ben, who played my son Tom, and some of the stagehands. With Baumann's help we actually got the ram alone, isolated on a rocky promontory. We formed a large circle around him. Baumann had already positioned himself at the most crucial balance point. We had him trapped. All we had to do was advance on him slowly to close in on him and . . . well, I hoped someone would grab him by the horns when we got close enough. To be honest, I hadn't really thought it through quite yet. But I perceived a slight gap in our circle. So I signaled with my hand as I spoke to one of the stagehands, asking him to move across the circle. Baumann, ever vigilant of my hand signals, moved over too. The ram, immediately sensing the change in balance that Baumann's move had caused, made a dash for the weak point. As he went past Ben, Ben ducked. The ram was gone.

In unison, Lee and I said, "Ben, why didn't you grab him by a horn as he went by?"

"He had a mean eye!"

I can't say as I blame Ben, though I didn't quite see it that way at the time.

Getting the ram off was a serious priority. If I left him on the island, there would be inbreeding, as he would breed his own lambs. Also, the sheep would be bred too early, which would mean lambs born in February or March. One way or another, he had to go. So, a few days later, Lee and I went out alone.

Lee was a seasoned hunter. I knew where the sheep hung out most of the time and we went there and waited, hidden by some trees. Eventually, they filed along in front of us, to the eastern rim of Blackbeard's Cove, and Lee shot the ram. It was a shame, a sad result of my shortcomings as a shepherd and dog handler, and I felt the failure keenly. It wasn't to be the last time.

⟿ *Fifteen* ⟿

The next summer's gather was to be the first one on my own and I wanted to be well prepared. Gerhard and Maartje Stroink, Dutch friends of mine who live in Halifax, had a whole raft of relatives visiting from Holland during the month of August, who thought it would be a great adventure to come down to West Green Harbour to help me catch my sheep. An island! Romance! Wild sheep! What fun!

I invited Dave Murphy, who had some sheep in Lunenburg County, to come too. He brought his Border Collie, so we had two working dogs. Ed Griswold, a summer person, like me, who had sheep in Connecticut, and Fiona Nettleton rounded out the group. I made sure to have a core of experienced sheep people. We all help each other, so it was no big deal for them to come.

I bought cases of beer and a lot of food. Most of the group were coming from Halifax or beyond and would be staying for a couple of nights. We would be fourteen in all. With one human to every two sheep on the island, how could we miss?

Early next morning we set off for the island in a dense fog. I had my trusty compass with the course written on the cover. Not being an expert navigator, I was taking no chances. I set the course for a little island that is in the middle of the harbor. When it loomed out of the fog I exclaimed, "Oh! There's Thrumcap."

Ed Griswold said, "You sound surprised."

I didn't say anything, but I must admit I was. I'm always surprised when my navigation turns out just right. You're going along in thick fog, unable to see anything, as if you were in a different world entirely from the one you know. Suddenly, there is the landmark you've been aiming for. I'm always relieved, but surprised, too. There's an element of magic in it.

As soon as we landed, the fog lifted. Fiona had brought along her Jack Russell Terrier, Sheila, who yapped the minute we got to the island and kept on yapping for quite a while. I regretted not asking Fiona to leave her in my barn. I was sure she would alert the sheep to our presence, as if they wouldn't be aware of the arrival of fourteen people, half of them kids.

To make things worse, Dave's bitch was in heat, which pretty much knocked Baumann out of any usefulness.

First, Fiona, Baumann and I went through the woods to arrive at the swamp from behind to see if there were any sheep there. There were fresh tracks, but no sheep.

Then we had a strategy meeting on the beach and decided that we should split up into groups. One group would go around the island clockwise with one dog, the other group would go counterclockwise with the second dog and the rest would go up the path in the middle. We planned to meet at Blackbeard's Cove and, depending on how many sheep we had been able to gather, we would decide where to go from there.

On the way down a grassy hill leading to Blackbeard's, I slipped and tore a muscle in my leg quite seriously. Everyone turned up on schedule. No sheep. Most of us hadn't even seen any. And here I was, scarcely able to walk. I was sure the day was ruined. I hobbled down the rocks to the shore and soaked my ankle.

"Fiona, would you take over? I can hardly walk and I wouldn't be able to run."

"Sure, Anne, I'd be glad to. C'mon Baumann. We'll just continue around the island, right?"

When my ankle was good and numb, I got up and limped back to the north end of the island. It was a long and painful journey, made much worse by the apparent failure of the day.

In fact, the others continued around the island without seeing a single sheep. They must have been hiding deep in the woods.

I rejoined the others and we ate our picnic, drank our beer, took off all our clothes and swam in the ocean. I felt much better. Dave Murphy was the only holdout in the clothes department. His underwear looked just like a bathing suit, so he kept it on. Then he got bitten by a huge greenhead fly on a strategic spot right through his underwear. We gave him a hard time about that one.

Being injured had its advantages. When we got home, my guests all bent to the necessary tasks, cooked a delicious dinner and waited on me hand and—yes, foot. I sat regally in a chair in the sun with my foot, very swollen by this time, elevated on a stool while everyone sat on the grass around me. The Dutch contingent very sweetly offered to get up at 4 AM to make another try at a gather, but since I could scarcely walk, it was out of the question.

I realized that my friends and I had seriously opposing goals. Theirs was to have a lark, an adventure, and if we caught some sheep, all the better. My goal was to catch the sheep first and foremost—and if I had some fun along the way, all the better.

Ten days later, Jonathan, Haleya and Nat came up for a visit. It was their first visit since the automobile accident and it meant a great deal to me. All three had moved back east. Jonathan and Haleya sold the school bus they had been living and traveling in and were renting a house in central Massachusetts. I took advantage of their visit to go out to the island to try to gather the sheep. The first thing we saw when we landed was a ram inextricably tangled in a heavy fish net that my friends and I had left across the path going up to the middle of the island. Things had become so confused with my injury that we had forgotten to remove it. The ram had been there for some days and was very stressed. With great difficulty, Jonathan and Nat disentangled him and took him by the horns over to the pen and closed him in. He immediately butted Nat in the solar plexus. Nat was very good-natured about it.

One of the ram's horns had grown towards the side of his face and had penetrated the bone just under his eye. Rams' horns that hug the sides of the face are not a good attribute for island sheep. Their horns can grow into their faces quite quickly, can prove to be fatal, and the condition can be passed along to their descendants. My sons named him Ramsey Eyeball. He continued to show his displeasure by butting the sides of the pen, trying to escape, so we decided to enclose him in a smaller pen, where he couldn't move much, using some extra pen sides that I had there just for that purpose. With Baumann's help we got him in and tied him to the side, then brought him water and some fresh grass.

We walked around the island and came across a small bunch of sheep, but because of my inexperience couldn't bring them in. We camped out there for the night and went home next day, taking Ramsey Eyeball with us. In the barn I was able to cut the end of the horn off and extricate it. I gave him some penicillin for a few days and his head healed well. Had we not brought him in, the horn would certainly have killed him. In that sense the heavy net saved his life.

The day after my family left, we had gale winds, but it was calm by evening, so I decided to set the alarm for 5 AM and try my luck at dawn. I lolled in bed until 5:30 and was in my boat by 7 AM.

I got to the island by 7:30 and set up a plastic fence from the corner of the holding pen down to the shore to block the sheep from running past the pen. I made sure the front gate was open to the pen (and the back gate closed) and went off with Baumann through the fields to the woods to skirt the swamp. The swamp takes up more than half of the north side of the island. It measures about 1,100 feet from west to east and is about 500 feet wide. The interior is all marshy with swamp grass, which the animals love to eat; the entire edge is a pile of rocks that acts as a breakwater. My modus operandi was this: after sneaking through the woods for about fifteen minutes so that the sheep wouldn't know I was there, I would come out at the western end of the swamp.

As Baumann and I approached the shore, but were still in the woods, I heard some bleating out on the rocks. It was some distance yet to the swamp and I didn't want to scare the sheep off, but I also couldn't risk by-passing them. We crept through the woods off the path and got to the shore, thus surprising a good bunch and cutting off their escape route. I kept Baumann out of sight behind me and as a result the sheep went slowly into the swamp. So far, so good. It was a huge bunch and I tried to suppress my excitement so I wouldn't blow it again. I kept walking slowly until the sheep were well out on the rocks and I was beyond the place where they could rush past me to freedom. They were well ahead of me at this point and I sent Baumann out to stop them. He did very nicely. They stopped dead, turned and ran back to me. I called Baumann back to me. He obeyed, passing them as he came, and stopped them before they could get past me. In this way we moved along in spurts the whole length of the swamp.

There was a promontory at the end of the swamp with huge jagged rocks along the shore that the sheep could negotiate, but I couldn't. Next to it was a path that wound through bayberry bushes. Beyond it was a possible escape for them up a path next to my cabin. The trick was to get them going so they didn't double back, but not to let them go so fast that they could escape up the path.

This section was usually accompanied by a great deal of yelling on my part at the dog, who couldn't be in two places at once. This time, Baumann stayed in perfect control and stopped them again at the end of the outcropping. I got him to run alongside the sheep to keep them on the beach and prevent their escaping up into the bushes, while I struggled to keep up. We got to the fence going down to the shore. They stopped and went slowly up the hill and into the pen. I closed the gate. I *had them.* Twenty-three sheep, including the big ram. What a great feeling. I tied a particularly athletic ram lamb to the fence and Baumann and I went back home to breakfast. It felt as if we'd be working all day, but it was only 9:30 AM.

The problem was to find help with the shearing. I could never line up help ahead of time because I never knew when I would be able to gather a large number of sheep. I called my friends the Griswolds. Karen was just leaving for Shelburne to do laundry. Enticed by the offer of my washer and dryer, she and Ed agreed to come at 3 PM, after Ed finished working on a staircase he had just torn apart. Bless them—friends in times of need. Another friend, John Davis, had a truck and said he would come to help and bring his truck. I needed one more strong man. I called Tim Murphy, another friend, and he agreed to leave work early to come and help.

We met at the harbor at three o'clock and went out to the island. Of the twenty-three sheep, eleven were adults and needed to be shorn. But two had lost their fleeces. Island sheep are under an unusual amount of strain, getting bred in December in the cold season, going through pregnancy with only seaweed and scrub to eat and then lambing in early spring, when the grass is only just coming in. This stress results sometimes in their wool simply falling out. I used to find great clumps on the raspberry bushes. A wild and woolly island indeed!

One ewe was one I had missed the year before. She hadn't lost any of her fleece from both years and it was matted and flapped against her flanks like an old boiled coat. There was only just enough space, less than half an inch, between the matted part of the fleece and her skin, for me to be able to slip the shears in so I could cut it. In addition, her horns were both growing into the sides of her head— one of them almost an inch. Imagine the headaches! I cut them off, using a special notched wire, sprayed the wound with antiseptic and gave her a shot of penicillin. When I let her out of the pen after shearing her, she leapt into the air, and on down the shore in great leaps. And no wonder. I weighed her fleece when I got back to the house and it weighed thirteen pounds.

All the animals had to be wormed, except the ram lambs that would go to the butcher. We had a lot of work to do. Ed and I were the only shearers. We managed to shear all the ewes but one, while Karen vaccinated and wormed them. John and Tim helped to grab them and bring them to the shearers. We loaded ten lambs and the big ram into my boat after tying their legs together and let the other sheep loose. It was six-thirty and beginning to rain. Five humans, eleven sheep and my dog got into my boat. Not bad for a seventeen-footer. The outboard had to work hard and we went slowly back to the harbor. We unloaded the sheep into John's truck at dusk, but by the time we unloaded them into the paddock behind my barn, it was pitch dark. Even so, I'm sure Ramsey Eyeball must have been delighted to welcome his friends.

Once again, in early September, I went to the annual Sheep Fair in Truro. At the dog trial I was sitting with Wendy Baumann (no relation to the dog, although she had owned him once, which is probably where he got his name). She had a litter of Border Collie puppies with her and naturally I couldn't resist holding one during the entire trial. That was it. I fell in love.

The time for having a dog of my own was long overdue, but I had procrastinated because of all the training involved, which loomed as being next to impossible. I was living in Manhattan. The only sheep I owned were wild ones on an island in Nova Scotia, completely out of the bounds of possibility for training a puppy. Still, I really had to have one. I couldn't rely on Baumann and the generosity of Van Buskirk forever.

I went to Wendy's and picked out the puppy I wanted. She was bold and friendly, just right for me. I named her Tess—I thought Tess of Blue Island sounded pretty grand. I took her home and she fell in love with Buttons, my dear old cat, who was remarkably patient with her. Tess wasn't even remotely under my control, but Buttons tolerated her and disciplined her with a swat when she came too close.

A few days later, I went out to the island to try again for a gather, not having caught all the sheep as yet. As I went up the hill past the apple trees I saw huge piles of half-digested apples next to each of the trees. I'd never seen such a thing before, but instinctively knew it meant *bear*. There had been four black bears on the mainland near my farm. Three had been shot by my neighbors. Clearly, the fourth had sought a safe haven on the island, an island that had beckoned to the bear with the aroma of delicious ripe apples, so it swam out there. What to do? I thought ahead to spring when, if the bear chose to spend the winter, my little lambs would provide several good meals after a long winter's nap. Contrary to public opinion, bears eat meat as well as fruit and berries.

I decided to take action. I called the Department of Lands and Forests. They had no one who could shoot or trap a bear, but recommended someone locally who could. Brian Cotter agreed to go out to the island with me and set some traps. He set out two of them, baited with rotten fish and a string of apples.

I went out the next day and found more droppings, but saw no bear.

Then the weather turned bad and I couldn't get out, but I could see the area near one of the apple trees where a trap had been set. The wind was blowing like crazy and I thought I could see a great black shape leaping about in all directions. I worried that a bear had been caught and was suffering, but the heavy winds prevented my going out to see.

Finally, after two weeks, I was able to go out. No bear. The bait was intact and there was nothing in the traps, which I sprung so the sheep wouldn't get caught. He'd eaten all the apples and there was no other food for him because the lambs, by then, were too fast for him to catch. I called the trapper to come get his traps and eventually he did.

I had auditioned for a movie, *The Bay Boy*, written and directed by Dan Petrie that was to be shot in Glace Bay, on Cape Breton Island, and I had been cast in the part. Liv Ullmann was starring in it and I was very excited, even though my role was very small. Shooting was to take place quite late in the fall, so I had to buy some clothes, as I hadn't brought any warm ones. Anyway, I didn't want to turn up on the set in my old overalls, not with Liv Ullman there.

I waited and waited for my contract to arrive. Weeks went by and I called and called some more, and was always told it would be sent soon. Then, finally, I was told the budget had been overrun and all the small roles had been cut out of the movie. This kind of thing happens and is one of the pains of my profession. But fifteen years later, I am still wearing the shoes and the overcoat I bought for the occasion. And I still get compliments for the overcoat. So there.

∽ *Sixteen* ∽

I had noticed, over the years, that hard as I tried to gather sheep in July and early August, I was never successful until *late* August. Finally, I realized that it was the fault of the seagulls! Seagulls nest on the open ground, making rudimentary nests, shallow hollows in the dirt or grass. They are therefore understandably annoyed and very vocal whenever anyone walks near their nests. In those days, there were multitudes of seagulls with nests all along the shore. It occurred to me that there was always a swarm of screaming seagulls a few hundred yards ahead of me whenever I went out in the early summer. The sheep thus had plenty of warning and were at least one quarter of the perimeter of the island ahead of me at all times. But by late August, the nests were all empty and the skies were quiet.

In late July of 1984, I got a call from Frank Kohler, Rodney and Phemie's son, asking me if I'd take Frank and his wife and two sons out to the island. When Frank was growing up, his grandfather lived on the point and Frank spent a great deal of his childhood there. He wanted to show the island to his sons. Rodney wanted to come too. I was thrilled. Rodney and Phemie had done so much for me all the years I was there and there were so few ways of returning the favor. At last I would be able to do something for Rodney.

We gathered down at the Government Wharf and Frank whispered to me that his Dad was in a foul mood. Then Rodney whispered in my other ear that it was his birthday. His eighty-first. I shouted "Happy Birthday" and gave him a hug and he cheered right up. Once in the boat, he held his arms out to the sides, closed his eyes and smelled the air with a look of bliss on his face. I was so happy to be able to give him such pleasure on his birthday. I thought of all the times he had taken me out fishing and all the years of teaching me about the waters and the local weather. It was the first time he had ever been in my boat and it meant a great deal to me.

We got out to the island. Three boys I had hired to do some clearing had set up a huge tent and Rodney decided to take a nap in it while the rest of us walked around the island. It was a wonderful day.

In late August, Brian and Martha Nettleton and their daughter, Mary, came down for a visit. Brian and Martha were home from Papua New Guinea for a furlough. Their time in the province was limited and they could only stay a couple of days, but I was honored that they took the time to come and see me.

I had some sheep in the pasture on the mainland, waiting to go to the butcher. Brian offered to get Tess started on her training. I had taught her to lie down and stay and to come when called. She was eager to learn and very obedient. Brian had brought a dog with him who gathered the sheep and held them for Tess. Brian got her to lie down and stay, then he went to the opposite side of the sheep and called her and she went around them very nicely. He did this many times, alternating

directions while saying the commands that went with each direction she was going in. Then he had me do the same exercise until I got it right. Tess did very well and he thought she
had good potential.

Shortly after the Nettletons' visit, I took my tape recorder
down to the rocks and set it close to the water to record the
sound of the waves. I wanted to play the tape in New York for
relaxation. I got busy with some task and forgot about the
recorder. When I finally went to check it, the waves were
splashing halfway up the machine. Not wanting to waste a
minute, I took it immediately to Shelburne to a repair man.
On the way to town I passed an ambulance and wondered
who it could be for.

Sadly enough, it was for Rodney. He had gone up to the
fish plant to wait for some fishermen to come in so he could
get some fish. No boats came in, so he got up to leave. While
walking out to his car, he collapsed and died instantly, probably of a stroke. The men at the fish plant called an ambulance
and also Rodney's son, Merrill. Merrill called me to ask me to
go see his mother and break the news to her, but because I was
on my way to Shelburne, I missed his call. Phemie learned the
news from a neighbor, who called to commiserate.

I felt terrible. Rodney and Phemie had both done so
much for me over the years and here was something that I
could have done that would have been very painful, but would
have saved her the shock of hearing it sideways. Rodney had
been healthy right to the end and we all agreed that he had a
death we would all wish for, but the loss was keenly felt.
Phemie kept saying for weeks afterwards, "I keep waiting for
him to come home from the fish plant."

In spite of our once-yearly fights, Rodney and I had loved
each other dearly. Phemie included me in all the gatherings
around the funeral as if I were part of the family, which

touched me deeply. After the wake at the funeral parlor, I was invited back to the house. I had put on a pretty blue cotton dress with large dark blue flowers on it. Phemie looked at me.

"What are those things hanging from the sides of your dress?"

I looked down at my sides and saw my pockets hanging out. After ironing the pockets I had forgotten to put them back inside. I heard giggles.

"Oh," I said, pulling the pockets straight out to the sides. "This is the latest fashion in New York. Didn't you know?"

Then she looked at my ankle supports. One was white and the other tan.

"Your ankle supports don't even match. And you went to the funeral parlor like that?"

I couldn't think of anything to elevate the ankle supports to a fashion statement, so I burst out laughing and so did Phemie and everyone else. I think we all felt better.

A few days later, down at the Government Wharf, a young fisherman told me his mother had said she was sorry she hadn't gone to Rodney's funeral.

"Why was that?" I asked.

"She said it would have been her one opportunity to see Anne Priest in a dress."

Phemie's eyesight wasn't good enough for her to stay alone in her house, which was quite isolated. She moved into an apartment in Shelburne and I visited with her every time I went to town, but it wasn't like being able to walk up the road, as I had done three or four times a week to spend the evening with them.

I have often thought, with some wonder, how it was that here was a couple whose lives were so different from mine and whom I would never have known had I not bought my piece of land. It brought home to me the fact that there are truly great people all over the world, living their lives quietly like the Kohlers, and it made me feel better about the world. Their deaths have left a huge hole in my life, but their friendship added immeasurable dimensions.

I went back to New York, deeply saddened.

One day in the late fall the phone rang. A very familiar voice said, "Anne, would you like to put a bit of training on Tess this afternoon?"

"*Brian!* Where *are* you?"

"Martha and I are at La Guardia airport. We have a few hours between planes. Our plane to Papua New Guinea leaves from Kennedy Airport. Would you like to come out and get us?"

Would I ever.

I popped Tess into the car and sped out to La Guardia and brought them to my loft in Tribeca. We spent a wonderful few hours together, which meant a great deal to them, since leaving their family in Nova Scotia had been a wrench. This gave them a transition which they said helped.

Brian described saying goodbye to their daughter Sarah, who was at university in Newfoundland. They took her to the ferry in Sydney, Nova Scotia, bound for St. John's. On the dock they all hugged goodbye and all were in tears. It would be four years before Brian and Martha would be back. Sarah was sobbing. Brian said people looked at them strangely as if to say, "She's only going to Newfoundland. It's not that far."

Their visit meant a lot to me too. I lived in two very different cultures—rural Nova Scotia and New York City. Brian and Martha did, too, between Nova Scotia and Papua New Guinea. Their visit was a touchstone for the three of us, each in our own way.

Living in Nova Scotia is like being thrown back in time, not because it is backward, which it is not, or because the pace is slower, which it is, but because people take time for each other. As hard as people work, they still take time to visit, whether on the street in a chance encounter, or in someone's home. For instance, I never rushed in to Phemie's kitchen to borrow something and dashed out again. I would be expected to stop for a cup of tea. There is a grace to the rhythm of life there that simply doesn't exist in the city. And I dare say that my neighbors accomplish as much work in their quiet ways as most New Yorkers do with their frenetic rushing about. It was this very frenzy that I was shortly to leave behind me.

∽ Seventeen ∽

Nineteen eighty-five would bring radical changes to my life. The cuts that the Reagan administration had made in the funding of the National Endowment for the Arts, plus the enormous rise in real estate prices in New York, meant that many of the theaters where I found my work were going out of business. I had been working in Off-Broadway and Off-Off-Broadway houses, most of them nonprofit, the very theaters that depended heavily on NEA funding. On average I had played in three shows a year, which I thought was very good, considering I spent every summer in Nova Scotia. But by 1985, there was so little work that even stars were willing to work for nothing or next to nothing. If a producer could get a big name, he wasn't going to hire me. It was a very low point in New York theater. I was performing in just one show a year, which wasn't enough to keep me in the city.

In March, my mother died. She was ninety-three and for ten years she had been slipping slowly into senility. My best

memories of her were the times we had spent in Europe together when she came over for her international meetings
while I was living in Paris. I had followed her lead into the
work of international peace and reveled in meeting her
friends. We lunched with her friend and colleague, Eleanor
Roosevelt, in Geneva and spent time in Rome and Florence
with Anna Lea Lelli, an extraordinary historian friend of hers.
We also visited other friends in Holland, the Dutch represen-
tative to the United Nations Human Rights Commission and
his wonderful wife. We toured and dined and giggled together,
just the two of us. It was extremely painful to watch her as she
lost her mind and I grieved for her then, year by year. Her
death was a blessed release for all of us.

By chance, a young cousin turned up one day for tea to
rest up from a house search he was conducting for himself and
his wife. When he walked into my loft, he gasped, "Do you
know how much this place is worth?" He told me, then *I*
gasped. He quoted a range of figures that were five to seven
times what I had invested in the loft in eight years.

For months I weighed what to do. I didn't want to give
up my career altogether. It was work that I loved more than
any work I'd ever done. But to spend nine months in a city
that I found wearing in order to do one show, and to stay
there in the hopes that things would improve in the near future, seemed out of balance.

Meanwhile, I tried to start Tess's training. I don't know
how many shepherds, if any, have tried to train a sheepdog on
Manhattan streets, but I thought I could at least begin. New
York City has a strict leash law, but I took chances. One block
away from my loft was a four-block, rubble-strewn open space
where I worked with her. (Shearson-Lehman has since built a
building there that occupies the entire space.) I imagined a

flock of sheep and assumed that Tess did too. I was able to teach her to run out clockwise and counterclockwise, to lie down instantly on command and to come to me when I said "That'll do, Tess."

She was so eager to work that I got away with more than I deserved to, but eventually I concluded that we had to find some real sheep for her to work. Besides, I was sick of paying fines for having her off leash. I gave her massive doses of exercise by going to a huge sandy landfill across from Chambers Street that was eventually to house the entire downtown Financial Center and Battery Park City. Years earlier that part of the river had been filled in with sand. It was ideal for us. A chain link fence surrounded it on the street side with a gate that someone had bent just enough for me to squeeze through. I took a tennis racket and ball and swatted them out as far as I could for Tess to fetch. She loved it and it gave her the exercise she needed so badly. She let me know when she'd had enough by lying down and refusing to bring me the ball. One day, though, I didn't agree that she'd had enough and urged her to go one more time. "Just once more, Tessie." She brought the ball to me, I swatted it as far as I could, she ran to fetch it, picked it up and kept on going. Next thing I knew she had dropped it in the river. She'd had enough and that was that. Still, there were no sheep on that landfill.

My friends, the Griswolds, who had helped me on Blue Island, live near Danbury, Connecticut, in winter. They had a flock of sheep and generously offered to let me come out whenever I wanted to train Tess. It wasn't easy. I had to drive for an hour and a quarter each way. It's not a good idea to work a young dog for more than fifteen minutes in a session, so it was a long drive for a very small dividend. In addition, the Griswolds' sheep were not dog-broke, which is to say they had never been worked by a dog. They were stubborn and challenged Tess, refusing to budge and even butting her. An experienced dog could have brought them into line, but Tess was just getting started and I was afraid the sheep might set her back.

After a few months of this, I decided to send Tess away to a woman who would train her in upstate New York. Barbara Leverett did a terrific job. After two or three weeks, she called and told me I could come up and work with Tess. She trained us both.

Tess was with her for two periods, totaling five months. By June she was really very good. I had improved too. Tess was the perfect first dog for me. She was hard-headed, to be sure, but when I blamed her for absolutely everything that went wrong—when 90 percent of it was my fault—the scoldings rolled off her back. Part of Barbara Leverett's training of *me* was to point out (with admirable tact) that it was fine to make a correction to Tess, but once I had done so, I must return my voice to a normal tone instead of maintaining the angry tone I was using. By staying angry, I was getting Tess all riled up and anxious. Get angry—fine—but then drop it. It has worked wonders not only with my dogs, but in my human relations as well.

I decided to put Tess into a dog trial and entered her in the Novice Class at the Pennsylvania Open Championship. She came in second. I was ecstatic. "We can only go up from here," I thought. I'd quite forgotten there was another direction.

Actually, Tess didn't do too badly in her very limited trial career. Since I was spending pretty much the span of the Border Collie trial season in Nova Scotia, we only entered two or three trials a year. She won her share and did well in many. She rose through the ranks of all the novice classes, but never got to the Open Class. Where she was to excel was on Blue Island.

By early spring I had made my decision to sell my loft and move to the country. Where to go? I wanted to find a place close enough to the city to be able to continue my work in the theater. At the same time, I seriously wanted a sheep farm in the country.

Martha Nettleton had once made a suggestion when I was complaining about the heavy losses that I experienced on Blue Island with the ewe lambs. There was no way of keeping the ram from breeding them, since there was no fencing on the island, and I couldn't isolate one group from another in any case, since all had to have access to the seaweed on the shore. So the lambs got bred along with the ewes. They had to learn how to survive on an island all while carrying their first lambs, experience lambing and survive lactation—a heavy load for a young lamb. Martha had suggested taking the ewe lambs off the island in the fall and getting some 4-Hers to care for them over the winter.

It was a wonderful idea except for the fact that there was no 4-H organization anywhere near me. But the idea stayed in my mind and blossomed into a plan for what I would do if I left the city. I would buy a farm and bring the ewe lambs down to New York each year from the island. I would keep the ewe lambs on my farm in New York until they were old enough to breed—at a year and a half—then bring them back to Blue Island after their lambs were weaned. The lambs would stay in New York until they were old enough to breed, and so on. Meanwhile I would bring more ewe lambs down from the island and repeat the process. In effect, I would be trafficking in sheep.

In order to be within striking distance of the theater, I drew a ninety-minute circle around New York and started looking. With my mother's death I had inherited some money that I could use to put a deposit down on a farm before selling the loft. I needed a minimum of ten acres. A house and a barn would be nice, too. Everything I saw was either too expensive or the town too developed and I got very discouraged. Farm land was disappearing.

I told some friends in upstate New York of my search for a farm and also of my desire to find some sheep for Tess to work. Now that she had some training on her, it was important to keep up her skills by working her regularly on sheep. They referred me to a friend of theirs, Rayna Walters, who had actually seen some sheep near where she lived in Nyack. Sheep in Nyack? That close to New York? Would the owner let me work Tess on them? They didn't know, but they gave me Rayna's phone number. When I called her, she told me to come up and we'd go see for ourselves.

Nyack is a very pretty town on the west side of the Hudson River. The houses get progressively bigger the farther they are from the center of town. Rayna and I drove out to where she had seen the sheep. It was one of the last houses on the street and was very large. There was a big field in front of the house bordered by a sweeping driveway that went up a hill to the house. Behind the house we found a sports car with a pair of legs sticking out from underneath it. The owner of the legs emerged from under the car and I asked him if those were his sheep, which we could now see in a field behind the house. When he said they were, I asked him if I could work my dog on them.

He picked something up off the ground and, as he stuck it into his belt, I saw it was a pistol.

I backed off. "We mean no harm, sir."

"Nor do I," he said. "Let's go see what your dog can do. Is she trained? Does she lie down?"

I assured him she did a lot more than that.

We started into the field and I saw that many of the sheep had small lambs in tow. Sheep can be quite aggressive when they have small lambs and I strongly suspected they were not dog-broke. I didn't want any trouble.

"You know, since the sheep have lambs, I don't think this would be a very good idea."

"I insist on it," he said.

Mindful of the fact that he had the gun, I decided to go ahead, but I was really worried that he might shoot Tess if she got too excited and tried to bite a sheep.

As we walked through the gate, the sheep all rushed down the hill to see what was going on. Tess hid behind a tree. I was quite relieved.

"I really don't think this is going to work," said I, hopefully.

"Go ahead." The guy was relentless.

I called Tess to me and we drove the sheep away from us and up the hill. Grateful that nothing had gone wrong, I decided to stop there.

"Thank you," I said. "That was just fine."

He wasn't fooled. "Can your dog get those sheep into that pen?"

I rose to the bait. "Of course."

I went up to the pen, which was about half way up the hill, and opened the gate, which was so narrow only one sheep would be able to get through at a time. Couldn't be worse. I sent Tess around the sheep and gave her the commands to drive them into the pen. She was terrific. About half of the sheep went in; the other half broke away and ran up the hill. Unbeknownst to me, there was a little passage above the pen which they ran through and were able to escape into the next field.

"We got half the sheep in. I think that's enough," I said.

"I want you to get them all in," said he. The guy had no mercy.

Rayna offered to stand and block the passage and I accepted gratefully. I sent Tess into the next field and she brought the sheep down the hill and through an opening at the bottom of the field we were in. They came up the hill again, I opened the little gate and all the other sheep came out. Tess went around them all and in minutes they were all in the pen.

The owner was delighted, as was his wife, who had watched the whole thing from an upstairs window. I was relieved beyond words and lavished praise on Tess. She was well on her way to being a very useful dog.

Rayna reminded me as we left that there had been a hold-up of a Brink's truck in Nyack, not too long before, where at least one man was murdered. Thus the gun.

I told her of my search for a farm and she said, "Oh, you belong in Greenville," a small town in Orange County, New York, where she grew up. "It's far enough from New York City that it isn't developed because the train service is very slow. There are still some working farms too. I have a good friend there and I'll introduce you."

Shortly afterwards she and her friend, Marc Suffern, and I met for lunch in New York. Two weeks later, Marc told me to come out to Greenville, as he had lined up a dozen pieces of property.

The Appalachian Ridge goes through Greenville. The two best pieces were on the ridge. One had 200 acres and was beautiful, but it overlooked Interstate 84 where the hum of trucks night and day was not something I wanted. The other piece was 116 acres. Route 84 was located behind the mountain, so it was quiet. About 50 acres were open fields, the rest wooded. There was a good-sized house and barn near the road and it was in my price range. The land rose abruptly to a ridge about two hundred vertical feet above the main road. The view was glorious. I could build a new house and barn on top of the ridge and sell the existing house when the new one was finished. It was seventy-eight miles from New York City—well within my circle.

I had found my farm.

I hired an architect to design a solar house on top of the mountain and while all the paperwork for the property was going on, I went up to Nova Scotia for the summer.

~ Eighteen ~

I needed a new ram for the island and bought three sheep from friends in Connecticut, but I had no way of getting them to Nova Scotia. They said I could borrow their truck to take them up, but how to get it back to them? I offered Jonathan a large sofa in Nova Scotia that I didn't need anymore and we worked it out that he would pick up my friends' truck with the sheep and meet me in Portland, Maine, at the ferry. There was a large, gorgeous ram called Big Boy and two two-year-old ewes, both of whom I had named Big Bertha. They had different markings, so I knew which was which. Since sheep don't know their names, it didn't matter anyway.

Taking animals other than dogs or cats into Canada was complicated. The sheep had to be tested twice for one disease and once for another, all within a specific number of days before departure. The vet then had to fill out papers which had to go to the USDA office to be stamped. It was always tricky, not knowing if the papers would get back in time for my scheduled departure, so I often drove them to the upstate office myself.

Then, once in Canada, a Canadian federal vet had to come and check the paperwork. Presumably he was supposed to check the animals too, but neither he nor any other vet ever did.

That year we arrived on a Saturday when the vets were off duty, but one kindly volunteered to meet the boat and take his day off another day. He was about two hours late, however, as he was nursing a severe hangover. This was my first experience with John, who was a very nice and amusing person, originally from New Zealand, but he did love his drinks. Once "inspected," Jonathan and I drove the sheep to my farm and let them out into the paddock behind the barn. Next day, Jonathan drove the truck back with the sofa I had given him.

I had stored the boat in the barn for the winter. I got it out, scraped and painted the bottom and put it in the water in three days—a record. I didn't have any time to waste, having arrived so late in the summer. While the boat was soaking up water, I went to Bridgewater and bought a pickup. If I was going to live in the country permanently, keeping sheep on land, I was going to need a truck. My little VW Rabbit just wouldn't do anymore, so I bought a bright red, four-wheel-drive Toyota.

My sheep-gathering was a disaster that summer. The sheep simply didn't come into the swamp and I had learned the hard way that to try to gather them on the far side of the island and bring them around without their bolting into the woods was next to impossible. In the early years, the sheep, having lived on a farm, were still domesticated, which meant that they were accustomed to being handled by humans and to being gathered by a dog, but by 1985 the original sheep were all gone and the ones born on the island were as wild as deer. They only got handled once a year and that wasn't enough to tame them. They were only gathered with a dog that one time and that wasn't enough to teach them how to be worked. Peter had warned me, when I bought the sheep back from him in 1982, that there wasn't much point in trying to gather the sheep unless they were in or near the swamp and he was right.

Finally, in late August, Tess and I succeeded in penning twelve sheep on the island. I decided to take the three ram lambs back to my farm right away. I got them into my punt, one of them going under water in the process, but no harm done, and heaved them up into the *Betsy*. I left the ewes loose in the pen, realizing that it was much too late in the afternoon to shear them all, particularly since I had to recruit help, and they would have a bit of grass to eat.

Martin Le Blanc is a man whose father has sheep on islands near Yarmouth, Nova Scotia. I met Martin in New York that spring, oddly enough, when we were both at a nightclub where a mutual friend of ours, Noel Harrison, was singing. He offered then to help me shear anytime I needed him. I needed him now.

I called that evening and he said he'd be delighted to come and would arrive by one-thirty in the afternoon. I borrowed some shears for Martin and waited. Shortly before 3 PM, he pulled into the driveway. I was concerned, as the forecast called for rain and the weather looked threatening. In truth, I was pretty frantic that he was so late. Another cause for concern was his clothes. He was dressed in a business suit. A business suit to go out and shear sheep? He said there was no problem; he would put on his rain suit. There was no time to argue, so we set off for the island.

The sheep were in the pen, good as gold. As we were penning the sheep in a corner, Martin said, "You know, I've never cut a sheep!" I was amazed, as it is virtually impossible to avoid cutting one or two in a lifetime of shearing. "No," he said, laughing, "my father does the shearing and I hold the sheep." He didn't know how to shear! I thought of the whole day wasted waiting for him. Well, nothing left but to teach him to shear.

I picked out a sheep and sheared it, showing him how to hold the sheep for each step of the process. Then I picked one out for him with a nice easy fleece. I took a particularly matted one for myself and sheared it. Meanwhile, Martin was hacking about one inch of wool (out of about five inches) off the sheep, who was lying there quietly. A good shearer would have shorn the wool clean to the skin. I had brought worming medicine and vaccine. After worming the sheep I had just shorn, I turned to worm the one Martin was shearing. With dismay I saw that she had parrot mouth, which is a serious overbite resulting from inbreeding, a sad consequence of the rams I had failed to catch in earlier years who then bred their mothers and their sisters and their cousins and their aunts. Luckily, she didn't have a lamb.

I was grateful that Martin was such a miserable shearer. There was plenty of wool left on her to make a decent sheep-skin. (In fact, it has graced the floor in front of the fireplace in my study in Greenville all these years!) I sheared the rest of the ewes myself, wormed and vaccinated them, and we took the parrot-mouthed ewe to be butchered and two ewe lambs off the island for me to take to New York later in the fall. It looked like a rotten day at the time, but compared to the rest of the summer it turned out okay.

Big Boy and the Berthas were still on the mainland. I had noticed Big Boy lifting his lip towards them, a sure indication that they were ready to breed. I didn't want them to lamb too early on the island and decided that I would take them back to New York in November, when I would come back for the island ewe lambs and some lambs I had bought from Peter. Dave Murphy agreed to take Big Boy for the winter along with some ewes I had also bought from Peter. I saw no reason to put Big Boy on the island as I had planned, since there were some rams I had missed out there who would have bred the sheep well before the time when I would have put him out.

I had to go back to New York to close on the house in Greenville and move out of my loft. As much as I loved the loft, I was more than ready to move out of the city. I had noticed that, when walking in New York City, my fists were always clenched. One summer in Nova Scotia, I went to a massage therapist who remarked on how tense my body was. A month later, during a massage, she noticed how much my body had relaxed. I was looking forward to a new kind of life away from the frantic rush of the city.

An old farm house came with the Greenville property, badly mutilated by the former owner with fake wood paneling indoors and asbestos shingles above fake stonework outdoors. But it was sound and roomy and would serve me well while my new house was being built on top of the hill. Nat was in the area temporarily and helped me move, which was a godsend. Once moved in, I had to get the barn ready for sheep, get in some hay for winter and set up some temporary fencing around the pastures.

There was a little orchard behind the barn which would do very nicely for the winter. It was at the same level as the hay loft, which made feeding very convenient. The sheep were sure to find their new lifestyle a luxury, after having lived on an island in the Atlantic all their lives, scrounging for food all winter.

Now came the next big move. I set off for Nova Scotia

on November 20 and, once there, set about lining up the butcher and checking with my lamb customers. All went well.

I was taking ten sheep down to the States and was concerned that they would be overcrowded in my truck. So I loaded them into the back of the truck and took them on a trial run for about an hour. It went fine, but the sheep pretty much destroyed the covering I had put over the open windows to keep them from climbing out. I went out and bought some hardware cloth and taped it to the window frames with that most wonderful of substances, duct tape.

Hardware cloth isn't cloth at all. It's a strong wire mesh with half-inch-square openings. It worked well. For added air circulation when the truck wasn't moving, I hung three narrow boards from the hinges at the top of the truck cap door. When the cap door was open, the boards hung down and looked like a fence. I was pretty sure the sheep would assume it *was* a fence and not challenge it. Brian had taught me the value of "visual barriers." Like the plastic fencing running down to the shore on the island, which looked substantial, the sheep accepted that it was. My little "fence" in the truck worked. Never, in the ten years of transporting sheep to and from my farms, did they challenge it.

Before I could leave, John, the federal vet, had to come to my farm to tag the sheep. We had an appointment, but he forgot it and was almost four hours late. It was dark by the time he arrived, so I brought a bridge lamp out to the barn, but John spurned it and tagged the sheep in the dark. So much for the inspection!

Because Reagan had done away with all the inspectors on the United States end, I was going to have to drive all the way to Houlton, a town on Maine's northern border with New Brunswick. There a private vet would leave his practice and come to the border to take the list of my sheep, check to make sure the ear tag numbers were the same, and send me on my way. This ridiculous process meant a whole extra day's drive for me and served nothing. My sheep were healthy, but they could have been sick with the most contagious diseases known to the sheep world and the process wouldn't have detected them. The extra day's drive was as hard on the animals as it was on me.

Because of having to go to Houlton, I took the ferry from Digby, Nova Scotia, which landed in St. John, New Brunswick. I was going to stay with friends outside of Augusta for the night.

The friends I was visiting in Maine came in to my life in a wonderful, rather roundabout way. A couple of years earlier, I had spent the day with a friend, Clayton Karkosh, a professor of theater design at the University of New Mexico, who summers in Lower Argyle, about an hour's drive from my place in Nova Scotia. After a long day of visiting friends and going to Frenchy's, a *major* thrift store chain in Nova Scotia where everyone I know buys their clothes, Clayton invited me back to his house for supper before my trip home. As we drove down the road from Yarmouth to his house, we passed a couple on their bicycles, which were piled high with camping gear. It was just beginning to rain.

"Oh those poor people," I said, "just off the ferry. It's raining and they still have to set up camp."

We went on to Clayton's and he started to cook dinner.

"Anne, go out and stop those people on the bicycles and invite them for dinner. There's plenty. Hurry. There they are!"

I rushed out, unprepared with what to say, so I said, "Helloooo!"

They said "hello" back but kept on going. This was obviously getting us nowhere, so I shouted, "Would you like to come to dinner?"

Without a word they made a graceful U-turn and came in the driveway. They had no sooner parked their bikes under Clayton's roofed porch when the heavens opened up.

The cyclists were Margie and Steve Knight, both teachers in schools near Augusta, Maine. They stayed at Clayton's overnight and the next day bicycled down to my place for their second night. We have remained good friends ever since.

Now, when I called the Knights to tell them I was coming through for the night, I asked them if by any chance they knew of a fenced-in field where I could put the sheep to give them some room and fresh grass. Miraculously, they had friends with sheep who were kind enough to let me put mine in their pasture with theirs. Next day the Knights recruited six friends to help get my sheep back into the truck.

The Knights were expecting a baby shortly after this event, so I sent them a lambskin as a thank-you present for all they had done. Their little boy, Kyle, became very attached to it, curling up in it whenever he felt sick or low. One day, years later, Kyle said to his mother, "Mom, have we thanked Anne Priest lately for the lambskin?"

I drove on to Greenville and let the sheep out of my truck into the newly fenced field. I was home.

～ Nineteen ～

I had owned sheep on Blue Island for ten years by this time, but had never taken care of them on a day-to-day basis. I thought I knew a lot about sheep, but in many ways I was starting from square one.

The ewes had been with Big Boy in Nova Scotia and I had no idea when he had bred them, whom he had bred, and even *if* he had bred any of them. Starting in early February, I examined the sheep to see if there were any signs of mammary development. I sheared around the crotch area of all of them, and saw no signs whatsoever of pregnancy. A month later I got the same answer. Finally in late March I saw some signs that three of them might be having lambs—sometime. But when was anybody's guess. I didn't even know what to look for to recognize when they were about to lamb, since they had always lambed on their own on Blue Island. Although they had managed to do this successfully, the whole point of bringing them to New York was to save those that might have died on the island. I had a new responsibility to them, but I really didn't know what I was doing. My long-distance phone bill to Betty Levin in Massachusetts that spring was very high.

On the last day of March one of the Berthas disappeared. There was an old abandoned icehouse on the property within the fenced area where I found her looking spaced out. I had been told this was one of the signs to look for, so I got her into the barn, penned, and went indoors to watch the news. Afterwards I went into the barn to check on the ewe and found her with a fine little ewe lamb. I checked the mother's teats to make sure they weren't plugged up; she seemed to be nursing so I went to bed.

It was a full two weeks before another lamb was born and then two ewes lambed the same day. First, the other Bertha had a nice ram lamb, just what I wanted. He would stay in New York to be my breeding ram for the following couple of years. Since I would be taking the Berthas back to Nova Scotia in the spring, he would be unrelated to those staying behind.

The second ewe lambed after midnight. I spent some time in the barn to be near her, but it was very cold, so I went to the house thinking to sleep for an hour or so. Came out to the barn to find that she had had a tiny little ewe lamb. The ewe was only a year old herself and very skittish. I hadn't put her in a pen and she ran around all over the place to get away from me when I tried to catch her, jumping over her lamb. The lamb had seemed to be sucking vigorously, so I gave up and went to bed. It was a mistake.

Next morning the lamb was so weak I thought she was dead. I got her mother into a pen and milked out her teats. They were completely plugged up, so the lamb hadn't gotten any milk, even though she was sucking noisily. It was crucial that I get some colostrum (the mother's first milk) into her, as it contains all the anti-bodies and can only be absorbed by the lamb within twenty-four hours. Usually, one tries to get the first colostrum into the lamb within a half hour or so of birth. I had frozen some from the earlier Bertha and quickly melted it. Too quickly. It curdled, but never mind, it was all I had. The mother's teats were so tiny I couldn't get any milk out of her. So I fed the curdled, lumpy milk to the lamb, squeezing it through the rubber nipple into her mouth. It took several hours. The colostrum had probably lost much of its immunities from being heated too fast, but it still had plenty of energy. The lamb came to life little by little, like a rag doll in a children's story. First, her eyes opened, then her legs got some life in them. She kicked them one by one, then I felt her body liven.

A while later, I got more colostrum from the Bertha who had lambed twelve hours earlier and fed it to the lamb from the bottle again. This time she was able to suck and I knew she would be all right. I had learned the hard way how important it is to make sure the milk is really flowing and that the lamb is really sucking. I named the lamb Pipsqueak. She grew to be a big, healthy sheep and lived out on Blue Island for many years.

That was my first lamb crop in New York. Three lambs weren't many, but it was a start.

Jonathan came for a visit in early May and helped me shear the Berthas and the young mother ewe. That is to say, he sat on one of the Berthas who wouldn't keep still! First, he sat on one side of her, then we rolled her over and he sat on the other side. The other two went well. A few days later I sheared the rest by myself.

I own about seven acres of pasture across the road and hired a man to bulldoze the brambles, as they were too thick to cut by hand. The day he was doing this, Clayton Karkosh was at my house, having spent the night on his way from New Mexico to Nova Scotia. We were having breakfast out on my little front porch when I heard the bulldozer start. I explained to Clayton what was going on. At the end of breakfast he said, "Let's go out and see how he's doing."

We walked over and found, to my horror, that the man had bulldozed two of my apple trees as well as the brambles. Thank heavens he hadn't gone very far. I yelled at him to stop and ask him what he thought he was doing. He said he'd been told to bulldoze everything in the field.

"This is a pasture, not a parking lot. Don't take down any more trees. Only the brambles."

I was relieved he hadn't gotten to the lovely big oak and maple farther on or the rest of the fruit trees. My concerns were not only aesthetic, but practical as well. Sheep need shade in the summer and spend much of the hot days under trees, coming out at dusk to graze. Too, they would enjoy the apple drops in the fall.

I spent most of the month of June installing an electric fence around the perimeter. The dealer who sold me the fence helped me set in the posts for the gate and showed me how to lay out the fencing and install the posts along the way. Nat, having been in the solar electric business for a while, supplied me with a solar panel that charges a battery which powers the fence. When it was all finished, I moved the sheep across the road into the "summer" pasture.

In July, I loaded the Berthas and three of the biggest yearlings into my truck for the long trip back to Nova Scotia. I hired a high school girl to keep an eye on the sheep that I left behind and to fill a tub with water for them daily. I crossed my fingers that all would go well and left. I had made reservations on the ferry leaving Portland for Yarmouth, which left at 9 PM and got to Nova Scotia at 8 AM the next morning. Once loaded into the ferry, I prevailed upon the loading crew to find me a spigot. I filled a bucket with water and hoisted it into the truck for my sheep. There was fresh hay in the front of their space, the windows were open, covered with my hardware cloth arrangement, and they were quite comfortable.

The men were intrigued with the sheep. For the nine years that I took sheep to and from Nova Scotia there were always crew held over from earlier years and they were always excited to see me and my sheep. "Oohhh, it's the sheep leddy. How are you?" Even now, five years after bringing my last load of sheep on the ferry, the men still remember me and ask "Where are the sheep?" in their wonderful Jamaican accents. This same ferry spent the winters as a cruise ship in the Caribbean.

While my boat was soaking up water in her seams, I went to Kingsburg to pick up the sheep that Dave Murphy had wintered over for me. I brought home Big Boy, the ram, seven mature ewes and one ewe lamb. I gave Dave the only other lamb that those sheep had borne. I put them in my big field on the mainland to await just the right time to put them on the island. Ever hopeful of catching all the male sheep on the island, I planned to keep Big Boy ashore until December, even if it meant making a special trip back up—or perhaps getting someone to take him out.

Now that I had my own dog that was reliable and keen and, more to the point, I knew how to work her, my summers settled into a fairly repetitious routine. I no longer went out to the island unless I could see sheep in the swamp or elsewhere on the front of the island. Some summers were more successful than others. I became less obsessive about catching them all, realizing that they did pretty well on their own. When I came across lambs with overbites I took them to the butcher. I didn't want them to breed or be bred. I caught eighteen sheep that summer in only three gathers. In one, I caught ten sheep that included five mature rams and a ram lamb. As exciting as that was, it didn't hold a candle to the gather that Tess made on our first try—even though only four sheep were involved.

On that occasion, we went out very early in the morning after seeing some sheep in the swamp. The outboard stalled in the harbor and I thought the day was doomed, but I finally got it started again and we went on.

Once on the island, I set up the fences as usual—one down the rocks to the ocean, the other across the wide path going up the hill through the black alders. Then Tess and I crept through the woods for about twenty minutes to get to the back of the swamp. We sneaked out into the swamp only to see that the four sheep were way down at the far end. If we showed ourselves, they would have such a head start on us that they would be long gone before we would have negotiated the thousand feet or so of rocks to where they were. So we beat it back through the woods to my cabin and sneaked out into the swamp from the east.

There is a big, broad spruce tree at the edge of the swamp and we kept it between ourselves and the sheep, but they must have heard us. They turned and trotted down the rocks away from us. I sent Tess out on a wide "away to me" (counterclockwise outrun) and she went so wide she disappeared over the pile of rocks. The sheep were racing by now and had passed a curve in the rocks and were on the last short leg remaining in the swamp when Tess shot into view over the rocks and stopped them dead in their tracks. I then raced along the rocks myself—or more like stumbled—to give her support. The sheep had the advantage: they are descended from mountain goats, evolutionwise, and this breed certainly showed its early ancestry.

When I got nearer the sheep, I noticed that they had drifted towards the water and were considering it as a possible escape route. I slowed down and edged towards the ocean myself and they moved away from the water. Tess was still behind them and we were able to turn the sheep and start driving them back in the right direction. We crossed the rocks, skirting the swamp in the usual stop-and-go fashion.

At the large rock outcropping, I let the sheep go along the water's edge while Tess and I walked through the bushes. The sheep came out the other side and Tess went berserk and split them. One pair went up into the bushes and the other pair came back towards the swamp. I sent Tess up into the bushes to get the first pair. She flushed them out and they joined the second pair. Then I sent Tess around all four of them and they all turned. We crossed the long beach with the sheep eyeing the water the whole way until we reached my little punt, which was pulled up on the beach. They shot up the beach as if to go into the bushes. The tide was so low that my fence going to the water ended before the water's edge, so I took the opportunity to hurry myself down to that opening while Tess kept them from going into the bushes. They looked at the pen and seemed to decide against it, but Tess flanked nicely and they changed their minds and went in. She waited for a pat and a thank you while I closed the gate, and threw herself into the ocean to cool off. Tess was now an indispensable asset to me, my right arm.

There were two very young ewes and two very small lambs. The ewes had lost their wool so I had no need to shear, but I had to go ashore to get ear tags, vaccines and worming medicine. I was back on the island by twelve-thirty in the pouring rain. They were so wild it was hard getting them into a corner, but with Tess's help we finally managed and closed them in with a gate. After doing the medicating, I tied the lambs' feet together and lugged each one down the rocks to my little punt, loaded them in, and went back to the pen to let the ewes go. Then I rowed Tess and the lambs out to the *Betsy* and loaded the lambs into her.

Arriving at the harbor, I realized just how tired I was when I noticed with pleasure about half a dozen teenagers swimming from the wharf. I asked them for help unloading the lambs and they graciously agreed. But when I commented on the filthy water they were swimming in, one of them said, "Would you rather I didn't touch your sheep?" That broke me up. I took note of their names and phone numbers for the future!

They loaded the lambs into my waiting truck and I put the lambs' heads close together so they wouldn't be frightened while I put the boat back on its mooring. Lambs like to snuggle up next to each other. On my return I found that the boys had placed one of my sneakers under the lambs' heads as a cushion. That broke me up again.

The following week I took the two Berthas and three other sheep out to the island. The Berthas had made two trips to Nova Scotia without getting on the island, so I was pleased to get them out there at last. Big Boy missed them, though, and mooned and bleated outside the barn. But the Berthas fought against their leg ropes and one of them limped when she got ashore. It is common practice to tie the legs together, but this was the first time one of my sheep had suffered from it. Later on that month, I saw her again and she was still limping. I hadn't liked tying their legs in the first place and this confirmed my feelings.

I decided to have a barge built that I could pull behind the *Betsy* so that I could load the sheep into it standing up. I designed a barge to be made of fiberglass that would have wooden fence sides and a high hinged transom (stern) that would drop down to form a ramp. I took the drawing to Sherman Williams, who had built the *Betsy*, and he said he would build me a barge over the winter. I called it *The Baa-rge*.

As successful as I was in gathering sheep that summer, I still missed a few, including two ram lambs. Therefore, it only made sense to put Big Boy on the island in the fall before going back to New York. At least, being a mature ram, he would have precedence over the young ones and would get to breed most of the ewes himself.

~ Twenty ~

I was delighted to find, upon my return to Greenville, that the sheep I had left there were in top condition in my new pasture across the road.

One of the yearlings that I had brought down from the island the year before captured my heart. I named her Misha, after Mikhail Baryshnikov. One warm winter day, after feeding them outdoors, Tess and I stood in the doorway of the hayloft and watched the sheep frolic. Spring must have been in the air. They ran the whole length of the field with Misha at the head. Suddenly she leapt into the air and, while still airborne, kicked her rear legs out behind her in a perfect ballet kick, giving her feet a bit of a twist at the end. We watched for half an hour as she did it again and again, each time racing the length of the field, finishing with a cabriole, the rest of the sheep following behind. It was entrancing. She was pregnant besides!

Lambing went well. Sometimes it was quite difficult to get the mothers into the barn when they lambed outdoors. What worked best was to hold the lamb in front of me and let the mother smell it and follow it into the barn. It didn't always work, but using my dog was difficult because the ewes were so protective of their newborns that they would attack her. One sheep was so wild that even after I had penned her, she would jump out of the pen each time I climbed into it.

Misha had a lovely little ewe lamb. What a fierce mother she was. If I rested my hand on the top of the pen side, she would butt it away—hard. When her lamb was about ten days old, I got a call from a local farmer whose son was in kindergarten. The boy had planned to take a baby goat to school the next day for "show and tell," but his grandfather had sold it that day. Poor Jason was broken-hearted, so his father asked me if I had a lamb I could bring to school for Jason. I took Misha's lamb and she was an angel. I held her on my lap while 210 adorable little children, all dutifully in line, each patted her. She didn't wet my lap and was quiet and good (doubtless terrified). Misha was probably going crazy in the barn.

Tess had her first litter of puppies in June, three males and a female.

In July, I was to perform in a summer theater in Westport, New York, on Lake Champlain. My hopes of continuing my career after leaving New York City were paying off. The parents of the producer had a big house where the actors stayed, surrounded by gardens and outbuildings. Tess and her puppies were happily ensconced in an outbuilding that had once housed turkeys and that had an outdoor run for them. Talk about benefits! After rehearsals, I would take them down to the lake for a swim. Once the play was running, I had more time to exercise the dogs.

We were performing a very funny play called *The Foreigner* by Larry Shue. One night during the opening scene, when I was on stage alone with one of the actors, I could hear some whispering in the audience. I looked out to see that every face was in profile. Not a single person was looking at the play, so I broke character and whispered to the actor "What's going on?" "A mouse" came the reply.

I looked again. The theater, located in the old baggage department of a railroad station, was more than sold out and folding chairs had been placed in the outer aisles.

A man, sitting in one of the folding chairs, had noticed a mouse running along a rafter just above him. Next to the man was a vertical pipe which he was tapping on. He would tap on the pipe just as the mouse reached it and the mouse would turn around and run the other way. The mouse would then turn around and try to run back and the man would tap on the pipe again. And so on. *And so on.* Another play was going on besides ours, and the entire audience was watching it.

My character was the owner of a hotel in the Georgia hills that the building inspector was threatening to close down. So I said in a loud voice, "Wayull, we may have rats and maas, but this old hotel is perfectly safe." Every head snapped forward and I had my audience back.

Another night when most of the cast was on stage and the "foreigner" was telling the story of Little Red Riding Hood in broken English, a bat flew right over his head. "Ooohh, batksy watsky" he said, and brought down the house. My dogs weren't the only theater animals that summer.

The show over, I drove back to Greenville and packed up to leave for Nova Scotia immediately. I noticed that Misha seemed to have diarrhea, but I loaded her in with the four other sheep in the back with Tess and two puppies in the front with all my bags.

We arrived in Nova Scotia with Misha looking very sluggish. I called the vet and he said he'd come the next day. But she died that night.

I took her body to the vet's for an autopsy. I had vaccinated her in the spring, but perhaps the needle went through her skin to the outside or maybe the vaccine was weak, but she had died of one of the diseases that I vaccinate for. She might have died anyway in New York, but the stress of the trip made it inevitable. I was desolate. My beautiful dancer who gave me so much pleasure, my beautiful, tough, excellent mother. Only two years old.

People ask me how I can bear to have my lambs slaughtered when I clearly love my sheep so much, and even more seriously, how I can eat them. My answer to the second concern is easy: I know what they've eaten. Or more importantly, I know what they *haven't* eaten. My lambs are given antibiotics only if they are very sick, never given hormones, and are wormed minimally. I pay close attention to withdrawal periods for any medication and usually double the time. But in fact, most get no medication. Many large lamb producers routinely put hormones and antibiotics into the feed and these lambs end up at the supermarket.

But there is a broader answer to both questions, which is that I raise lambs for food. *They are not pets* and I studiously avoid making them pets. I find them as cute as everyone else does and I take care of them and delight in their progress, but I know right from the start that most of them will go to the butcher and I don't name them or become attached.

I remember the first time I had lambs butchered in Nova Scotia. The butcher insisted on coming to the farm and slaughtering them there. (I never did that again.) I took the dogs into the kitchen, closed the doors and turned on the radio as loud as I could stand so as not to hear the lambs being shot. But when it was over and I went out to see, I was surprised at my reaction. I felt proud that I had raised food in a hungry world. Taking lambs to the butcher isn't fun, but it has to be done and I'm always glad when it's over. The praise I get from my meat customers makes it worthwhile. By the time the sheep are grown, though, it is a different matter. Like every other animal, human or otherwise, I like some more than others and I do become attached, sometimes deeply so.

In early September, Betty Levin came with her two dogs, Kelty and Mab, for a visit. I hadn't seen any sheep in the swamp yet that summer and had no particular hope that we would find any, but we went out anyway. We set up my fences as usual and crept through the woods to the back of the swamp. There, right in front of us, were twenty-one sheep. With all that wonderful help they were brought into the pen in no time. Having three dogs and two humans to keep the sheep under control at the tough spots made all the difference.

An old friend of Betty's, who was not well, lived near the Bay of Fundy in Nova Scotia. For several years, usually just after Labor Day, Betty would spend a couple of days with me out on Blue Island helping to catch my sheep before going to visit her friend. As was the case when I was alone, sometimes we found sheep and sometimes not, but we always had a good time. I really appreciated her help.

While we were shearing my sheep the next day, we noticed that one old ewe had a very stuffy nose. Betty said it was one of two things: either a tumor (she had just had a similar one in one of her sheep) or a nose bot, which is a larva from a particular kind of fly that lays its eggs in the nostrils of animals. Nasty habit. The tumor would soon be fatal if that's what it was, but the nose bot was treatable with a wormer that I had in stock.

Betty suggested taking her back with me to New York because, as she said, "You might get another lamb out of her." Not only did I get another lamb out of her, she had triplets for three years in a row, then slowed down to twins until she died at thirteen! She was an extraordinary mother, feeding all of her lambs with no help from me. I named her BOTILO, after my Nova Scotia zip code, B0T 1L0, or Botty for short.

Because of Betty's good advice, I named Botty's first ewe lamb after her, then felt badly because she turned out to be a pain, stubborn and uncooperative. I called Betty to apologize. "That's all right," said Betty, "just think about the things you don't like about me that you can associate with her."

The first time I sheared the lamb, she kicked so much I had to sit on her and shear her backwards from the usual pattern. The result was that I nicked her all over the place. I treated her with Blucoat, an antiseptic which I keep on hand for cuts. I made the mistake of holding the bottle in one hand while I used the dauber to apply the Blucoat. Betty (the lamb) kicked the hand that held the bottle and it splashed all over her, her horns, her body, her legs, everywhere.

When Blucoat hits the air, it turns purple. The lamb looked awful and it served her right. It would be weeks before the color wore off.

That day on Blue Island was truly a bonanza. Of the twenty-one sheep that we caught, eight were lambs and three were rams, including Big Boy. We had three young men to help. Betty and I sheared seven of the ewes. We would take twelve sheep off the island—the lambs, the rams and Botty—enough to use my new barge. No longer did we have to tie their feet together and lug them down the shore, but instead led each sheep separately, on foot, down the rocks to the *Baarge*'s ramp and in. I had specified that a gate be placed across the inside of the barge, halfway in, so the sheep would be secure while we got more.

~ *Twenty-One* ~

In Greenville my new house and barn were nearly finished. The house is on top of a ridge with views of the Ramapo Mountains to the east and the Catskills to the north. Facing due south, it is solar-heated, with a greenhouse and a stone wall inside to collect the heat from the sun. It works well and is a wonderful house to live in. The barn is a two-story building with a large space for sheep down below, where I can set up pens for ewes and their newborns, and a shepherd's room in the corner where I often sleep during lambing. Upstairs is a huge hayloft. Since the barn is set into a hill, the hayloft is at grade level for convenience in unloading hay and in feeding during the winter months.

Nat helped me set in posts for an electric fence that would enclose the field the house is in. It extends into the woods behind the barn for the sheep to be able to get into the shade in the hot weather. I rented a gas-powered post-hole digger and Nat and I went at it to get the holes dug for the gate and corner posts. The soil is shale and clay and even the powered digger wasn't very enthusiastic about getting through it. Nat and I held onto it for dear life and several holes got dug. Luckily, Jonathan came for the weekend and he and Nat finished the job.

By the end of November the house was ready and my sons helped me move the furniture and boxes up the mountain to my new home. After they were gone, I moved the animals with Tess's help. They came up the driveway pretty well, went into the barn, then went out the other end into the field.

No sooner had I moved into my new house than I had an opportunity I couldn't resist. By a happy coincidence, several friends of mine were living temporarily in various countries close to the equator in Africa and the South Pacific, so I planned a three-month trip around the world

I was able to arrange with Cathy Cook, a friend who used to live in Nova Scotia, to come and take care of Tess and my sheep while I was gone. Cathy had never worked with sheep before, but there's not that much to do between breeding and lambing, so when, on New Year's Day, my ram butted me, I became concerned. This could be dangerous. I had gone out with hay to put into the hay feeder, as usual, and he charged me out of the blue. As I ran to the barn, he butted me in the rear end, good and hard, and then butted me a third time. I pulled down the garage-style door in the barn and he butted that. As I watched, the door pushed in a good six inches.

I really didn't want to leave Cathy with such an animal. There was only a week to go before my departure. At the same time, I wanted to give the ram a chance just in case his behavior was a fluke. I tried feeding him on the ground, thinking that maybe his wide horns were keeping him from getting enough hay out of the feeder. I tried raising the door just a few inches and shoving the hay out through the gap. Still, I didn't think the ewes were getting enough and I had to get to the feeder somehow. One day, I went out with an armload of hay. The ram came at me and I ran around the feeder, first one way then the other. We played keepaway for a while until finally I gained enough distance on him to make a dash for the barn. Slamming down the door, I kept right on running to phone my fence supplier, who knew a butcher. Bob, the fencer, kindly arranged with his butcher to meet me at Bob's farm. Somehow, I got the ram into my truck with some neighbors' help and got him to Bob's place. By this time the ram had dented the body of my truck considerably. It could have been me. I asked the butcher to slaughter the ram, hang him for two weeks and then freeze him whole. I was planning a huge barbecue party after my trip. The butcher sent the skin to a tanner. It lies on the floor in front of the fireplace in Nova Scotia and the dogs love to lie on it.

My trip was better than my wildest expectations. I alternated each hectic week visiting friends with a week alone by the sea. I went on safari with friends in Kenya and visited other friends in Zimbabwe. In Australia I stayed on a sheep farm with friends of the Nettletons and then went to Sydney to spend a few days with a cousin of mine. My last destination was Papua New Guinea to join Martha and Brian Nettleton in Mendi, where they were living in the Southern Highlands.

Papua New Guinea (PNG) is a country of extremes: steep mountains that look like upside-down Vs all bunched together, steamy, impenetrable jungles below. Temperatures in the highlands are a pleasant seventy to eighty degrees by day and quite chilly at night. The lowland jungles are tropical. Because of the terrain, roads are few and travel is still largely by plane.

Unfortunately, Martha was quite sick with a malaria-like illness. Their daughter Sarah was visiting them while I was there. I'm very fond of Sarah and we were able to take over many of the chores that Martha was too ill to do. The Nettletons were in PNG with CUSO (Canadian University Service Organization), rather like our Peace Corps. Their original aim had been to set up a marketing system for livestock, but by the time I got there, they had been in PNG for six years and their focus had changed completely. Concerned at the lack of protein in the local diet, they wanted to introduce sheep. Some years earlier, some New Zealanders had tried putting sheep into the country. They had simply dumped—there's no better word—a thousand sheep into the provinces, providing no help whatsoever in how to care for them. The sheep all died and the project was considered a failure. The lack of communication lines within the country made this inevitable.

Brian and Martha tried a different approach. They introduced a few sheep at a time into the school system, where the children were taught how to care for them and how to shear. The sheep grazed on the abundant grass outdoors all the school day, then the children shut them up in a barn at night at the school. By 1988, when I got there, there were small flocks of sheep in sixty-five different schools. Those children who showed a keen interest in shepherding were given a small flock of three ewes and a ram at graduation, so they could start their own flock.

Brian felt that sheep could be beneficial to the Papua New Guineans in two ways. First, the meat would provide more protein in their diet, since the only meat they ate was pork. Domestic pigs roamed free in the countryside and were slaughtered only for special occasions. The pigs did a lot of environmental damage, which infuriated Brian, so he was trying to encourage a different meat animal.

Second, the sheep would provide health benefits. Although PNG is a tropical country, the highlands are high indeed and the nights are very cool, so that wool would be a welcome commodity. Families live in small huts with a fire in the middle and only a small hole in the roof to let out the smoke. To keep warm, they huddle around the fire at night and, as a result, there is a high incidence of lung disease. Brian suggested that it would be much better to sleep warmly on sheepskins and not be exposed to smoke all night long.

He was a sheep missionary, finding ways that sheep and wool could improve people's lives and even their land.

Sarah and I went on a two-day trip with one of the Nettletons' local colleagues to deliver some sheep to one town and to pick some up in another. We spent the night with another CUSO couple, Jim and Lorna Logan, who were teaching at the Nipa Vocational School. Next day, we visited the school and watched the children learn how to shear sheep. Sarah went to a classroom taking some raw (unspun) wool. She made a spindle by piercing an apple with an arrow and taught the children how to spin yarn. Out came some more apples and more arrows and pretty soon all the children were spinning very successfully.

Later, back in Mendi, Brian showed me a letter he had received from Alf Wight, aka James Herriot. Because, under British law, the use of a vet's actual name could be considered advertising and therefore illegal, Dr. Wight had been obliged to change all the names in his books. Years earlier, Brian had been one of Dr. Wight's young vets that came to the practice to get his start and Dr. Wight was now writing Brian asking permission to use him in his next book, to Brian's great delight. Dr. Wight pointed out that he had already put Brian into the latest TV series under the name Calum Buchanan. The book, *Every Living Thing*, was published in 1992 and was Herriot's last.

Brian left PNG a week before I did to be with his daughter, Fiona, in New Zealand while she competed in the International Golden Shears competition. Fiona won first place in the Junior Class, the first Canadian and only the third woman ever to win it. I flew down to be with them both. I was delighted to see Brian's old New Zealand friends, Anne and Philip Woodward and Kent and Pam Wright again, whom I had met that night so many years earlier when Brian had lost his shoe at the sheep fair in Nova Scotia. I asked Brian if he had seen the James Herriot series in which he was a central character. He said yes, and then ran his finger down his cheek to show me he had shed a few tears.

I stayed there for a couple of days and spent most of one day in a shearing shed where Fiona, Philip and two others were shearing. They work a nine-hour day with two fifteen-minute tea-breaks mid morning and mid-afternoon and an hour and a half for a huge lunch at noon. Between the four of them, they sheared fourteen hundred sheep. Fiona broke two hundred that day, which meant she had to buy a case of beer for the others. I don't think I ever sheared more than fifteen sheep in one day—but then, I never had to. It takes a lot of practice to get to be that fast and that good as well.

I went down to the South Island and stayed on a sheep farm that was a B&B, owned by Kate and Ron Shaw. I joined Ron in hiking up their high fields to gather sheep. Because the terrain is so huge and the hills so steep, they use a dog called a Huntaway to spook the sheep out into the open. Ron signaled to the dog and he galloped out, barking like mad, finding sheep under bushes and in gullies. How different from the Border Collie, who works quietly and uses her eye to control the sheep. Still, the Huntaway was very effective that day and his stamina was extraordinary. Then Ron called in his Huntaway and used his header dog, a Border Collie type, to round up the sheep and bring them in.

Ron had given me a ski pole to negotiate the rugged slopes. We had already climbed one hill and Ron wanted to look on the other side of another. Sensing that I was near the end of my energy, he gave me the task of looking for stray sheep in the fields where we were. In the course of my search, I heard the bleating of a young lamb. I climbed to the bottom of the hill and found the lamb, too weak to stand, but otherwise a nice fifty-pound lamb. I lifted him over my shoulders and started climbing the mountain to our meeting place. It was too steep to walk sideways—I kept slipping like Sisyphus's stone—so I climbed straight up, slowly, slowly, using the cleats on my climbing boots and the ski pole when I could spare that hand from holding the lamb. At the top I met Ron.

"Oh, thank you, Anne. I'm so grateful to you. But the gate is down at the bottom of the mountain you just climbed up."

"Here, you take the lamb," I said, laughing.

Ron told me that a heavy worm infestation had caused the lamb's weakness. Because the fields are grazed intensively, a worm build-up occurs and lambs must be wormed every three weeks.

The Shaws received busloads of people daily. Ron would demonstrate his header dog's work, shear a sheep and give a little talk. Then Kate would give them a plate of homemade goodies and tea. It was another way for farmers to bring in some income.

They invited me to join them at a dinner party with some friends of theirs, also sheep farmers. At the time, President Bush (the first) was making a big fuss over the subsidies that foreign countries gave their farmers. The Shaws' friends wanted to know if sheep farmers in the United States received any subsidies. At that point, the only subsidy we received was a price-support program for our wool, financed by duties levied on imported lamb (mostly from New Zealand). The New Zealanders resented this hypocrisy and I didn't blame them. But they were curious about how the program worked.

Using my own wool as an example, I started to explain

how much I was paid for my wool and how much the government kicked in. "For instance," I said, "I took one hundred pounds of wool to the wool pool—"

The entire table exploded in laughter. "One hundred pounds!" They repeated this and were convulsed all over again.

Finally, to ease my confusion, someone explained that an average New Zealand farmer will sell *ten thousand* pounds of wool each year. They are sheep farmers and I just raise a few sheep. There is a vast difference.

But it's not the only difference. At the time, a N.Z. farmer would receive $9 per head for his lambs. That was nine N.Z. dollars, which was then around five U.S. dollars. I netted $150 (U.S.) per lamb. But I had to feed hay for at least six months of the year, which cost a lot. Most N.Z. sheep are on grass year-round. In the eastern U.S., it takes roughly six hundred sheep to support a family, assuming the farmer grows his own hay. In N.Z. it takes two thousand sheep. I was told that the human population of New Zealand at the time was around six million. The sheep population numbered sixty million.

When I arrived home in Greenville, I found to my astonishment that all the sheep except Botty had lambed. Three sets of twins and a single. Was my timing ever off! I had failed to separate the ram from the ewes early enough in the autumn. Different breeds come into estrus at slightly different times. Scottish Blackface come in quite late. Still, I had misjudged it. Fortunately, poor Cathy had done a super job. I had left Betty Levin's phone number for her and Betty talked her through all the births and told her what to do afterward. Everybody was fine, including Cathy. The lambs were big and healthy too. Strangely enough, all were males.

Three weeks later Botty gave birth to triplets amid loud shrieks and groans. The sounds were disturbingly human. She was so exhausted after the first lamb that she didn't get to her feet at all for the second one. I pulled the lamb around so she could lick it off and wiped away the mucus from its mouth. Taking a break for dinner, I returned to find that a third lamb had been born while I was in the house. Only one of the triplets was a female, the purple ewe, which was another good reason to have got rid of the ram. It's a slow road to build up a flock if only one lamb out of eight is a ewe.

～ *Twenty-Two* ～

For two summers I had been catching sheep on the island that had been born in New York and were used to the dog. I called them my 'New Yorkers.' Over the years, I found that I caught my New Yorkers over and over again throughout the summer, but they helped me because on each of those occasions they brought in some island sheep that hadn't yet been caught that year. I was always glad to see them, relieved that they had made it through another winter on the island.

Big Boy's horns were extremely close. One of his horns was resting so hard on his head that it made a wound, which was being attacked by maggots. I had to sedate him and, with the help of a friend who held him, I sawed slices off the bottom side of this horn with a wire saw so that it no longer touched the top of his head. But the genes for close horns were still there, of course, and I felt I shouldn't keep him anymore. I deeply regretted having to make the decision. Big Boy was a magnificent animal and easy to handle, which was certainly not true of many rams. He would stand still, untied, while I gave him a shot or wormed him orally. Furthermore, he was a calming influence on the flock, making them much easier to handle when he was with them in the barn or the field.

Dave Murphy needed two new rams. He kept his sheep on a peninsula on the mainland, near Lunenburg, where he could keep an eye on them, so he was willing to take a chance with a ram with close horns. I took Big Boy down to Dave's at the end of the summer, along with a yearling ram.

Before taking Big Boy away, I caught a young ram on the island and brought him off, but intended to take him back out again later for breeding. Aware that Big Boy might fight him (his "calming influence" stopped when it came to other rams), I intended to keep them apart, but Tess fouled up the process of separating the sheep and Big Boy went after the young ram. The latter was soon bleeding from his mouth and nose.

The new tenants in my cottage, Val and Ray Schuler, came to my assistance. Ray helped me get the young ram away from Big Boy. As we led him to the other pasture, I noticed that his horn was loose and assumed that Big Boy had broken the bone that runs inside the horn. What you see of a sheep's horn is a hollow sheath that covers a heavy bone extending about halfway up the inside of the horn. Beyond the bone, the horn is solid down to the end. Unlike deer's antlers, which are entirely made of horn and which are shed each year, sheep horns are permanent. They keep growing until the ram is fully mature at about five years of age. Oddly, they don't use their horns as weapons, but a horned sheep's head is very heavy and the horns add to the force exerted when they butt each other for primacy.

What to do? I didn't want to take him out to the island, feeling that he might not make it through the winter. I approached Val and Ray with the idea of leaving him in the pasture for the winter with a ten-year-old ewe for company.

They were delighted to have two sheep to take care of. Val named them Blossom and Sam. Sam's horn mended over the winter; he bred Blossom and she had triplets. I took her to New York the following fall where, like Botty, she had triplets two more times and then twins.

~ Twenty-Three ~

Nat and I made plans to go up to Maine to spend Christmas with Jonathan and his fiancée, Marnie Cooper, who were to be married three days afterwards. Each had a child by a former marriage. Marnie's son, Clay, a blond bundle of energy, was six and Jonathan's little girl, Liz, was four. Marnie was living in an old house on a property owned by her parents. Several years earlier her father, a large-animal vet with a practice in the area, had bought four hundred acres of woodland on a peaceful lake. Marnie's sister and one brother also lived on the place with their families. I was very happy that Marnie and Jonathan were to be married.

In mid-December, Elizabeth Hyde called me from Nova Scotia with the terrible news of Brian's death. He and Martha had come home on three months' leave from Papua New Guinea to spend Christmas with their family. Brian was driving to the airport at ten-thirty in the morning to pick up Martha and Sarah, who were flying in from Ontario. He ran head-on into another car and was killed immediately.

The driver of that car said Brian had suddenly switched to the left side of the road and crashed into him. Chili, the Jack Russell terrier who had so won my heart, was with him on the front seat and was killed too. Martha thinks that after driving on the left in PNG for all those years, he had gotten mixed up. I wonder if he hadn't seen an interesting bird through the windshield and, while trying to view the bird better, leaned down and inadvertently pushed the wheel over to the left. The loss was terrible for his family and his many friends. He was always talking about the impact of sheep on Blue Island and elsewhere too. Well, Brian himself made an impact on our world, all right.

No one was neutral about Brian. He felt so strongly about his issues that people either loved him or were enraged by him. He was very generous, passionate about getting a healthy sheep industry going in Nova Scotia, devoted to his family, impatient with short-sightedness and rightly intolerant of betrayal. He helped many of us get going and keep going, many people besides me.

Although I was sure he had been notified, since he and the Nettletons were still close friends, I wrote to James Herriot because I wanted him to know how pleased Brian had been when he got his letter asking permission to put Brian in his next book. Mr. Herriot wrote back a lovely letter, describing Brian as a born naturalist, "larger than life," and remembered his arrival at the clinic with a badger around his neck. His letter reminded me of the day Brian and Sarah and I were climbing in the highlands of Papua New Guinea. A bird flew by about 50 feet away. Brian was ecstatic. "It's a merlin!" he cried happily. "It's the first one I've seen."

After Jonathan's wedding I went up to Nova Scotia to spend a few days over New Year's with the Nettleton family. It was a warm and painful reunion. I asked Martha what her plans were. She replied that she had signed a contract just before leaving Papua New Guinea to teach for a year in Mendi, the town near where they lived. She wanted to honor that contract, and besides, she had no real work to do in Nova Scotia. But she wanted to wait for a month until the mourning period for Brian in PNG would be over. He was much loved there, she said, and the people would cry all the time and she couldn't stand that. As it was, when she went back, they said to her they were so glad she had come to tell them of Brian's death because they wouldn't have believed it otherwise. She was very touched, but it was not easy. They cried anyway.

Because Brian was "larger than life," he dominated the scene, but Martha was his anchor to windward. Each time he came down to help me with my sheep, he would always phone "the boss" as soon as he arrived. I don't think he could have functioned without her. True, he was intelligent, an extremely competent veterinarian and farmer, forceful and even bloody-minded at times, very knowledgeable about plants and all sorts of animals not in his practice. But I always felt Martha was crucial to his very being.

It wasn't until after Brian's death that I came to know Martha and to enjoy our growing friendship. Also, with six children, aged from eight to fourteen when I met them, she was heavily occupied at the time. She's the kind of person that gets things done without seeming to—she just does them. Her sense of humor is understated and quite wonderful. When she was in PNG after Brian's death, she wanted to get away for the Christmas holiday, so she and a friend went to Thailand and traveled up into the hinterland where most tourists don't go, sleeping in cabins on wooden floors. She described her friend to me: "Anne-Marie was the perfect traveling companion. She never complained about anything, even when she got her leg caught between two elephants."

Children are attracted to Martha because she genuinely likes them without making a fuss—she's very British. She's firm with them and they appreciate it. Upon her return to Nova Scotia after her final year in Papua New Guinea, she wanted a job where she would be needed. She found it, in spades. She worked for a family for a year where the father had terminal cancer, but was still functioning, the eldest son was autistic and seriously retarded, and the five-year old twin girls were healthy with the exception that one of them was profoundly deaf. Martha stepped in and became the lifeline they all needed. A decade later the twins still visit her in Cape Breton for a month each summer.

⁓

I returned to New York after the New Year to some devastating dog kills on my farm. I was wintering my six ewe lambs in the summer pasture, which was a half-mile down my driveway and across the road. Dogs got in and chased three of the lambs out through the fence and killed a fourth one. The morning it happened, my neighbor, Bill Koselnak, called to tell me that a wounded lamb was in his yard and he had caught it. My four-year-old granddaughter, Liz, was staying with me, so I strapped her in the front seat of my truck and rushed down the mountain, passing my summer pasture on the way to Bill's. There, in the pasture, lay a lamb on the ice. I went in to the field to get her. She was still alive, but had been disemboweled. I went on to Bill's and asked him to come shoot the lamb in the field. He loaded the wounded one in the back of my truck and came with me to put the other one down. That left only two in the field. I penned them and brought them up to the barn where I had isolated the wounded one.

For days I looked for the two missing lambs. That first day, Bill's two older children tramped through the thick woods with me, looking for signs of the lambs, while Bill's wife, Bunny, and her youngest boy entertained my little granddaughter. We kept finding bits of wool hanging from twigs, evidence of their passage. After Liz went home, I looked through all the surrounding woods for many more days. One neighbor said he had seen the lamb and that his German Shepherd was "playing" with it, running around it in circles.

"Your dog may have been having fun, but it was most certainly not fun for the lamb. It was sure to be terrified," I said.

He had another dog, an Akita, who roamed the woods all day and all night. This dog had killed a neighbor's cat and harassed other dogs who were tied up.

"Your Akita runs all over town, threatening your neighbors' animals. You ought to keep him home. There's a leash law in this town."

"I have four hundred acres and my dog can run where he likes. Besides, a veterinarian told me that dogs don't kill sheep."

"That's pure baloney and you know it. I suspect your dog killed my lamb."

"Get out of here."

Months later he came into the ATM lobby of the bank where I was, alone.

"Somebody shot my Akita," he said. "Was it you?"

I was quite frightened. The bank was closed and there was no one about. His tone was menacing. At the same time, his news made me want to shout for joy!

"No," I said. "I don't know anything about it. I've been away in Canada."

He nodded and left. I learned later that others had been victimized by this dog.

One day, Bill Koselnak's daughter, Mary, phoned to tell me that she and other kids on the school bus had seen a dead lamb from the bus. She described where it was and I went to look. I found great clumps of wool on the ground every ten feet or so until I found the dead lamb, horribly mutilated. I wept bitter tears.

Dog owners simply don't understand how their beloved,

sweet-tempered dog—"He is sooo good with children"—could hunt down sheep. I point out that dogs' instincts towards sheep are quite different from their relationship to children. Dogs will see sheep in a pasture and be attracted to go in. When dogs chase sheep, the sheep's flight arouses the feral instinct in dogs. They attack them just as a wolf would. It is a basic instinct in a dog—he doesn't kill to eat, he kills to kill. Dogs will often leave a wounded sheep and go on to the next. It's all in the fun of the chase.

Sheep can die of fright too. Their hearts just stop. Furthermore, even if they aren't killed, they may reabsorb their fertilized eggs if they are pregnant. Then, the loss is in not having any lambs in the spring.

But there was still one lamb left to be found. I continued the search, finding bits of wool on a barbed wire fence right next to the road leading south. Another neighbor, John Wieboldt, said his wife had seen a sheep across the state line on a horse farm in New Jersey. My heart raced. That farm was south of me, over two and a half miles beyond where I had seen the bits of wool on the barbed wire, a long distance for a lone lamb to stray. I followed the road into New Jersey, one mile from my driveway. It had been a month since the attacks and I held out little hope for finding the lamb, but I just had to keep on looking. Perhaps the sheep John's wife had seen was my lamb.

About a mile away from my house I saw a man leaving his house, leading a small boy by the hand. I stopped, willing to try anything.

"Excuse me, sir, but by any chance have you seen a lamb going by here within the past month?"

The man, who introduced himself as John Anderson, seemed astonished at the question and I explained what had happened. He said he hadn't seen my lamb, but he had grown up on a farm, his brother raised sheep in Idaho and he had some experience. If I needed help, I was to call him. That was a welcome offer.

I kept on going for another mile and reached the horse farm where a man was feeding his horses. I asked him if the lamb was there.

"No," he said, pointing, "but there is a sheep down that road in a pasture with a horse and some beef cattle. It's not a lamb, though. Too big to be a lamb."

My heart racing even more, I continued down the road, and there she was, my young lamb, standing on top of a manure pile in a field near a horse, who was sharing his hay with her. The cattle were in a separate space.

How to catch her? She was alone and a single sheep will panic. In any case, being a lamb off the island, she wasn't used to my dog. The fencing left a good deal to be desired, being designed for cattle and horses. She had come in through the fence with no trouble and wouldn't hesitate to go out again.

The horse and cattle belonged to someone who lived in the city and kept them as an investment, but by chance the man hired to feed them was there. I thought up a plan and asked him if he would mind if I fed the horse for a few days. He didn't mind. "Do what you have to do!" he said with a smile.

For a couple of days I brought hay for the horse in the field and got him used to me. There was a small lean-to in the same field. A few days later, I put the hay in the lean-to. The horse went right in and the lamb followed. My plan was working. Next day I brought some portable gates from home and attached one to each side of the lean-to. I put the hay inside. The animals went in and I closed the gates.

Now to get some help. I drove back up the road and

found John Anderson, the nice man with the little boy. He suggested we let the horse out so he wouldn't kick us. We did that and the lamb scooted out behind him before we could catch her. Now the animals were wary and didn't want to go in. I hunted around in the barn, found some grain and led the horse back in. Again the lamb followed. I went in and grabbed the lamb while John held the horse. John took over and carried the lamb back to the truck and I drove her home. I named her Magic. The other lambs seemed very glad to see her. They surrounded her and gave out quiet murmurs. John Anderson and his partner, Susan Sanford, and I have remained good friends.

My friend Betty suggested I put a bell on one of my sheep. Then, if a dog were chasing the flock, I would hear the bell. It seemed like a good idea, so I put a bell on Botty because she was my oldest sheep and the other sheep respected her. She was quite bossy and I figured that if she ran for shelter the other sheep might follow her.

I decided I needed a guard animal. There are three kinds of animals that guard sheep: donkeys, several breeds of guard dogs and llamas. I didn't know anything about llamas and a dog was impractical for me, since I was away in Nova Scotia for three months in the summer. A donkey made the most sense, since they eat grass alongside the sheep. Donkeys protect sheep in several ways. Their imposing presence alone is a strong deterrent to intruders. But if a dog or coyote should manage to get into the pasture, the donkey will chase it down and stomp on it.

A friend had bought a guard donkey from John Conter in Montana and was delighted with her purchase, so I called

John. His specialty was spotted asses—they are quite small and very expensive. Cute as they are, I didn't need an expensive spotted ass, so I settled for a six-year old white jennet (pronounced jenny—a female). Donkeys have an instinctive hatred of all canines—dogs and coyotes alike. I would have to protect my dog until the donkey got used to her.

One day there was a message on my machine. "Your little white ass is on a truck on its way to you." John gave me the name of the truck driver, Randy, and a phone number where I could reach him to arrange for delivery.

I called the number and was so excited that, when a woman answered, I blurted out, "My little white ass is on a truck coming east and I need to talk to Randy."

"We-yull, thet syounds interestin'," she observed. I was relieved to find that she wasn't Randy's wife!

John had told me the donkey's name was Blanca, because she was white, but I didn't much like the name. It sounded too much like Blank. I played around with several other names, but when the truck arrived and I saw my donkey, I knew at once who she was. Eeyore!

Eeyore spent the first week staring into the woods. I figured she was dreaming of Montana. She was very shy and it took a while for her to let me touch her. She had been sold to some people in Montana for a while and I think they must have beaten her, as she would jump away if I even raised my hand. Even now, more than ten years later, she runs away if I'm carrying a stick and she doesn't like men at all. But we're great friends and I hug her almost every day.

Now that I have had several donkeys, I know how affectionate they can be. Eeyore has had three babies over the years and they love being hugged, and even demand it by coming over to me and leaning against me. And they are effective. Friends have ridden by the field on horseback and observed

Eeyore shadowing them the whole length of the fence until they were out of sight. A man who walked his dog on the road told me the same thing.

⌒

In the spring, I decided to buy another Border Collie puppy. Tess was still healthy and useful, but since I couldn't run my farm without a dog, it seemed wise to get another dog started that would be ready to take her place in case anything happened to her. With the huge challenge of gathering sheep on the island, I needed a long time to get her properly trained.

Betty recommended a litter of puppies out of a bitch whose work she liked very much. Since I admired Betty's bitch, Kelty, enormously and loved the quiet way she worked, I took the recommendation seriously and went to see the puppies at Mike Canaday's farm in Altamont, New York. I wanted a female and there were only two females in the litter. They were two weeks old, an age at which absolutely nothing shows that's of any use, but I chose the one that licked my nose and seemed to enjoy being on my tummy. I would return in a few weeks to pick her up.

Meanwhile, I took all the sheep down to the summer pasture in my truck, but had to lead Eeyore down. She didn't want to go. I pulled on the lead, I talked to her, I offered her some corn. No go. I called Bill Wieboldt, my elderly next-door neighbor, and he drove up to my farm. He clicked his tongue and she followed him down. But once she was in the summer pasture, she wouldn't cross the wet places. John Conter told me that donkeys are fearful of getting stuck in mud and don't like to cross streams or muddy areas. I tried getting on her back and riding her across. No way. Finally, I had to bring some boards down to build a bridge for her to walk on. Even then, I had to lure her along with grain. Then she came to another wet patch. No go. This was becoming ridiculous. I got Tess to gather some sheep and drive them across the wet place so that Eeyore could see for herself that it was safe. She followed the sheep happily and has never again had any problems with the wetness there. Donkeys come by their reputation for stubbornness honestly.

The sheep have never shown the slightest fear of the donkey from the moment she arrived. Lambs run under her belly and between her legs, apparently without thinking twice about it, not that lambs think twice about anything very much. Eeyore gets impatient with them sometimes and kicks at them, but not hard. More of a nudge than a swift kick.

Now that I had a farm in New York, I could raise sheep with beautiful wool, wool that I could knit into garments. I bought my first two from Betty, two black Border Leicester lambs. Their wool is soft and crimpy, quite different from the straight, coarse, hairy wool of the Scottish Blackface sheep that I had on the island. The Scottish Blackface were perfect for island living, being very tough; they were able to live on very little, give birth to twins, get fat during the summer even when nursing lambs and be ready to breed again in the fall. The Leicesters, on the other hand, couldn't survive a winter on Blue Island. They need more to eat than the Blackies, so I would have to keep them in New York.

On the way back from Betty's with the lambs, I stopped to pick up my new puppy. During the ride home, Tess was in her usual place on the floor in front of the passenger seat. The lambs were in the back of my truck and the puppy, whom I named Nell, was in my lap for most of the ride. I wanted her to bond with me right from the start. After a time, she decided to investigate Tess. She seemed to think Tess might have a bit of milk down there. Tess nearly took her head off, so she beat a retreat to my lap. Tess sat up, with her body facing me but her head facing the door. She remained that way for the rest of the trip, reminding me of nothing so much as a wounded wife whose husband has brought his mistress home.

I let the new lambs out in the summer pasture where the other sheep were. But the sheep were all at the other end of the field, way out of sight. So I got Tess to drive the lambs across the long pasture, so that they would know there were other sheep to be with and wouldn't panic and perhaps try to get out through the electric fence. The little lambs bleated all the way. When they were halfway to the end and were clearly going to continue in that direction, I ran back out onto the road. I wanted to see what would happen when they met the main flock.

When the little lambs appeared, all the heads of the sheep shot up. For a moment they stared at these two little black creatures coming towards them. Then they took off and ran away, with the two little lambs in hot pursuit, bleating at the top of their lungs. The sheep thought the lambs, being black, were dogs. It was very funny and quite poignant at the same time. The lambs wanted nothing more than to be with other sheep.

Tess continued to be jealous of Nell until one day, shortly after bringing Nell home, we all went for a walk down the driveway. Nell took off. The driveway is a third of a mile long, yet I irrationally panicked, fearing that she would bolt all the way to the end and out onto the road. I sent Tess on a "go-bye" (clockwise around the sheep). She understood at once and went neatly around Nell and stopped at twelve o'clock. Nell promptly turned around and came back to me. That cured Tess of her jealousy. She had found out who was boss.

I usually ran Tess in three trials a year. This wasn't enough to be in the running for the finals, but I did it because it was fun and a good way to keep in touch with other Border Collie people. Mainly, though, it was an excellent way to find out what the dog's weaknesses were and my own as well. No excuses, no glossing over. We often overlook our dog's failings because we're in a hurry to get a job done, then forget to go back another time and correct the problem.

As keen as Tess was in the toughest island situations, she had one serious problem with the sheepdog trials. She got so excited that she would start trembling as soon as my truck swung into the trial area. When she felt threatened by sheep bolting away from her, she often cut in and nipped them. In the Border Collie world, this is called "gripping" and is strictly forbidden. Often, we would be disqualified in less than five minutes, having driven for hours to get to a trial. Occasionally, however, a judge would announce that gripping would be allowed if the sheep being used were unusually stubborn or difficult to work. At one trial that we went to in Pennsylvania, the judge announced that gripping would be allowed because all the dogs, thus far, had gripped. The sheep had never been worked in small groups before and they broke away from each other constantly; sometimes one would even lie down. The contestants, several of them top handlers, were having a terrible time of it. Tess was in her element. These were like Blue Island sheep! She gripped, all right, but finished the course better than any other dog and took first place.

On the trip up to Nova Scotia this year, my truck was more crammed than usual with two dogs and all my belongings in the cab and five two-year old sheep in the back. Four of them had been born in New York, the fifth had come down from Nova Scotia as a lamb and was going home again. They would join a growing number of my sheep that had been born in New York and were easier to catch than the island-born ones, accustomed as they were to being handled and worked with a dog.

⌒ Twenty-Four ⌒

Finding a good butcher in Nova Scotia was always difficult. Vincent Buchanan was a young man in Shelburne whom I used for several years. He had no butcher shop or cooler, but he had the use of a shed on someone else's farm where he could butcher the lambs. He did a good job, killed the lambs quickly and mercifully and skinned them well too. I would then take them to a store that had a cooler, where they could hang for the required amount of time.

I took some lambs to Vincent late one summer. I drove into his field and backed up to the shed. I always took a dog along in case one or more sheep jumped out of the truck while another was being removed by the butcher. One by one, Vincent took the lambs out of the truck, shot them, cut their throats to let the blood out and got a second one while the first was bleeding out. Then he started skinning the first lamb, followed by gutting and cleaning.

My job was to salt down each skin. The salt would preserve the skin and keep it from rotting. The skin would be salted for at least five days, the salt scraped off and the skin dried before sending it off to the tanner. I spread the skin out on the grass and covered every inch with granulated salt. I couldn't put it in the truck, as it was still full of live sheep. Then I went back to the truck to continue reading my book.

I had just started to read *Billy Bathgate*, E. L. Doctorow's engrossing and violent novel about a boy caught up in the mob in New York in the 1930s. The early section of the book is set on a small boat leaving the city, steaming down the East River. Billy watches through a crack in a door as a man dressed in evening clothes, who has betrayed the mob, is being fitted for cement "shoes" before being tossed into the sea. I, the reader, was pressed up against Billy, watching what was happening inside.

Every fifteen minutes or so Vincent would shout, "hide," and I would run out to spread salt on the skin, piling each skin on top of the previous one, getting salt and blood all over my hands. Rushing back to the book, I squeezed in next to Billy once more and watched while a man whom I thought of as "the dresser" meticulously rolled up the victim's trousers, careful to make each roll match the earlier ones. This job done, the cement was poured into the tub where the victim's feet rested. Before the body was thrown over the side of the boat, I had to go out and finish my job of salting. By the time I got back to the book, the boat had made its way through New York Harbor into the Atlantic and the body was resting comfortably on the bottom of the ocean. There was no running water in the shed, so when Vincent had finished killing and dressing all the lambs, the early pages of my book had salty, bloody fingerprints on them, a fitting accompaniment to the text.

Sam had grown into a fine ram under the care of my former tenants, Val and Ray Schuler. I wanted to put him out for breeding and I didn't want any competition, so I asked the son of one of my friends to go out with me and shoot the mature rams still left on the island. It was a horrible decision to have to make, but I had to do it for the health of the flock. Chad Bower, still in high school at that point, did a lovely, quiet, clean job of it. He shot five rams, dropping each in place exactly where it stood. No suffering, no running around. It took all day and we went back to the mainland in the dark.

Earlier that year, another friend from Lincoln, Ellen Raja, had taught me how to clean rams' skulls. Now, I had five skulls available to get started on. I have sold many to artists, both to use as models and to hang on their walls. I offered a finished one to Chad and he accepted with pleasure.

I was taking one of the live rams I had caught, plus a very large ram lamb, back to the States for two sheep breeders. Blossom and a lovely little lamb with a black face were going as well. That took up all the space in my truck, so I had to leave four ewe lambs on the point to be taken care of over the winter by the new tenant in my cottage, who was eager to do it. He knew nothing about sheep, so I wrote a detailed page of instructions for him. I had built a wooden hay feeder outdoors and asked him to use it. The hay was to be delivered after my departure.

Alas, he decided to ignore my instructions and fed the sheep inside the barn. The hay was extremely moldy and the area where he fed the sheep was small with a low ceiling, so the mold hung around in the air. Sheep are very sensitive to mold and can develop pneumonia or, worse yet, listeriosis, from exposure to it. As a consequence, one of the lambs died of pneumonia over the winter and two of the others died the following winter on the island. They had been coughing earlier, so it was clear that they had pneumonia too. The experiment was over. From then on I took all the lambs back to my farm in New York.

⌒

Beverly Lambert is one of the top Border Collie handlers in the country. She had asked me to bring down a Scottish Blackface ram for her and he was one of the rams in my truck. I stopped by their place in Maine, where she and her husband, Doug McDonough, were living at the time.

After unloading the ram, Beverly said, "Let's work the dogs for a bit."

"Okay," I said, expecting only to work Tess after she had worked some of her own dogs. The sheep were nowhere to be seen, but Beverly sent one of her dogs out and soon sheep were popping out of the woods. We spent some time driving the sheep around with our dogs and then Beverly suggested that I let Nell work them.

"She's really not ready," I remonstrated.

"Come on, you have to start sometime and I want to see how she does."

I knew that if things got out of hand, Beverly would be able to deal with any situation, so I got Nell out of the truck and brought her into the field. The sheep were all quite close by.

I let her go and she ran around the sheep, keeping them in a tight circle.

"Boy, for a five-month-old, she shows a lot of promise," said Beverly.

A tragedy awaited me in New York. Three days before my return, my next-door neighbor's Akita had killed one of the little black lambs I had bought from Betty in the spring, the second Akita to attack my sheep. He had pushed his way through the electric fence, ignoring the three-thousand-volt shock he would have received, and chased them. The adult ewes had taken refuge behind the donkey, who stood guard in front of them in a corner, but the lambs had exploded over the field and the donkey couldn't be in a dozen places at once.

Annie Wieboldt, Bill's wife, had seen the whole thing from her kitchen window. She sent her daughter Karen to my field with her gun. Karen shot over the head of the dog, who fled through the fence again and up his driveway to home, thus positively identifying him. Because Karen had identified the dog, the owner was hauled into court, where the dog was declared to be a "dangerous dog," and she was required to keep him tied up.

There was a lot of damage. One of the black Border Leicester lambs was killed. Karen saw her lying where she had been downed, but didn't realize her wounds were fatal. I found her body a good hundred yards away where she had crawled, trying to rejoin the flock. I was able to claim compensation, funded by dog licenses. Every single lamb was wounded. Huge wads of wool were stripped off their backs. One had his entire tail bared, leaving just a string of vertebrae behind. All the wounds were infested with maggots. I was able to clean them all, but it was gruesome and heartbreaking. I named the surviving lamb Nancy Harte after my roomate in boarding school.

In early winter I had another tragedy with dogs. Heavy snow and ice had pushed my electric netting fence to the ground, so I brought the adult sheep into the barn with the donkey, left the lambs loose in the front yard and turned off the electric fence.

It's hard to find reasons for doing truly stupid things, so I won't try. I do remember thinking that the electric fence was probably grounded out because so much of it was on the ground and why waste electricity when it wasn't doing any good, sort of thing. One can say, "If only, if only . . ." only so many times. But it gave a green light to a couple of dogs—another Akita, number three, and a black Lab cross. They were in the woods, probably hunting deer, saw the lambs and came through a fence that had no power in it. The lambs crowded around my front door and I rushed out to see what was the matter. I saw the dead lamb immediately. It was the sweet ewe lamb with a very black face that I had brought down from Nova Scotia in the fall.

I ran to the house and got my gun and some shells. The dogs were chasing a large ewe lamb and I chased them around the barn. The dogs then chased the lamb through the fence into the next field and knocked her down while I was climbing over the ice-encrusted gate. As I landed, they left the lamb and started to run into the woods. I shot at them, just barely nicking one of them. They ran off and the lamb bolted down the field. I got Tess and we followed her tracks in the snow down the hill across the road and into my summer pasture. She was freaked out enough that Tess was able to corner her and I grabbed her by the horns. Then, what to do? I didn't think I could make it up the hill for a third of a mile, dragging a large lamb, but I was able to pull her to the gate. Just then Bill Wielboldt came along and held her for me while I went up and got my truck.

I called the dog officer. He came and we followed the dogs' tracks through the woods for an hour and a half. There was blood in the snow at first, but not for long. When we saw from the tracks that they were chasing deer, we gave up. Later I learned that lots of people had seen those two dogs from time to time. The Akita "disappeared," most likely shot by a hunter. I saw the big Lab a few weeks later and he was safely tied up. I couldn't prove that it was he, so there was nothing I could do. At least he was tied.

All barns attract mice or rats because of all the feed and my barn was no exception. I wanted an animal to control them. Buttons notwithstanding, I'm not particularly fond of cats. Brian told me once that Sheila, their first Jack Russell Terrier, had killed thirty-nine rats in their barn. I had loved Chili, Sheila's daughter, because of her spirit and sweetness and went about looking for a Jack Russell. A bunch of calls during the summer in Nova Scotia had failed to turn up any. I called Sarah Nettleton in Ontario, asked her if she knew of any breeders and hit the jackpot. She had just put a deposit down on a JR and suggested I send her a check so that she could put a deposit on another puppy from the same litter.

Early in February I went up to Ontario to pick up my puppy. I fell in love with one of them right from the start and decided to buy her. I stayed overnight with Sarah and Paul McLean, her husband-to-be, and got up for an early start next morning for the eight-hour drive with the two Border Collies and the ten-week-old puppy. It was very cold. I tucked the puppy inside my down coat on my left side. She spent the whole trip with her nose pressed against my armpit. I stopped every few hours to let her and other dogs pee and she never had a single accident.

This little pup was going to be the smallest coin of the realm and I decided to call her Penny. She fit nicely into a cardboard box in the front hall where the dogs eat and spend the night. I put an old pair of woolen pants into the box; she burrowed inside to keep warm. She was home.

～ Twenty-Five ～

My next anxiety was waiting for Eeyore to have her baby. When I had bought her a year earlier from John Conter, he had told me she might possibly be pregnant. He had put her in with a jack for a few days and didn't know if she'd gotten bred. Early in the fall, curious to find out whether she was pregnant or not, I asked my vet to make an examination. He put on a long, plastic glove that reached up to his elbow. He pushed his hand up into the donkey to investigate and while his arm was in there, he signaled "thumbs up" with the other hand. I was thrilled. I knew she had been bred around the end of April '89. With a gestation period of from twelve to thirteen months, she should be due in April or May.

April, and then May, 1990, came and went. Eeyore was huge, but she wasn't producing. Never having had a donkey or a horse give birth before, I was very nervous, especially when she seemed to be overdue. I called Bruce Blacklock in Nova Scotia, as he had bred donkeys.

"Is she eating and drinking okay?"

"Yes."

"Well, let nature take its course." I waited a week and called John Conter, the man I'd bought her from, in Montana.

"Is she eating and drinking okay?"

"Yes."

"Let nature take its course, then."

I waited another week and called the vet.

We had the exact same conversation.

June came.

One day, I went out to the barn after breakfast. The sheep were all inside to get out of the sun, which was already hot. And there, in the middle of the barn, surrounded by sheep, was Eeyore and her little gray baby. I burst into tears of relief. The baby was all legs and bony knees and had a huge head and ears. Funny-looking as she was, she was utterly adorable. I hugged her and called her Bambino, or Bambi for short. Eeyore was a fine mother and I left them alone, once I was sure she was nursing.

By the end of the month, I was ready to go to Nova Scotia. During the ensuing summer, I was moderately successful rounding up the sheep, but an annoying case of flu, followed by five weddings to attend, slowed me down. Betty and Liddy Fitz-Gerald, a friend of Betty's from Maine, came in September, but we only caught three sheep together.

Nevertheless, the *Baa-rge* got a good workout. A memorable trip was made with two brown Scotch Highland cattle. The island was becoming overgrown again. The sheep paths in the woods were only open to the height of sheep and this made walking around by humans difficult. One fall, after a summer of literally running in a squatting position, I returned to the theater, where one of the actresses said to me, "My God, Anne, your legs are made of iron. What have you been doing all summer?" I laughed and explained about the trees.

Since cattle eat a lot more than sheep and eat different things, they would create new paths and widen the old ones. It had been many years since my disaster with the first pair of cattle and I felt it was safe to reintroduce them at this point. The local people knew me better now and understood that I really cared about my animals.

The Scotch Highland steers were thirteen months old and were trucked down to my farm from Cape Breton. With shaggy hair covering their eyes and hanging down their sides, they were quite endearing. They were fairly tame, but wouldn't let me touch them. I named them Gus and Charlie, Charlie being the blonder of the two and also the friendlier. Gus was very shy. Penny, my Jack Russell puppy, thought they both were great and they seemed to like her too.

I asked my butcher, Vincent Buchanan, who was used to handling cattle, to help me load them into the barge from the barn. It worked well. The big opening to the barn with its sliding door is raised about a foot or so above the ground. The barge was already on the trailer; we backed it up to the barn door and let down the stern ramp. It was just the right height and the cattle could simply walk on. All I had to do was to drive it to the harbor, back it down the ramp at high tide and she floated off.

When the cattle were on the *Baa-rge*, I joked that I should change its name to the *Moo-ge*. My investment advisor later suggested *Stock Moo-ger*, but my friend Naomi Hamilton topped us both, saying they traveled by steerage.

I had hired two local boys to help me unload the cattle at the island. I wanted to photograph the landing, hoping the cattle would walk around on the rocky shore for a while, but they galloped off into the bushes and disappeared before I could even aim the camera.

Later, I started Nell's training in earnest. When Betty came for her annual visit in September, we worked our dogs on the sheep in the field in front of my house. We walked out with our dogs and she sent Kelty out to bring the sheep in closer to us. We took turns sending out the dogs and getting them to turn the sheep this way and that, driving them away, bringing them back, turning them around us.

Nell was able to go around the sheep and keep them together. Sometimes she stopped at the far end of the sheep and sometimes she didn't, but she was eager to work. Betty gave me some good tips on how to train her. I took Nell out to the island once, but she slipped her collar and chased the sheep. That was the end of work for that day.

Tess was very jealous and didn't work well when Nell was there. Since I needed Tess to focus on the work, I left Nell at home, but continued to train her on the sheep on the mainland. She learned very quickly and was loads of fun to train.

Betty had suggested using Nell to get the sheep into the barn. One day I needed to worm them, so I followed Betty's suggestion. She had never driven sheep before (pushing the sheep away from me), but caught on quickly. It took some time because they were afraid to go into the barn, a strange place for them, but she got them in. She was going to be a very useful dog.

Tess loaded the sheep I'd brought from New York onto the barge. Two local boys, Malcolm and Michael, went with me to the island. They paddled the barge to the shore, turned it around and we lowered the ramp to let the sheep off. The ones that had been born on the island started eating immediately. Betty, my purple ewe, looked around, her mouth agape, as if to say, "Where the hell have you brought me?" We all laughed.

It was time to return to New York. I took four nice ewe lambs and a ram lamb down with me.

Back in Greenville, I was pleased to see that Bambi, the baby donkey, had grown a lot. She was very friendly and regularly came to me for hugs. It makes a big difference in the ease of handling of a mature donkey if it has been raised with physical affection and contact.

One day, after training Nell on the lambs for quite a while, I sensed that the donkeys were feeling hostile towards her, so I pulled her back. The lambs felt the release of pressure and ran down the field to where the donkeys were grazing. Bambi went over to them and methodically put her nose on the back of each lamb, apparently checking them to make sure they were all okay. I was delighted, as it showed me that she had bonded to the lambs and felt some responsibility for their safety.

I had been concerned for some time about Tess's hearing. She seemed not to hear my commands a good part of the time. Friends teased me and said she just didn't want to hear me, but I knew her well enough to know how keen she was to work. She was stubborn, to be sure, but a reliable dog, and she wasn't behaving according to her character.

I took her to Tufts Veterinary School for testing. The results were not good. She had lost 70–80 percent of her hearing in one ear and 50 percent in the other. It was a comfort to me that Nell was coming along so nicely, but I felt badly for Tess who had been my right arm for so long and found occasions for her to work whenever possible from then on.

One day in early March of the following year, I heard loud noises, accompanied by a frantic ringing of a bell. I rushed out of the barn to see Eeyore shaking Botty by her leather collar. She was lifting the ewe off the ground with her teeth, shaking the devil out of her and slamming her to the ground. I climbed over the gate and rushed into the field, yelling at the donkey. She dropped Botty, who sank, exhausted. Eeyore then attacked Blossom, biting her wool. I ran at her again and she ran off into the woods. Blossom was down and Botty was freaked out, but when I approached them to examine them, they both got up and seemed to be okay. I went into the woods and grabbed Eeyore. Her face had a look of pure rage. When I took hold of her halter, her ears went back and she backed around. I was afraid she would kick me, so I let her go.

I stayed there awhile to observe the animals. After a few minutes, they all calmed down and Eeyore started grazing. The sheep approached as though nothing had happened. Still, I decided I couldn't take the chance of leaving the donkey with Botty. Something was going on between those two and I had no idea what it could be. I got Tess to drive the sheep into the barn, closed the door and went to fetch Eeyore. I managed to get her into a separate section of the barn with the help of some grain and closed the door. Later, I led her across the driveway to join the lambs in another field.

I called John Conter in Montana, who asked about the relationship of Eeyore with Botty. "Not good," I replied. "Botty's very bossy and is inclined to butt any sheep away that try to share her food."

"Get rid of her," was his advice.

"Not on your *life*," was my response. She had already earned me $1,000 in three years, not counting the lambs that she was carrying. "I'd get rid of Eeyore first!" but of course I wouldn't do that either. I'd have to work it out.

Two days later, just before sitting down with a drink to listen to the evening news, I went out to check on a sheep that I'd been watching every two hours all day. I found her behind the barn, licking off her newborn lamb. But Billy Fitz, Nancy Harte's enormous new lamb, was nursing from her, stealing her colostrum. I chased him away in order to bring her into the barn. The new mother became very agitated at my chasing Billy and started to run off a bit when I noticed a loud sloshing noise at her rear. Sure enough, lamb number two was on its way. I let her lick it a bit, then picked up both lambs, one under each arm and backed down to the barn with lamb number one yelling all the way. That caught the mother's attention and she followed me in with Billy Fitz in hot pursuit. What a little piggy.

As it turned out, the mother had so much milk that I was able to milk her out, after she had fed her lambs, in order to save some colostrum for a future crisis. I froze it in an ice cube tray and later put the frozen cubes into a plastic bag, possibly not to be used until the following year.

Whenever I thought a sheep might lamb in the middle of the night, I would bring her into the barn, put her in a pen, and then sleep in the shepherd's room, where I could keep an ear open for sounds of labor without even having to get out of bed. I had, next to the head of my bed, a Dutch door which led to the part of the barn where the sheep were. Whenever I heard a noise, I'd turn on the light in the barn, hike myself up and look over the bottom half of the door to see what was going on. I would sleep in a sleeping bag with my clothes on, admittedly not as well as I would in the house, but I could jump into my boots and get to the sheep very easily.

One night I was sleeping in the barn, waiting for Botty to lamb (she didn't). Every time she took a breath, the bell around her neck would "ding," and with every exhale, it would "ding" again. It drove me mad, so I went into the barn and removed the collar and bell.

Botty lambed a few days later at 11 AM. She had twins. It was a very hard birthing and she didn't get up between lambs. I had to bring them around to get her to lick them off. Later, I felt that the little ewe lamb was weak. Botty had always had plenty of milk and colostrum, so I milked her out by hand and put her milk into a bottle to give to the lamb. To my horror, there was blood in the milk from one of her teats. That side of her bag seemed much hotter than the other side, but other than that there were no symptoms of mastitis, that is, no hardening of the bag. Mastitis is a bacterial infection which can be dangerous. If it is a severe case, it can render that side of the bag useless forever. I called the vet, who recommended stripping all the milk out of that side. He also said that the lambs' sucking on that side would help clean out the rest of the blood. I wondered if Eeyore's ferocious banging her up and down had brought this on.

I sheared all the sheep in April. True to her breed, Nancy Harte's fleece was spectacular and I was thrilled to have it. It was like chocolate mousse. But Botty was so thin that she looked like the Picasso sculpture of the goat. All bones. Blossom was thin, too, and their lambs, while healthy by now, had had a rocky start. I was very concerned. I put Botty's bell back on her.

A few days later I saw Eeyore attacking Botty again. Once again, she had grabbed the sheep by the collar and was shaking her. The bell was dinging loudly. The bell, my God, the *bell*! It was driving the donkey just as crazy as it had driven me that night in the barn. Both times, Eeyore had grabbed Botty by the collar. What a fool I'd been not to have put two and two together earlier. I rushed into the pasture and removed the collar and Eeyore never bothered her again. I've never used the bell again, either.

～ Twenty-Six ～

To spend a whole year in Nova Scotia had long been a dream of mine and I finally decided to do it in 1991–92. I rented my house in Greenville and sold all my female sheep except Nancy Harte, four Scottish Blackface yearlings and Botty's lamb to go to Nova Scotia with me. I would leave Botty and Blossom and Eeyore to take care of the ram lambs over the summer.

With a heavy heart, I had made the decision to put Botty and Blossom down at the end of the summer when I would come south to take the ram lambs to the butcher. They were both thirteen years old and bone-thin. Their last lambing had been a torture for them and I felt it was unfair to lug them up to Nova Scotia again. Had I been staying on in New York, I might have softened and kept them until they died a natural death. To complicate matters further, Eeyore had been bred in April. She would foal the following spring. What to do with her? I had all summer to decide what to do. I was renting my house to a family that seemed responsible and considered asking them to take care of her for the winter.

I needed a new boat trailer for Nova Scotia. The old rusty one I had used for several years had collapsed the last time I hauled the *Betsy* from the Government Wharf to my house. Thank God it hadn't collapsed under Gus and Charlie. I drove up to Marlboro, New York, about forty-five miles away, to buy one. Having never owned a *new* trailer, I was looking forward to the prospect, but driving it home was a ghastly experience. The trailer, having no load, bounced all the way, even on the interstate, and it made the truck bounce and all my bones too. The prospect of six hours of hauling it up to the ferry in Portland was unbearable.

Nat solved the problem neatly by cutting down a couple of ash trees and trimming them to size to fit onto the trailer. He then secured them with chains and heavy rubber ties. It worked beautifully.

I loaded up the truck with the three dogs, provisions for the summer, suitcases, and a thermos picnic box full of frozen food into the cab of the truck, the six sheep in the back, followed by the boat trailer with the two or three enormous logs on it. It cost a fortune to take the Portland ferry with the trailer, but Penny, my Jack Russell, was pregnant, due in a couple of weeks, and I didn't want to take the time to drive up to Bar Harbor to take the quicker, cheaper ferry with all the animals.

The ferry took us to Yarmouth, where John, the government vet, met us at the boat. But we hit a snag. The customs wouldn't let me take the trailer into Canada with the trees on it. They were afraid that there might be diseases on the trees and didn't want to introduce any to the province. I tried to persuade them otherwise, pointing out that I was going to burn the trees for firewood forthwith, but they were adamant.

Despite my protests, I understood their position. We were having infestations of gypsy moth in the northeastern United

States and I would have felt terrible were I to introduce the pest into Nova Scotia. But it meant leaving the trailer behind for a few days so that the Department of Agriculture could come and take the trees away. I had to make a 150-mile-round trip just to pick it up and it bounced on the highway, treeless, all the way home.

Once at the farm, I put the sheep in the enclosure behind the barn for a few days until I would have time to make repairs to the electric fence.

Penny whelped ten days later, two little roly-polys, one each sex. Penny weighed about ten pounds and the puppies weighed a half-pound each. In a week they had doubled their birth weight and in three weeks they had quadrupled their weight. She was a super Mom. She was to have six litters during her breeding life and took wonderful care of all her puppies. I often get cards and photos from the many people who have bought her pups. I believe strongly in keeping puppies until they are eight weeks old. Penny used the last two weeks to teach her pups manners, putting her jaws right around their heads to discipline them, growling at them or nipping if they did something wrong. She was terrific.

I went out to the island to explore without any attempt to catch sheep. I always liked to do this on my first trip of the summer. It allowed me to observe the changes in terrain and any storm damage and to assess the feed potential for the year. The coastline always changed. Sometimes I had a sandy beach, sometimes not. Newly fallen trees were always blocking the paths here and there. Behind Blackbeard's Cove had been a small pond. Little by little, each year, the pond filled up with rocks, thrown thirty feet back from the shore in winter storms, until, after twenty years, the pond was no more.

This year was not good. There had been a drought and the grass was very dry and short. I decided to bring a lot of sheep off the island for the summer, as I had plenty of grass on the point, and it would allow the island grass to grow better for the fall and early winter.

That day, I decided to explore the interior of the island, starting from Blackbeard's Cove. Following a brook up a steep hill, I was surprised to see it disappear underground after a while. I wasn't on any path but was beating through the underbrush. I came across a place where the brook was running underground and the air above was strangely cold. More climbing brought me to an open spring with clear water. I leaned down and took a drink. There were no hoofprints near it, so I knew it would be clean. I walked on, heading towards the shore, when I came across Gus and Charlie, my Scotch Highland steers, keeping cool in the woods. I sat down so as not to alarm them and talked to them for about ten minutes, telling them how beautiful they were (they were, too) and marveling at how much they'd grown. Their horns had doubled in length. I wanted them to get used to my voice, so I chattered on about nothing very much. Charlie was standing next to a branch that was dangerously close to his eye (or so I thought). I warned him about it (part of my chattering) and the next thing I knew, he had turned his massive head so that the branch was behind it. He leaned back a little and scratched his head behind the ear with the end of the branch. I got up and walked slowly towards the steers. Charlie met me halfway and smelled my hand. I was thrilled, but also praying that Scotch Highland cattle were as gentle as people said they were. No one would ever have found my body in those woods.

I started working Nell on Blue Island that summer. Her training had been coming along very well and I felt she needed the experience. She was slower than Tess, but very keen and more responsive to me than Tess had ever been. But Nell was more sensitive than Tess and I was glad that I was more experienced now that I was working with her, not blaming her for everything that went wrong.

One day we penned four ewes and a ram lamb. I could have taken the lamb off by myself, but one of the ewes, Number 234, had mastitis on both sides of her mammary, which meant she could never nurse again. Amazingly, the lamb was hers. How she was able to rear a lamb with double mastitis is a mystery. The infection in one of the sides must have occurred late enough that the lamb was able to get its milk. I needed help to get her off the island.

My "boys" were all in school, but Peter Burke, who was now grown up, was available and willing to come and help me. I sheared the ewes and we prepared to lead Number 234 down to the boat. Peter and I each took hold of a ewe's horn and I handed him the rope I'd put around her head as a backup.

Before we started down the rocks, Peter said, "Anne, if those bulls come at us, I'm going to let go of this sheep, Okay?"

"Okay, Peter."

The steers had never even thought of attacking anyone, so I was full of confidence. Just as we got started down the steep part of the rocky shore, the steers popped out of the bushes and galloped toward us. Peter let go of the ewe's horn and, I must admit, I let go of mine too. But, bless his heart, he hung onto the rope. The steers stopped at the top of the rise. I went towards them and came across a heavy white birch stick across my path. I picked it up and shook it at them and said, "Shoo, shoo." To my relief, they wheeled around and ran into the bushes again.

I pondered why the steers had taken it into their heads to rush us like that. Then I remembered that that very morning, when Nell and I had gone up the hill through the little orchard to get to the woods behind the swamp, I had come across Gus and Charlie. They were under an apple tree, but had eaten all the apples within their reach. I jumped up and caught a branch, pulled it down and pulled off some apples for them. That afternoon, when they rushed us on the beach, all they wanted was more apples. I decided to let them wait for drops after that.

My friend Dave Murphy had some Bluefaced Leicester sheep. They are a different breed from Border Leicesters and have even softer and more lustrous wool. I decided that it would be a waste to breed Nancy Harte to a Scottish Blackface ram with his wiry, coarse wool and asked Dave if I could bring her over to his farm in Kingsburg, about ninety minutes away from mine, to be bred to his Bluefaced Leicester ram. He said fine. So, before going down to New York, to deal with my market lambs, I took her to Kingsburg and left her there.

Since my New York house was rented, I stayed with friends in Greenville. My tenants had bought some horses and I decided not to leave the donkey there for the winter to foal. I wasn't very impressed with the way they were handling their animals. Their horses, to whom they had given the run of the place, were busy eating my flowering trees when they weren't chewing on the sides of the barn. I laid down some rules (which were not followed) in an effort to try to protect my property.

If I was going to take Eeyore to Nova Scotia, I would have to buy a horse trailer. Also, she needed to have a blood test to cross the border. By good luck, I found a used trailer for a reasonable price. Meanwhile, I had taken my New York lambs to the butcher and had to wait for five days for them to hang in the cooler before they could be cut, wrapped and delivered. In early October, with the help of my neighbor Bill Wieboldt, I loaded Eeyore into the trailer and drove north.

On my return to Nova Scotia, I learned the shocking news that my old friend, Elizabeth Hyde, had been operated on for a brain tumor. She hadn't even been diagnosed when I'd left three weeks earlier. I was glad that I had chosen this particular year to stay up there so that I could be with her often. Her sheep needed to be vaccinated and the lambs removed, so I made plans to organize a gather of her sheep on McNutt's. By chance, Betty Levin and Liddy Fitzgerald were coming up much later than usual, so I asked them if they would be willing to gather Elizabeth's sheep instead of helping with mine. Of course they agreed. Martha Nettleton swung into action too, and drove down from Truro in the livestock truck from the auction barn. We all met at the wharf in Carleton Village and were taken out to the island by one of the Van Buskirks.

The gather went very well. Betty brought Kelty and I had Tess. At one point, I saw a group of sheep in the woods. Finding a path to run on, Tess and I went after them. My goal was to get ahead of the flock on the beach so that my group could join them well ahead of the people and dogs on the shore. I was thankful to be in good physical shape as I sprinted through the woods after Tess and we succeeded in bringing the sheep down to join the others. The island is two thousand acres, but the sheep stick pretty much to the west side where the terrain is flatter than on Blue Island. We vaccinated and wormed about a hundred adult sheep, and loaded about forty lambs onto the boat to be taken to Truro. It was quite a day. Martha accompanied the truck up to Truro and Betty and Liddy came home with me. Elizabeth was out of the hospital by that time. She was very grateful, and happier still when she got the check from the auction house.

I was still trying to gather sheep out on Blue Island and

having a devil of a time doing it. Because of the drought, they didn't come into the swamp—it was all dried up and the succulent grasses they came for weren't there. One day I went out with Nell and found five rams chewing their cud in front of my little cabin. After setting up the fencing, Nell and I walked softly towards them, but they bolted into the swamp. I sent Nell on a 'way to me so that she would go around them to the right, skirting the ocean to prevent their running into the water. I followed after as fast as I could go. All the animals were out of sight for a while because of the large rock outcropping. When I emerged into the swamp area, I could see the rams running away as fast as they could. No sign of Nell. I looked closer by and there she was, patiently waiting for me. She hadn't the experience to keep going if I was out of sight. I sent her out anyway and she stopped one of the rams, who immediately made for the water. I called her off and the ram joined his pals.

We needed to do some specific training on the mainland to get her to work out of my sight. The trouble was there was no place for me to hide on the point, it being a large field. But I found a small, round rock that stuck up about eighteen inches. I flattened myself down behind it and yelled "away" to Nell, feeling like a complete idiot. Nell was certainly smart enough to know where I was, but she couldn't see me and that seemed to have made the difference. Thank God no one was there to see me. She went in the wrong direction a few times and I corrected her and started again. Finally, she did it right twice and I quit for the day.

Dave called and said that Nancy Harte had been bred, so I went to Kingsburg to pick her up. When I brought her home, a very sweet thing happened. She had been separated from Eeyore all summer and into the fall. Eeyore happened to be near the barn when I unloaded her from my truck. They went toward each other slowly, Nancy Harte bleating very softly and Eeyore making little breathing noises. They both stopped and touched noses. Who says animals don't feel emotion?

I went out once more at the end of October and caught a few sheep, delighted that one of them was one of the Berthas, eight years old by then. Another was Number 544, Pipsqueak's mother, who had been such a flighty young sheep my first year in New York. She was six. They were both in super shape. Number 544's fleece was in multiple clumps. I sheared them off and she looked as though she'd been attacked by an army of moths.

Halloween brought a major storm. It was the biggest in a hundred years and led to the book *The Perfect Storm*. My house is set about fifty yards away from the water on the northeast side. I felt each wave break against the shore. Every single major wave shook the house under my feet, about once every five minutes, for three endless days. By the end I was exhausted. Luckily, the local fishermen were all safe in the harbor. They call it the Storm of the Century.

During the summer I had rented the small cottage on my farm to a woman, Brenda Conroy, who had a five-year-old son, Galen. She had come to see the place one day, sent by a mutual friend, and was seriously considering renting it but felt the pull of Halifax, where she had lived for several years. The day she came, I was working Nell on some sheep in the field. A friend of mine was also visiting and together they watched the work from outside the fence. Nell drove the sheep away from me, then, on command, ran neatly around them and brought them back to me. Again, I told her to drive them away, and, with several re-directing commands, to push them through a gateway I had set up in the field. After a while,

Brenda turned to my friend and said, "How can I *not* move here when this kind of thing is going on?" She and Galen moved in and we became good friends.

⌒

After a two-month trip to New Zealand over Christmas, I returned to Nova Scotia to some good news. Nancy Harte had had her lambs, a gorgeous pair of twin rams, one black, one white. Brenda had named them Ebony and Ivory. Unfortunately, the father was not the Bluefaced Leicester ram for whose wool I had gone to so much trouble, my second breeding failure with her. Dave told me that she had jumped the fence out of the field where the BFLs were and into the field where the Scottish Blackface were and had been bred by his Scottie ram. Clearly the BFL ram didn't have the sex appeal of the Scottie.

The scheduled lambing started in mid-March. The first one went well, birthing two lovely ram lambs—no problems. The second one gave me two more ram lambs and a big problem. It was quite cold and the ewe had lambed outdoors, so I was eager to get them all into the barn. She resisted, but finally went in. I put her in a pen and was watching to see if everything was okay when, to my horror, she started to attack one of the lambs. I moved her into a corner pen and tied her head to the wall. Immediately the little abused lamb started nursing. Gutsy little tyke.

That evening, I released the mother's head, as she seemed quite relaxed. Next morning the little lamb was in terrible shape. His ears were all bloody and there was blood all over him. He had only survived by hiding in a little niche in the corner. I tied her up again. Again, that evening, I released her. I had never had such a thing happen, so I called Betty Levin in Massachusetts and told her what was happening.

"Tie her up at once," she cried.

"For how long?" I asked

"Two or three weeks."

"Two or three *weeks*! Lord, Betty, what a prospect."

"Well, that's what it takes, sometimes."

What happens is that occasionally a ewe won't recognize a lamb as being hers and will try to kill it to protect her milk supply. Instinctively, all ewes repel lambs that are not their own. Sometimes, if a ewe dies giving birth, we have to graft her lamb onto another ewe and the process is the same. It takes as long as two to three weeks for her to accept the lamb. I called the ewe Murderous Millie, the Monster Mother, and her lambs Beloved and Despised. Despised was very smart. He waited for his brother to nurse and then sneaked behind him to nurse on the far side where his mother couldn't see him because her head was tied to the corner.

A few days later my sister called to tell me that my aunt, Dot Davison, had died. She had always been my favorite aunt. I walked down to the shore for a moment of meditation, listening to the waves, at the same time that my family was attending her funeral in New York. When I got back to the barn, I found Brenda, who had come over for a visit, holding a new lamb. She held it up for me to see.

"It's a girl!" I shouted, "I'll name her Dot. She's the first ewe lamb born this year."

Later on, another of the new lambs seemed to be hypothermic, but I pulled him through with a heat lamp and a dose of molasses and yoghurt.

In late March, Eeyore gave birth to a lovely little gray female. She had a black stripe going down the length of her back and across her withers, so I called her Noelle, as she had arrived "gift wrapped." Eeyore was a super mother and I had no worries about either of them.

It had been a week since Murderous Millie, the Monster Mother, had lambed and she was still tied. The lambs were doing well, but I had limited barn space and having her there constantly was a nuisance. From time to time I let her loose in the barn but was forced to tie her up again as she tried to attack Despised. Eventually, she gave in and accepted him.

By this time lambing was over for the year and the lambs were all out in the big pasture with their mothers. They were a happy sight, for at around six in the evening something wonderful would get into them, as happens with most lambs. They started to race around the field, some leaping as they went, running back and forth, jumping and cavorting. I noticed that the little hypothermic one was usually at the tail end of the group, but he waited for them to turn and then he was in front.

Shortly afterwards, I went down to Massachusetts for a quick visit to pick up my new Border Collie puppy, Kate. When I got back I found that a Husky dog had gotten into the sheep pasture, killed a lamb and dragged it back to the barn, where it proceeded to eat it. I can only assume that Eeyore had been busy with her baby, or perhaps the lamb had been isolated from the rest of the flock, making him an easy target.

Worse yet, the lamb was the little hypothermic one that I had worked so hard to save. Brenda heard the ruckus and photographed the dog eating the lamb—a brilliant move. She then called the dog officer who came and took the dog away. I called him at once and he told me who the dog belonged to. He had talked to them and they had pled with him to let them keep the dog, promising to put him on a cable at all times. Would I agree to this? Against my better judgment, I said yes. Ten days later, I was sitting at my table in the kitchen. I looked out the window and saw the donkey and all the sheep in a cluster, looking at something. I knew immediately what it was they were looking at and ran outdoors. Sure enough, it was the Husky. I got hold of him, put him in the barn and called the dog officer again. He came and got him. Later, three generations of the family came over and pled with me, giving lame excuse after lame excuse. They even blamed the direction of the wind, which didn't explain why the dog was off his cable. I told them they had had their chance and they'd blown it.

⌒

Because of a record snowstorm in the winter of 1992, Blue Island was a disaster. During the following summer, I found the dead bodies of a ram and six ewes—two of them Pipsqueak and her mother. A third was Betty, Botty's daughter, my purple ewe. I also found the bodies of eight lambs in various places. I suspect that the heavy snowstorm prevented the ewes from getting to the shore and their seaweed for too long a period. One day, though, Nell showed her mettle. She and I had brought two large rams and a tiny ewe most of the way around the island. We got to the swamp and were running along the rocky shore when suddenly the sheep stopped on a rock and eyed the ocean. They were very tired (we all were) and very spooked. I was afraid they would jump into the water, which would have been the end, so I sent Nell on a go-by (circling in a clockwise direction), thinking she would approach them from the left and get them to turn by virtue of the pressure she was putting on them. She surprised me by jumping into the water and swimming right at them. They turned, all right, and went down the shore. Later they did it again and once again Nell jumped in the water and drove them in the direction of the pen. This time I was worried, as the waves were breaking on the rocks, but she negotiated them handily and came ashore. We penned the sheep. She had become a very valuable three-year old.

Later in September, I went to pick up Barney, the Blue-faced Leicester ram I was buying from Dave Murphy. I felt that his fine, soft wool, typical of his breed, would improve the quality of my fleeces. I was planning to buy more Border Leicester ewes in New York to join Nancy Harte. Barney would also breed the Scottish Blackface ewes that I would be taking to New York, but their lambs wouldn't be tough enough to survive the winters on Blue Island because Blue-faced Leicesters are too tender, but I could sell them locally in New York. I looked forward to having some nice wool that I could play with, as I had taken up spinning.

In the fall, my house and I were both in a movie. It was a joint production of Heritage Films, a Nova Scotia production company, and the American producer who had written the film. It was titled *Mary Silliman's War* (the title for the video release was changed to *Way of Duty*). It was set in Connecticut during the American Revolution and was about the efforts of Mary Silliman to free her husband from the hands of the British, who had kidnapped him. It's a true story, much of it taken from Mrs. Silliman's diaries. One of the colleges at Yale University was named after the couple's son, Benjamin, a famous scientist. My house was built sometime between 1775 and 1794, so it was chosen to be the Sillimans' farm.

I auditioned for the role of the tavern keeper and got the part. My scenes were all shot elsewhere, but the cast and crew shot at my farm for about three days. The cast was first-rate—some of Canada's best actors—and I enjoyed it immensely.

One of the scenes had my sheep in it. One of the Silliman children came around the house, pushing a wheelbarrow full of grain and set it down outside the fence. (My electric fence had been shoved out of sight to the ground and replaced with a wooden one.) Then he took a tub of grain and climbed through the fence to feed the sheep. Nell and I had brought the sheep to the fence and Nell was holding them there. They were a motley crew of sheep that no one in their right minds would have had on a farm—four rams, one ewe and two lambs—but who would know?

We brought the sheep to about twenty feet from the fence. I asked the Assistant Director if we were close enough.

"Not quite," he said.

I edged them in a bit closer. "Close enough?"

"Just a bit more, Anne."

I was really tense. The Scottish Blackface rams had all just come off the island and were anything but tame. I didn't know how long they would stay around. Finally, we were near enough. The sheep relaxed and munched on the grass.

"QUIET!" yelled the A.D. It was *so* loud, but my sheep didn't budge.

"CAMERA?"

"ROLLING!"

"SOUND?"

"ROLLING."

"ACTION!"

The little boy brought the wheelbarrow around the house, stopped—but something was wrong.

"CUT!"

They had to start all over again. I was really nervous by this time. The boy wheeled the barrow back behind the house.

All of the yelling, starting with "QUIET," began all over again.

As the boy was coming around the house, Nancy Harte decided she'd had enough and wandered off to the right. One of the lambs followed her. The sound was rolling, so I couldn't call to Nell. Furthermore, we had to stay off camera. I whistled, very softly, the command to go to the right. She went. I whistled a "lie down." She lay down. I whistled the "walk up" command. She walked up. Slowly, Nancy Harte turned with the lamb and rejoined the group, just in time to get in the picture. Whew. I whistled Nell to come to me.

It was a "take."

Afterwards I told the A.D. what had happened and asked him if he had heard my whistle.

"Yes, I heard it," he said, "but I thought it was a bird."

Alas, the scene had to be cut from the film because the camera was out of focus. The camera was on a trolley, the "best boy" running alongside, focusing the camera as it moved along. A very difficult task on a bumpy lawn. In any case, Nell, never on camera, was the star of the scene.

∼ Twenty-Seven ∼

Because I had by now spent a year and a half in Nova Scotia, I was returning to the United States with many more animals and a great deal more baggage than usual.

Penny was very pregnant. I had scheduled the trip carefully, leaving her with a six-day leeway period in New York before her litter was due. Eeyore and Noelle would ride in the horse trailer along with the three adult Scottish Blackface rams that I was taking back to sell to people who had requested them. I had planned that both donkeys would be in the same half, so that Noelle could nurse. I needn't have bothered planning it: There was no way they would be separated. Noelle turned herself around so that she was facing her mother's teats and that's where she remained for the whole trip.

I backed the trailer up to the barn and loaded the rams into the other half of the trailer. In the back of the truck I loaded Nancy Harte, the two ewe lambs that had been born in the spring and Barney, my Bluefaced Leicester (BFL) ram. In the cab, besides the four dogs, was all my stuff. I had taken apart my dog carrier and set the bottom into the top to make a little nest for Penny on top of a picnic box in the front seat. Tess occupied the floor in front of the passenger seat. The other two dogs were on top of the duffel bag that rested on boxes that were themselves on top of the jump seats in the back of the cab.

It was a long drive pulling the trailer. I had to stop periodically to let the dogs out. The deadline for meeting the vet at the border was 5:30 PM. I tore down those roads. Meanwhile, Penny didn't like her little nest and wanted to be in the back part of the cab with the other dogs. She climbed back there all right, but Kate kept lying on top of her, which I didn't think was a good idea. I didn't have time to stop, but reached back from time to time and pulled Kate off Penny. It was a strenuous trip. I made it with one minute to spare.

The vet, a very nice man named Dr. Patrick Covill was ready and waiting. He checked the papers; all were in order and I was free to go. Before leaving his office, I asked permission to let the dogs out to pee and Pat said sure. I went back to the truck and let them out, lifting Penny so she wouldn't have to jump. She squatted on the paving and a large amount of goo came out, then a *head*. I panicked. I picked her up and ran to the building, frantically shouting, "Help, help, Penny's aborting. Help, help. "

Pat was wonderful. He said very quietly, "Put her down on the floor here and we'll see what's going on." The puppy was out by then and Pat got a towel and dried him off.

"He looks full term to me and in fine shape. And by the way . . ." looking at Penny squatting in a corner, "I think she's going to have another one pretty soon. Do you have something to put them in?"

I went to the truck and got the dog carrier, in two pieces, and together we assembled it. Penny was installed with her puppy, we loaded them in the front seat, the other dogs in their places. After thanking Pat warmly, I took off.

Just beyond the border there was a gas station with a restaurant attached. I pulled in and ran inside. "My dog is having puppies in the truck. Could I have some napkins please?" I asked the woman behind the counter. Without looking at me, she reached behind her and, also without looking, plonked a pile of napkins on the counter. Without a word! I wondered how often people came in who had puppies being born in their vehicles. They were excellent napkins, though, big and thick.

A short way down I-95, Penny gave a heave and produced another puppy. As she was licking it off, I grabbed a couple of napkins, reached into the box, scooped up the afterbirth, swung into a rest area, flung the napkin in a trash can and kept on going. She had a third pup a little while later and that was that. I had started the day with thirteen animals and ended it with sixteen.

When I got to my farm, I let the animals out into the barn. It was too late to set up the temporary fencing for them to be outdoors, but they would be fine in the barn overnight.

At the Sheep and Wool Fair in Rhinebeck, New York, in October I bought two Border Leicester ewes, a two-year-old and a lamb. Both were colored, both with one black parent and one white parent. They had coal-black heads and legs and beautiful, silver wool. The two-year-old looked just like Queen Elizabeth I with her elegant neck ruff. I named her

Queen E. The lamb was to be Rosemary. I now had the beginnings of a flock with beautiful wool.

In February, I went to Massachusetts to the memorial service for my Aunt Margery, my mother's last surviving sister. Nancy Harte's lambing was imminent, so I penned her and left very detailed instructions for the young man who was to take care of my sheep while I was away. She lambed before he got there. Luckily, he read my instructions carefully and called his father, who had cattle, to come and milk her out. Good thing, too. One of her teats was plugged up and she had had triplets. The two ram lambs were white, the beautiful ewe lamb was black and I named her Margery. Nancy Harte raised the lambs entirely herself and they grew extremely well. I was able to sell one of the ram lambs for a breeding ram, which pleased me. And Margery lived on my farm for years and had many beautiful lambs herself.

I put the lambs outdoors when they were three days old, as I usually do, and Noelle immediately attacked them viciously. Horrified, I put myself between them and got hold of her halter. She was clearly upset. I isolated the lambs and penned them in the barn. Then I brought Noelle in and held each one up to her face, stroking her neck as I did so and talking very gently to her. I felt that she was frightened by them and perhaps considered them to be dangerous little aliens to be stamped out. Thereafter, before letting any new lambs outdoors, I introduced each one to Noelle, let her get the scent, and also let her know that I cared about them. The following year she was fine with the new lambs.

Dot lambed at the end of the month. The weather forecast was very bad, so I had brought her and all the lambs with their mothers into the barn for the night. At ten-thirty, I checked the young ewe before going to bed. She was in labor. The lamb's head and one leg were out, but the other leg was back and still inside. I tried pulling on the leg that was out, which was a mistake, as it made the opening more crowded than before and didn't have the result I was hoping for. So I put on a plastic glove, spread dish soap on it, and went inside her. The opening was so small that I had a terrible time. I finally found the other front leg, but the foot was under the lamb's body and there was no room to get my fingers around it. The lamb looked dead, its tongue hanging out. I pushed the head back in, thinking that I could then start over. As I was pushing, I heard a tiny "meh-h-h." The lamb was alive!

I got a piece of string, made a noose which I managed to push in with my finger and manipulated it around the lamb's foot. With my free hand I pulled on the string and got the foot out. I grabbed it and pulled. The shoulder appeared and the lamb followed. I made sure it was still breathing, wiped the gooey birth liquid from its mouth, and put it down next to its mother. She had collapsed with fatigue and was totally unresponsive. I put the lamb up to her nose. Nothing. I went to the kitchen and got some frozen colostrum, thawed it and stomach-tubed the lamb after adding about another ounce that I had milked from its mother. I squirted about two ounces of molasses and some water into the ewe's mouth, laid the lamb next to her, set up a heat lamp and went to bed. It was 1 AM. My hands were swollen for two days from being crushed by her birth contractions.

At times like this, a little voice in my head says, "Why on earth are you doing this?" I blame all those idyllic books I read as a child about the romantic farm life. When I was about four or five years old, I had a phonograph record of "Little Bo Peep." There was even a picture of the little girl shepherdess on the record itself. She had black curly hair, a long dress with little flowers on it and a big sunhat. In one hand she carried a crook and she was shading her eyes with her other hand. She was very, very pretty. It was my favorite record and I loved it so much I took it to bed with me for my nap.

Naturally, since it was an old 78 rpm record, it was in pieces when I woke up. I was desolate and cried bitterly.

I'll bet Little Bo Peep never stayed up lambing in a cold barn until 1 o'clock in the morning

Next morning at six, I went out to the barn. Both ewe and lamb were on their feet, but the mother had no interest in letting him nurse. In any case, he thought I was his mother, so I milked her out and fed it to him in a bottle. They straightened things out between them after that. I dosed her with penicillin for five days and all was well. But it was a good reinforcement of my intention *not* to breed my lambs when they were so young. Ewes aren't fully mature until they are two years old. If bred at the age of six months, their growth is apt to be stunted and their lambs often have a low birth weight. I hadn't intended to breed the two lambs, but had been unable to keep them separate from the rams during the movie shoot. Sure enough, two weeks later, the other young ewe gave birth to a tiny but vigorous little lamb whom I called Tinker Bell, since she was nearly invisible.

∼ Twenty-Eight ∼

In April, I went to Israel with Peter Hagerty, the head of Peace Fleece. I had first read about Peter in *Harvard* Magazine in the 1980s. He had formed Peace Fleece as an attempt to forge peaceful ties between the United States and the USSR by importing Russian wool and mixing it with American wool, dying it pretty colors and selling it as Peace Fleece. By 1993, having solved the problems of U.S.–Russian relations with wool, he decided to try to bring peace to the Middle East!

Having accompanied him and a group of fiber spinners to Moscow in 1990, I decided to join the group again.

Our purpose in Israel (short-term anyway!) was to organize a wool festival, as we had done in Moscow. Peter chose an extraordinary village called Neve Shalom/Wahat al Salaam, which means Oasis of Peace. It is an intentional bicultural community with an equal number of Arab and Jewish families. Established in 1984 with just a few families, it has grown quite quickly. There is a Peace Center, where outside groups come to work out their differences. While we were there, some grandchildren of Holocaust survivors and grandchildren of SS officers met for the second time to share their guilt and try to resolve their anger. There is a school where the children are taught in both Hebrew and Arabic. At the time of our visit, about a hundred families from outside the community sent their children to the school because they wanted them to have an integrated education. Working out differences and striving for a peaceful coexistence is full-time work, but that is another story. Enough to say that we were welcomed warmly by the whole community, who were eagerly anticipating the first wool festival ever put on there.

The village is situated at the top of a high hill, overlooking bright green fields and orchards with both olive and orange trees. Beyond is a wide plain that goes all the way to Tel Aviv, whose lights we could see at night, the Mediterranean on the horizon. I was surprised at the greenness of everything, but learned that it was so because the rainy season had just finished.

At the base of the hill, on land belonging to the village, lived a Bedouin shepherd, Abu Abed Ajami, and his wife Fatma. They owned about 150 sheep, which they called Arab sheep. Historically, Bedouins are nomads, moving from grazing area to grazing area with their sheep. This was not so with Abu

Abed and Fatma. There was enough grazing to keep them at Neve Shalom/Wahat al Salaam year-round. Unlike most sheep breeds, their sheep produced more milk than their lambs needed, so Fatma milked them daily and made cheese, which she sold. They also sold the wool and butchered lambs for meat.

We arrived on April 14 in the evening and had a good night's sleep after the exhausting twelve-hour flight from Boston to Tel Aviv via Frankfurt. We were housed in a dormitory with six to a room. I was curious to see what the food would be like. We got up in time for an eight-o'clock breakfast, which was delicious—cold cereal, cottage cheese, a yoghurt/sour-cream mixture, some kind of cold fish and excellent coffee.

Our task the first day was to wash the sheep with the aid of the school children. Wash the sheep? I'd never heard of such a thing, but every place does things differently and we were there to help, not question. I was to find out why.

The children were let out of school for the day and we planned to have a picnic together. We meandered down a long hill through olive orchards, with their grey-green leaves, to the river, the children, ranging in age from about eight to twelve, full of excitement. I looked at them carefully to see if I could tell which children were Arab and which Jewish. I couldn't. They were just a bunch of lively, happy kids.

A dreadful path had been made by a tractor and the swampy places, muddy and sloppy wet, were hard to cross. There were areas of wildflowers blowing in the hot wind, none of which were familiar to me. I kept asking the children, "What's this? What's that?" (Most of them spoke English, but their knowledge of botany wasn't so hot.) We got to the river and waited and waited. And waited. Finally sheep appeared.

Most English sheep breeds have short, prick ears and long, skinny tails, but the Bedouin sheeps' ears are long and floppy, rather like a bassett hound's. Their faces are light brown and white, and the tails big and fat. The tail holds moisture and nourishment, much like the hump of a camel, and is well suited for the desert. Close behind them came Abu Abed, riding his little donkey. Quite the entrance. No squishing through the swamp for him.

Each sheep was dragged into the river by the men in our group, whereupon an army of squealing children grabbed its feet and dunked it up and down, being careful to keep its head above water. Of course this required the children to be in the water, too, so they had a great deal of fun. The amount of dirt and lanolin that washed off was amazing. It was a hot day and by the time the sheep had climbed up the hill again they would be dry.

Once we had eaten our picnic lunch, most of us rested in the afternoon in a desperate attempt to overcome jetlag.

That was my last chance to sleep in for a while. The next morning at 5:30 AM Peter woke me up and we went down the hill to Abu Abed's place. He and Fatma lived in tents—huge, roomy ones. They kept their clothes and possessions in one tent and lived, cooked and ate in the other. Fatma was a large woman, quite dark-skinned, with a huge smile. She rose each day at 4 AM to milk the sheep. Her dress was a typical Bedouin style—long, black, with intricate, colorful embroidery across the bodice.

Peter and I were the only shearers in the group, but others had come down with us to catch and turn sheep up on their rumps for us, especially for me. I was then sixty-five years old and recognized my limitations. If I had to catch and turn up the sheep, I wasn't going to have much energy left to shear for very long.

There was a group of sheep in a large paddock where Abu Abed and his son, Suliman, had spread out a huge plastic sheet for us to shear on. Someone brought me a sheep but didn't turn it up, so I started to do so. Immediately Suliman insisted on doing it for me. He reached over the sheep, grabbed its legs and flipped it over. Whump! He went to get a rope to tie its feet, but I shook my head at this and started shearing. It's lucky we were shearing with hand shears because when I got to the tail I found to my surprise that it was divided into two halves. I took my time and sheared it carefully. To my further surprise, there was a small bone that curled up right where the tail divided. This little bone was completely hidden by wool. Had I been shearing with electric shears, I'd have cut it off. The wool sheared easily until I ran across a sheep that hadn't been washed for some reason. What a difference. Sticky, gummy, *impossible*. I avoided any unwashed ones whenever I could after that. We sheared until eight o'clock, then went up to breakfast. I am not at my best before breakfast, to say the least, so shearing for over two hours on an empty stomach was a major accomplishment for me.

By nine we were back down again. Peter had arranged for small groups of school children to come and watch during the course of the morning. It was obvious to us that the children, while they knew of the Bedouins' existence, had no real contact with them. The sheep-washing had been their first experience with the sheep. Since a great deal of what was planned for the wool festival centered on the children and their school, we thought it made sense for them to be in on every stage of the process.

By this time it was very hot and Abu Abed had put up a canopy for us to shear under—a most welcome addition. We took turns shearing so as to be able to talk to the children. I am a slow shearer anyway and explained each step of the process. At the end I took the fleece and put it over a child like a coat. They were fascinated by it but pretty repelled by the dirtiness. They giggled and wriggled and we had a lot of fun. Peter had a long, funny story about how the Vikings brought shearing to England. The result was that we each took forever to shear each sheep, but the children were interested and entertained and it all seemed fine. Each group of kids stayed for twenty to thirty minutes.

During the third group of kids, I noticed that Abu Abed seemed pretty anxious. Finally he came over to my sheep, grabbed the shears out of my hand and shoved me rudely aside. He did the same thing with the next sheep. Naturally, being a strong feminist, I assumed that the fact that a woman was shearing *his* sheep in *his* country in front of children had gotten to him. I went over and plopped myself down on a couch at the edge of the canopy next to Meg Wadsworth, an old friend of mine, who was part of our group.

"My nose is seriously out of joint," I said.

"I noticed," she laughed.

Hmph. No support there. Next thing I knew Abu Abed had done the same thing to Peter. "Ah," I thought, "it must be because we are Americans." I felt better. After all, what were two Americans doing "helping" a Bedouin shepherd to shear his sheep, someone whose ancestors were undoubtedly the shepherds present at the birth of Jesus? I noticed Peter wasn't nearly as put out as I was. By 11 AM the temperature was in the 90s and we quit for the day.

That evening Peter told me we wouldn't shear next day because he wanted to find out what had caused the "incident" and would go down alone and talk it over with Suliman, who spoke English. Perhaps Peter was a bit more upset than he had seemed.

At breakfast, Peter admitted what Suliman had told him and what we both, being shepherds, should have figured out for ourselves. Abu Abed was worried about his sheep. Some were about to lamb, some had just lambed, some were being weaned and he was concerned because it was so hot and we were taking such a long time to shear each sheep with our endless stories. I was relieved and glad that Abu Abed felt protective of his sheep, just as I would have under the same circumstances.

The next day we started shearing at dawn again and worked until breakfast. Abu Abed was busy with other things and didn't shear with us, but after a while, he came over to me, pointed at my arm and said what sounded like "Tuff, tuff."

Thinking he had said "tough, tough," I felt somewhat embarrassed and mumbled something about shearing not being *that* tough. I found out that "Tuff" means "Good." It was a nice compliment. Later, Fatma appeared with glasses of sweet mint tea and little pieces of sheep cheese. The tea gave me the energy to continue and the cheese was delicious too.

Abu Abed sheared with us after breakfast. I had just started to shear a ewe when he came alongside with a rope and calmly tied the sheep's feet together. Those of us who shear the New Zealand method don't tie the feet together because it makes reaching the belly and the crotch impossible. Also, with the New Zealand method the shearer can hold the skin tight to prevent nicking. "Okay," I thought, "let's see what happens."

He started shearing the back end of the sheep. I started shearing the front end. We rolled the sheep over and continued the process, and we continued to shear in tandem for the rest of the day. It was quite restful and rather fun. My friends teased me that this was a pre-nuptial Arab ritual, but I countered that I had Fatma to protect me. We had achieved Arab-American peace.

One day a group of us who were weavers went on an expedition to a town in the West Bank. First, we went to Jerusalem to the home of a nun who invited both Arab and Jewish students to live in her apartment, the only place in all Jerusalem where students of both religions lived together. She worked for an organization called The Ark. She arranged our trip and came with us. One stipulation was that there be no more than six of us, for we had to go by taxi and the nun didn't want more than one vehicle for safety reasons. She feared that if two taxis were split up, there could be trouble. Also, we had to take an Arab taxi because an Israeli taxi might have been subject to attack. We passed through the checkpoint between Israel and the West Bank with no delay and drove through Hebron on our way to the village.

The first person I saw at the house we were going to was an old woman sitting on the stoop, a small stair with about six steps leading to the house. She was spinning with a drop spindle. The height of the stoop allowed the spindle to drop a long way before she had to stop and wind it up. She was wearing a kerchief on her head and a black dress with a beautiful bodice decorated with flowers. Around her neck she wore a large brass pendant with intricate designs hammered into it.

The young women of the family met us at the door, all of them wearing dresses in different colors with bodices similar to the old woman's. They all wore kerchiefs on their heads too. We had brought some makings for lunch, but when we followed the women into the kitchen and saw what a feast they had prepared for us, we were a bit embarrassed with our paltry offerings.

They invited us into the living room and we sat on the

linoleum floor, which, I was amused to note, bore a pattern of an Arab rug. After lunch they brought down a few of their rugs for us to see. They were very beautiful, handwoven, made with hand-spun yarn, dyed with natural dyes. Predominantly red, they had stripes of other colors—black, green, brown and white. The red dye was made from cochineal, a kind of dried bug. The black was made from Dead Sea mud, and the green came from an iron ore. Tassels adorned the corners.

I asked if I could buy one. Others wanted some, too, and there weren't enough to go around. They brought more rugs down from upstairs, but they weren't all for sale. Only one person spoke English, a young man, and he consulted with his wife. The rug I wanted to buy was hers. He came back and told us she had agreed to sell it. The nun explained that the West Bank was cut off from Israel at that point and the workers were not able to get to their jobs in Israel, so they were short of money. The rugs we bought would keep them going for quite a while.

Outdoors, we watched two old women set up a loom on the ground. They only weave in the dry season. As the rainy season had just ended, they were ready to weave again. The women sat about ten feet apart. In front of each woman was a pair of metal stakes, about four feet apart. The woven panel would measure ten feet by four feet. Two or more panels would be sewn together to make a finished rug.

They started warping their loom. (The warp is the longitudinal threads of a woven piece.) One tied the end of a large ball of wool yarn to a stick, which she held with her toes behind the metal stakes. A small child, sitting on the side between the two women, would grab the ball of yarn from one woman and hand it to the other. The second woman would pass the ball of yarn around her stick and hand the ball to the little girl.

In this manner the yarn warp would be threaded, held in place by the sticks at each end, which, in turn, were held in place by the metal stakes. Then, one woman started to weave. She took a narrow, flat stick and pushed it in and out of the warp threads, causing the odd threads to be on one side of the stick and the even ones on the other. Then she flipped the stick on its side, forming a gap through which she threw her shuttle with the weft threads. She used the stick to beat the thread down, then repeated the process of winding the stick in between all the warp threads, this time with the odd threads on the bottom and the even threads on top, and threw the shuttle again. It all happened in the twinkling of an eye. Within an hour, she had woven a foot of rug. I imagine rugs have been woven in this fashion for centuries.

One of our group had brought a home-made spinning wheel to the village. He had constructed it using a bicycle wheel in place of the traditional wooden wheel. He presented it to our host family. They were particularly delighted because the young men could copy it for other people in the village in the local machine shop, using old bicycle wheels. Skilled as the women were with the drop spindles, they could greatly increase their production with wheels, as they are much faster. We returned to Neve Shalom/Wahat al Salaam, happy with our collection of rugs.

The wool festival was held in the playground of the school. Earlier in the week, we had painted all the equipment in the playground, to the surprise of our hosts.

Some Jewish women attended who were members of a spinning guild in Haifa. They had never before participated in an event that included Arabs. Quite a few of their members were too scared to come, but the women who came had a wonderful time and vowed to persuade their friends to attend next time.

We set up some Inkle looms, used for making belts, and taught children how to weave. A weaver's cooperative from Beersheba also came. These were Arab women who had been organized by an English woman into a viable cooperative. They wove beautiful rugs in gorgeous colors (we later visited their cooperative and bought some of their rugs). Two women set up a loom on the ground, just like the women we had seen in the West Bank village, and started weaving a rug panel. Other people spun on the spinning wheels we had brought. It was festive and great fun.

Next day we were to leave, but there was one more thing I wanted to do.

Back in February, Peter and I had gone to a farm in Massachusetts to shear with Kevin Ford, who shears only with hand shears. Although I had learned to shear originally with hand shears and had done so for several years before I felt I could justify buying electric ones, it had been some time since I had had a blade lesson and Peter felt it would help us both. When Kevin saw my rusty old shears, he was shocked and doubted they could ever be sharpened properly. I thought I'd taken good care of them, but in fact, since I use them on the island, they had probably gotten rusty from all the trips in my boat.

I looked longingly at the shiny, new, razor-sharp shears Peter had and he explained that Kevin had beveled the edges for him and sharpened them too. Did I want to go all the way to Israel and then hamper my work with terrible old shears? The answer was no, so I asked Kevin to prepare a new set of blades for me and, incidentally, to sharpen the old ones if he could. Just for safety, I took both pairs to Israel and tried them both. Overwhelmingly, I preferred my old, comfy ones, which were now truly razor-sharp.

So I wanted one last chance to shear with Abu Abed. We went down at our usual 5:30 AM. I wore a warm sweater, since the heat wave was over. Abu Abed chose a nice big ram for us to shear, and shear him together we did. When we were finished, I presented him with my shiny new blades. He looked at them and smiled.

"Tuff, tuff," he said, nodding.

～ Twenty-Nine ～

Shortly after my return to Greenville, Joanna Hyde phoned me with the news that her mother, my good friend Elizabeth, had died. We had much in common and had enjoyed each others' company for twenty years, so it was a painful loss, although I'm sure it was a great release for her. I miss her sense of humor most of all.

Lambing started soon after my return. Queen E. had a spectacular pair of jet black twin ewe lambs. I sold one and kept one, whom I called Nefertiti. I remembered the bust of Nefertiti in my fourth grade history book, the most beautiful black woman I'd ever seen.

When I got to Nova Scotia, the first thing I did was to buy some old ewes to continue Kate's training. These were truly dog-broke and I was able to work with her very well all summer. She improved dramatically.

I didn't get out to the island until early August. The steers were doing a terrific job of opening it up. As usual, I caught some of my "New Yorkers" early. I was more successful that summer than I had been for years, catching twenty-two sheep. Nell was superb. She had matured to the point where I could trust her to use her own judgment.

Clayton Karkosh came over one day with Steve and

Margie Knight—the couple whom we had invited in for dinner when they were bicycling so many years ago. They brought their two children, Kyle and Emily, and we all went out to the island for a picnic. The day was perfect. We set off around the island, showing all its treasures to the children, and ate our picnic on the headland overlooking Blackbeard's Cove.

After lunch we set off again, to continue our journey. About halfway down the west side we noticed several local fishing boats steaming down the harbor towards Shelburne. I explained that there was a fishermen's blockade in Shelburne, which was a major port, to protest the foreign trawlers that were literally sucking up all the fish from local waters. Huge factory ships from Russia, Norway and Japan regularly dragged the fishbeds with enormous nets, catching all the fish, both immature and full-sized. They processed the fish right on the boats, throwing away fish that were too small—dead by that time. There were now several Russian trawlers trapped in Shelburne by the fishing boats.

The call had gone out to all fishermen in the surrounding towns to join the protest. We looked down at the rocks just below us and saw a man in his undershorts waving frantically to the fishing boats, who, in the unlikely event they had seen him, would have assumed he was cheering them on. There was another man with him, fully clad, who was lying down.

I called to him "What are you *doing?*"

He turned in great surprise to hear a voice calling from above. He explained that their boat had capsized and they had been in the water pushing it ashore for two hours. His friend had collapsed from the cold and they were desperately trying to attract the attention of the fishing boats to get rescued.

By a divine coincidence, Margie had visited Frenchy's in Yarmouth, a branch of the thrift shop chain, and had a whole bunch of sweat pants and shirts in her backpack. Clayton scrambled down the bank with the pack to help the men, while the rest of us continued on our way to get my boat. When we reached them, the man who had collapsed was warming up in Margie's clothes and feeling better. I looked at their boat. It was a silly little fiberglass thing, named by the manufacturer the *Andrea Dory*, of all things. They wanted to ride in their boat while we towed it behind the *Betsy* to Jordan Ferry. I told them nothing doing. Either they got inside my boat or they could stay on the island. They didn't have much sense.

In mid-August, I went up to Halifax and sheared a sheep on CBC-TV to promote the upcoming craft fair. I was acutely conscious of my shearing technique, not as far as the general public was concerned, but for my shearing friends who might be watching. Every time I made a second cut (where you cut the wool twice because you didn't get it close enough the first time) I could hear Martha Nettleton saying, "Oh-oh, second cuts, oh-oh, oh-oh."

I saw her the next day at a sheepdog trial in Pictou and she confirmed the exact scenario that I had imagined!

At that trial, Nell came in first place. The sheep were very challenging, not being noticeably dog-broke, and the area very small, a riding rink. Nell kept the sheep well under control, driving them through all the gates nicely and into the pen, whereas most of the competition sent the sheep flying over the fence, out of control, because they came on too fast and too close.

At Pictou, there was a tradition that the winner had to put on an exhibition run in the big arena in the evening. I put Nell through her paces while Bruce Blacklock, at the mike, explained what we were doing. I decided to try a "shed," which is a maneuver I had only just started to train her on, whereby the dog splits up the sheep into two groups and keeps them apart, driving one or two sheep away from the rest. It is no easy feat, as sheep, with their flocking instinct, do everything they can to reunite. After about four tries, she did it just fine. The crowd was pleased and I was, too, needless to say.

As an actress, I am constantly being asked to take risks while at the same time feeling the need to entertain. With those instincts in mind, I decided to show the audience the work of a "started" dog and brought Kate out into the arena. She was quite wonderful and drove the sheep here and there where I told her to. Then I decided to end the show. Kate had other ideas. She was having a glorious time and didn't want to stop. Luckily, I had left a thirty-foot lead on her and as I ran to catch up to her, I kept trying to step on the lead. She got away several times and the audience howled with laughter. I missed a few more times on purpose and finally stopped her.

The doors of the arena opened to reveal a livestock truck with its ramp at the ready. I called Nell over and she drove the sheep down the whole length of the arena, up the ramp and into the truck. Never mind that it was where the sheep wanted to go, the audience applauded wildly. I was so high on the experience that I got half way to Bill and Hilary Flower's place, where I was to spend the night, before exhaustion hit me.

Later on in the fall, Nell won first place in her class in a trial in Connecticut. It was a two-day trial and she earned more points than any other dog in her class for the two days. I was very proud of her.

Barney had died earlier in the summer, so I needed to buy a new ram for my New York flock and I wanted another Bluefaced Leicester. Dave Murphy, from whom I'd bought Barney, told me that he had sent six rams to Ontario a couple of years earlier to sell. Only two had sold and his friend

Gordon still had the other four. I got in touch with Gordon and arranged to buy one of them.

How to get it to New York? I called Sarah Nettleton, who was living in Ontario at the time and knew all sorts of sheep people. Some friends of hers who raised Merino sheep were planning to take some rams to Prince Edward Island. Perhaps they could pick up the BFL ram and we could arrange to meet in some convenient place during the summer? I called them and they were more than willing to do this favor for me.

We tentatively arranged to meet somewhere in New Brunswick or northern Nova Scotia later on, but their sale didn't work out and they never came east. Meanwhile, they had gone to see the rams in Ontario and were so appalled at their condition that they bought them all. Blessed people. The rams had spent the previous two years in a box stall, indoors, never going out to grass, never shorn during that period. Sarah came to shear them and said they were in ghastly shape. Poor things. The men set to work fattening them up. They planned to keep the three, but to take them down to friends in Maryland for the winter. We arranged to meet on a highway somewhere in Pennsylvania in October for me to pick up my ram. It was a godsend for me.

God, was he ugly! He had a long, giraffelike neck and huge bug-eyes way up near his ears. Nothing like Barney. I called him E.T. But his wool looked lovely, his back straight and strong and he seemed gentle. I wormed and vaccinated him and quarantined him for a while.

Finally, at the end of the month I put the ewes in with him. I had opened up the gate to the next field to give them more grazing. E.T. looked completely nonplussed. *Ewes! Help!*

He ran into the next field to join the donkeys. I had separated the ewes from their lambs and they yelled at each other all day across the driveway. A quiet day in the country.

Early next morning I called Betty to ask her to recommend a good sheep psychiatrist! After two years in a box stall with three rams, he must be totally blocked. She said to be patient, that it might take him a week to get in touch with his testosterone. I went outdoors to do chores and found he had bred Rosemary, my lovely colored yearling, and they were in love all day. Ugly or not, she loved him anyway.

Once over his initial shock, E. T. settled right down and bred all the ewes.

I also needed a new Scottish Blackface ram for Nova Scotia and had arranged to buy one from Bruce Blacklock. In December I made a quick trip to Nova Scotia to pick up the ram. A young British soldier was staying with Bruce, who suggested that Michael, the Brit, accompany me to the South Shore. My boat had long since been stored away for the winter and it was going to be a problem getting a fisherman to take me to the island, as lobster season was in full swing and all the boats were out all day until dark.

Luckily, one of the fishermen had a skiff boat, like mine, and finished his day early in the afternoon. He agreed to take me, the ram, whom I had named Michael by this time, and the human Michael out to Blue Island.

I was concerned about the ram, as he was very thin, and I wasn't sure he would survive the winter with so few reserves. Rams don't eat much when they are breeding, under the assumption that only one appetite at a time is to be paid attention to. When I complained to Bruce, the answer was "Well, he's been busy this fall." I thought he should have given him a bit of rest before I picked him up and said so.

The weather cooperated and we got Michael out with no difficulty. He looked a bit confused and didn't want to leave the landing area, but I figured his nose would lead him to the ewes before long. My lamb crop in the spring proved me right.

～ *Thirty* ～

Sometime during the winter, Betty suggested that I should think about taking the sheep off the island. I hotly remonstrated that I had caught more sheep the previous summer than I had done in many years.

"I know, Anne. But it would be awful if something happened to you and you weren't able to get out there any more."

I huffed and snorted and said I wasn't nearly ready to think of such a thing.

And I wasn't. It was hard work, but it had always been hard work. I was enjoying doing it and felt I was accomplishing something worth doing. Right from the start, I saw that my mission was to raise food in a hungry world on a farm where food hadn't been raised for fifty years. I have always felt that I was a steward as much as an owner, that I farmed on the island and on the shore with a respect for the integrity of the land. I felt pride in what I had learned and wasn't ready to quit. I dismissed Betty's suggestion out of hand.

In late January I went upstate to visit my best friend, Barbara Smith, who had just lost her husband. Bobbie lived on an old farm in a small village near the woods. There was plenty of snow, so I brought my cross-country skis. The dogs came too. They love to run alongside me when I ski cross country and got all excited one day when it was clear that I was going out and that they were coming too. But Nell seemed listless, even depressed, and I left her in Bobbie's care.

Over the few days of my visit, Nell seemed to sink lower. As soon as I got home, I called my vet and took her to him. He wanted to do some tests and told me to come back in the afternoon. When I went to pick her up, she couldn't walk and had to be carried to the truck. The vet told me he had called the Animal Medical Center in New York City, talked to one of the neurologists there and told me to take her in.

Early next morning, in the midst of a huge blizzard, I drove Nell into the city, putting her on a sheepskin on the front passenger seat. She was totally paralyzed and blind. During the trip I spoke to her every once in a while. She wiggled her ears, the only part of her body she could move. Even her tail was motionless.

Once at the hospital I went upstairs for help to get her admitted. An attendant brought a gurney for her and we went up in the elevator to the office, where I waited for Dr. Richard Joseph, the neurologist. After examining Nell, Dr. Joseph diagnosed her condition as granulomatous meningoencephalitis, or GME. The disease can be fatal within months and often renders a dog permanently blind. He was so sure of this that he wanted to start her treatment of heavy doses of cortisone before even getting the results of a CAT scan.

Dr. Joseph was a young doctor, very handsome and extremely serious. His concentration on the dog was fierce and I couldn't break through even with a limp joke about giving Nell a DOG rather than a CAT scan. He excused himself for a few moments, indicating that an attendant would come and get Nell shortly, but that he would return soon as well.

I was desperately worried for Nell but couldn't get the seriousness of the doctor from my mind. The attendant arrived and started to wheel Nell away. He was a plump, young man and from his face I could see immediately that he was retarded. I said to him, "Be careful, she's paralyzed and completely helpless."

The young attendant put his hand on my arm and said, "Don't worry, we take very good care of animals here." He was so sweet and so caring that after he left the room, I burst into tears. Ah, *now* I understood why Dr. Joseph was so serious: He had created a neutral, totally unemotional barrier between us that kept me from becoming emotional myself. He returned and told me he would call me later on in the day.

True to his word, he called and said he had heard a rumor from the ICU nurse that Nell had wagged her tail. I was thrilled and told him so. He said, "It's only a rumor. I didn't see it myself. Call me tomorrow."

When I called the next day, he said he had seen her wag her tail and that she had eaten from his hand.

The following day, he said I could come and get her. I was shocked. How could I care for her if she was paralyzed and blind? I went to the Animal Hospital, rode up to the waiting room and waited for a long time. I was listening for the wheels of the gurney that would tell me she was coming. I never heard the gurney. What I saw was a dog on a leash, staggering along the hallway. Nell. On her feet. I fell to my knees and hugged her. She was still on heavy doses of cortisone and Dr. Joseph gave me clear instructions. I would have to bring her back for a visit in a few weeks.

I got an attendant to bring a gurney, not wanting to risk the elevator and the long walk to the parking garage without one. Together we installed Nell in the front seat and I drove home. I carried her into the house and put her on the sheepskin for the night. She wet the pelt that night, but never did again.

Meanwhile the weather had warmed a bit, then sunk well

below freezing. My driveway was covered with smooth, thick ice all the way from the house to the barn and beyond.

I took Nell out in the morning with the other dogs. They were so glad to see her, they jumped on her and knocked her down. I realized I would have to walk her separately until she got stronger. She was too weak even to squat, so I had to prop her front legs on a snowdrift to enable her to pee. Penny was pregnant and I figured she wouldn't knock Nell down, so she came out with us.

I took Nell out every few hours for weeks. She was still blind, but remembered where the furniture was in the house and didn't bump into things very often. Gradually, she became stronger. Her walk was steady and she began to look more like herself.

One day, about a month after coming home from the hospital, I was standing behind the island in my kitchen and she was sitting in the dining room, facing me. She looked worried, the way dogs do sometimes. Without making a sound, forgetting for a moment that she was blind, I smiled broadly at her and cocked my head. Her face relaxed. Her face relaxed! She could *see*. I grabbed her and looked into her eyes, which I'd been doing regularly. Sure enough, at the edge of one eyeball, I could see some brown next to the opaque black that was her lens. I shone a light into the eye and the lens contracted a tiny bit. Light was getting in. I was ecstatic. About a month later, some brown was visible in the other eyeball. A wonderful way to mark her fifth birthday.

It took months for her eyesight to improve to where she could work well again. She has never regained her full powers of sight and has a hard time seeing black sheep in a dark barn or outdoors at dusk, but she works and she's all heart. Her back legs never regained their full strength, either, but she has compensated by strengthening her front legs. I'm convinced that Nell's will to survive was strengthened by the close presence of sheep that she could smell whenever she went outside. Working is her life. She'd rather work than eat or sleep. Passion is a powerful incentive.

Dr. Joseph was very pleased with her progress when I brought her to the hospital for her check-up. Her intake of cortisone was reduced little by little until her permanent present dose, which is five milligrams of Prednisone every other day. Prednisone is very hard on the stomach and the doctor told me that if I fed it to her with rice, the rice would go through her stomach quickly, pulling the medication with it as it went through. As a result, she has never had any stomach trouble from the pills. Dr. Joseph also explained that GME isn't always fatal. He pointed out that the cases causing death are in the textbooks, but those that survive are not.

In early March, Penny went into labor. Her first whelpings had been so easy, I wasn't worried at all, but I was there all day with her. After many hours passed, I became concerned and called the vet who told me to give her eight hours. It was already close to that, so shortly afterwards I took her in to his office. Her puppies were so big they couldn't get through the birth canal and she had to have a caesarian. Four puppies, three males and a female. The female was very weak and died within an hour of getting her home. But the males thrived. I took note not to use that stud again, as he was too big for Penny.

I had bred Nell to a dog whose work I admired just before she got sick. As the winter progressed, it looked very much as though she were pregnant. What to do? She was due to whelp in April. Giving birth at her stage of recovery would certainly set her back, but abortion for dogs is very risky, even for healthy ones. The vets were as uncertain as I was about the best course of action. Finally, I decided the risk of aborting was greater than the risk of birthing and did nothing.

I brought her into my bedroom the night she was due and she actually went into labor. Out came some black goo. Her puppies had mummified. It was sad, but clearly for the best. She was unaffected, so my choice had been the right one. Once she recovered, I had her spayed. Dr. Joseph felt that breeding her would "rock the boat."

With the warmer weather, I began working Nell gently on the sheep. She did well and I could see her getting stronger. But she was still too weak to do the island work. Tess was physically still strong enough, but she was so deaf that it would be impossible to keep her under control. Because she couldn't hear, she worked on her own and usually fouled things up. And Kate wasn't working out very well for me. She was so hyper that she got on my nerves and, as a result, we didn't have a good working relationship. Besides, she wasn't nearly ready to work on the island. I had her hips X-rayed when she reached two years of age, to ascertain whether she had hip dysplasia. X-raying for this has become routine in the Border Collie world and we urge people not to breed their dogs if they are dysplastic. She turned out to be very slightly so. I decided to offer her as a gift to Becky Peterson, who owned Kate's father, on the condition that she have her spayed. Becky agreed. In turn, she offered me a dog for the summer to use until Nell should be stronger. Gem was a lovely dog to look at, a bit shy, but a good worker.

⁓

We all made the trip up to Nova Scotia —four Scottish Blackface yearlings in the back of the truck plus one of Queen E's ram lambs, which I had sold and was delivering to a woman who had arranged to meet me at the ferry in Portland. The five dogs, all the luggage and I were in the front. I still had one of Penny's puppies left to sell. We arrived at the ferry in good time and the lamb buyer was there too. We transferred him to her truck with no problems. A woman came to watch and admired the puppy, whom I had called Badger.

After getting the tickets, walking the dogs, and getting my truck into the loading line, I found there was plenty of time left before the ferry was due to leave. I wandered up and down the lines of cars looking for the woman that had expressed an interest in the puppy. As I passed one car, the driver leaned out and exclaimed, "A Jack Russell! Where did you get him?"

I told him the puppy was from my breeding. He told me he had been looking for a Jack Russell for years and was very eager to buy one. At that time, the breed wasn't as popular as it is now, so puppies were harder to find. I put Badger in his arms and watched them fall in love with each other. Before agreeing to sell the puppy, I asked the couple a whole lot of questions to make sure they would provide a good home. They were on their honeymoon! They had left their dog behind in order to make the trip and were feeling very sad without him. From their answers I was satisfied that Badger would have a good home and agreed to sell him. They asked if they could pick him up on their way home from their honeymoon. Of course I said yes.

A couple of weeks later Doug and Heather Denton returned from their honeymoon to pick up Badger. I put him in Heather's arms, as Doug had disappeared around the house. I asked Heather where he was and she said he'd gone off to be privately sad about my having to part with the puppy. What a sweet man. I have corresponded with them ever since and have always been so happy that I found them for Badger.

The weather was ghastly all summer. We had thirty unbroken days of fog. I got out to the island once in July and once at the very end of August after nearly a month of fog. The rotten weather gave me time to do some necessary work on shore. The fences were in serious disrepair. I had bought a bag of fence insulators in New Zealand and most of them had broken over the winter. They were clearly not made for sub-freezing weather. Posts were loose, one of the corner posts out of the ground completely, having broken the wire in the process. Also, I wanted to work Gem on the sheep I had brought up from New York in order to get her used to me and to see for myself how she worked. We got along fine. She's a gentle dog and works quietly, so we got a lot of work done.

But out on the island it was a different story. There, tension prevailed! The sheep were wild and the dogs had to obey me instantly. I took both of them out and tried sending Gem out as the main dog. She was too slow, so I sent Nell out and she seemed to work well enough, but in moments of crisis, such as getting past the blind rock outcropping, I was very apt to yell. Poor Gem freaked out. I had never raised my voice when we were working on the mainland and she didn't want any part of it.

By early September, the weather had cleared and we were able to get out to the island regularly. I settled on a technique that worked very well. When we came upon sheep in the swamp, I positioned Nell at the back end to drive them. Then, with Gem on a leash, I took up the front end to keep the sheep from bolting past us. This meant that Nell didn't have to do the constant running back and forth, checking them, then running back to me to drive them, as we had done in years past.

We caught one nine-year old ewe that I had not seen

since 1986. She was born in '85, but I hadn't caught her as a lamb, so she had never gone to New York with me. She was wild and in super shape. It made me wonder why I worried so much about the sheep when some of them did so well without any help from me. But two others that I gathered gave me the answer. They both had serious parrot mouth from inbreeding, one with a full inch of overbite. They would satisfy my two mutton customers. I caught twenty-two sheep that summer in six gathers, which was as well as I had done the year before.

One of my great triumphs that summer was to catch my new ram, Michael, whom I had put out on the island the previous December. He was a recent descendent of a ram brought into Canada in the final importation of Scottish Blackface from the British Isles before the shutdown that was due to BSE, or mad cow disease. Having driven for forty-eight hours to pick him up in northern Nova Scotia at Bruce Blacklock's farm, spending forty-eight hours on my farm getting him out to the island, and then another forty-eight-hour drive back to New York, the prospect of losing him was depressing. On the first trip I took out to the island in July—no dog, no guests, just me with binoculars spying on the sheep—I came across a large bunch of sheep on a high point of land overlooking Blackbeard's Cove. There was a ram facing me, majestic with his huge horns. Was he my new ram? I couldn't see any ear tag. The ram turned around. Yes, it was Michael. How did I know? His tail was docked. Any ram I had left on the island would never have been caught before and therefore would have a long tail. I was relieved. New genes at last.

But I didn't pen Michael until my final gather of the year and it was a lucky fluke at that. Earlier in the month, I had failed to pen a group of wild sheep. There had been a ram lamb in the bunch and I was heartsick at leaving him on the island to compete with Michael. Now it was October and I had to get back to the States. I needed to take the yearlings that I'd brought back from New York in July out to the island, so I called a neighbor, Jamie Matthews, who worked for me occasionally, for help in loading them.

We went out to the island with Nell, much stronger now. I also had to remove my rolls of fencing and gather up my moveable posts, pull up the mooring and say goodbye to Blue Island until next year, always a sad moment. I had seen sheep in the swamp before going out, but by the time I got there they had left the swamp and had come around in full view of the boat landing. I left Jamie in the boat with the yearlings and went ashore with Nell. The sheep stayed there while I set up the fences, but scooted up the path by my cabin just before I was ready. Because they had hung around for so long, I assumed they were tame "New Yorkers" already caught earlier, but went looking for them all the same. They were nowhere to be seen. Despondent, I took one last peek into the swamp. Nearby were two sheep. I sent Nell out and who should it be but Michael and a huge ram lamb.

Gathering only two sheep is always a challenge because a sheep needs to have two companions to feel safe. Just as it takes "two to tango," so it takes "three to flock." These two were wired. I didn't dare check them too much because, if they had bolted past me in the wrong direction, we never could have stopped them again. Nell was absolutely brilliant, running and checking on her own. I was racing to keep up. They went into the pen and had the grace to wait in there until I had a chance to catch up and close the gate. I could satisfy another lamb customer and leave Michael as sole breeder.

Jamie and I unloaded the yearlings ashore, loaded the fencing and the ram lamb into the boat, let Michael go and went back home. For the rest of the day, I watched Michael and the yearlings through my binoculars, going from the swamp back to my cabin, up the hill to the orchard, down again, back to the swamp over and over. It was a great way to end the year.

But Nell's illness had taken its toll on us both. I was nearly sixty-seven, which might have had something to do with it too. I found myself looking out at the island, seeing sheep in the swamp, and thinking "Oh dear, there are some sheep. Do I have to go?" I didn't even notice that I was thinking this until the end of the summer when I finally listened to myself. I realized the work was no longer fun, that I was dreading it and that it was time to quit.

Betty's suggestion rang true. All of a sudden, all the reasons I had given for keeping going no longer applied. At my age, I simply didn't want to race along the rocky shore after sheep anymore. Although I would continue with the sheep on my New York farm, I decided to sell the Nova Scotia flock. The relief I felt after making the decision told me it was the right one to make.

~ Thirty-One ~

Three weeks before she was due to lamb, Rosemary, one of my beautiful young colored Border Leicesters in New York, developed a serious vaginal prolapse. I had never dealt with this before and didn't realize that what I was doing to correct it wasn't enough. By the time I did realize it, it was too late. I took her to the vet, who performed a cesarian section on her, hoping to save the lambs. One was born dead; the other, a black ewe lamb, had a heartbeat, but they couldn't get her to breathe and she died, too. Rosemary had to be put down.

It would have cost $120 for the vets to get someone to dispose of her dead body, so I took it home. I sheared her exquisite, silver fleece on the tailgate of my truck. Although I don't recommend it, I must say it is a lot easier to shear a dead sheep than a live one. Sadly, I took her body down to my dairy farm neighbors who regularly burn large bonfires and have been very generous about burning any sheep of mine that have died.

Years ago, when I was living in Paris with my former husband and my then young sons, I bought a gorgeous crocheted coat, made by Dior's knitter in her spare time. It was silver gray, mostly wool with a bit of mohair mixed in. It was a simple design with raglan sleeves and a voluptuous knitted collar that folded over itself. It was luxurious and soft and I loved it. It had been my favorite coat for over thirty years, but it was looking threadbare and rather shabby by now. I decided to spin Rosemary's silver-gray fleece, with some mohair mixed in, and to use the resulting yarn to copy the coat. It seemed a fitting use for her lovely fleece.

Because of Queen E.'s tendency to roll over during lambing, I decided to put her in the barn when she was due and to sleep there myself in my shepherd's room. It was well that I did. I awoke at 5:30 AM to the sounds of a screeching little lamb. I rushed into the main part of the barn to find Queen E. on her back again and a little lamb next to her. I got her into a pen where she wouldn't have room to roll over and she produced two more lambs one after the other. They were all females and I have kept them all. They have turned into beautiful, productive sheep, two of them white like their father, one colored like her mother. Fleeces from the colored one have won blue ribbons at the Maryland Sheep and Wool Festival more than once.

This year, I got to Nova Scotia in plenty of time for Penny to give birth to her puppies—five of them this time. No cesarian and no whelping in the truck either!

⌒

I had put out the word during the course of the winter of 1995, informally among friends, that my island sheep would be for sale the following summer. One of the people I called was Sarah Nettleton in Guelph, Ontario. Sometime during the winter I heard from two farmers whose sheep she had shorn. Both wanted to buy my flock. Since I was sure that one, if not both, would drop out before the summer, I told them both they could buy them all. In addition, a local Nova Scotian also called me, thinking he could get a small business grant from the government to buy the sheep as a start-up business proposition. I strongly doubted he could, especially since he had absolutely no experience with sheep, but I went ahead and told him he could buy them too. It was so uncharacteristic of me not to explain that there was another interested party that I still wonder how I could have failed to do it.

I was right about the local man. By summer he had disappeared. But the two Ontario men were both still interested. I had to tell one of the men he couldn't buy my flock and I called John Crawford, the last one to get in touch with me, to give him the bad news. He still wanted a ram, however, and I was sure that I would be able to supply him with one. To make it worth Dirk Randeraad's while to come all the way to Nova Scotia to pick up sheep, my summer's task was to gather as many of the sheep as I possibly could.

In my first walk around the island, I came across Michael, lying down. At my approach he got to his feet, but he was so lame, he could only walk a few steps before lying down again.

He was on a bluff overlooking Blackbeard's Cove, a hard place to bring a boat into, and for a week I tried in vain to recruit a crew of men to come out to the island to help me get him off. Either the winds were too fierce or, when they weren't, everyone was busy.

After a week, I went out alone with Nell to investigate. We walked to Blackbeard's, but no Michael was to be seen. I looked in the woods behind the bluff and under all the bushes, but he was gone. I took that as a good sign. As Nell and I progressed around the island, we came across Michael under a tree. Leaving Nell out of sight, I approached him. He looked all right, but I couldn't tell much without palpating him. I called Nell, whereupon Michael got to his feet and ran off, limping to be sure, but running. He looked to be very thin. Rams don't eat much while they are breeding. Then, when breeding is over, the grass is all gone because it is late fall, so, on an island, they have a hard time regaining their weight until summer, when the lush grass is available. Being lame, he probably wasn't eating as much as he would have otherwise.

Late in September I caught a bunch of wild sheep. When I returned to the island with help to get them off, who should be hanging about behind the pen but Michael. By crowding the sheep in a corner with a gate, I lured him into the pen. It was a fitting way to end my career on the island. Michael looked to be in better condition and was only favoring his ailing leg slightly.

I called Dirk in Ontario and told him the good news. I also called John Crawford to tell him I had a nice two-year old ram for him, which was what he wanted. Dirk drove down with a good-sized trailer and took sixteen sheep away plus the ram for John. I took the rest to the butcher.

∽ *Thirty-Two* ∽

In October, Nell took first place in her class in a sheepdog trial in New Hampshire. The competition was stiff and she had done a super job. Not bad for a dog who my local vet, eighteen months before, had predicted wouldn't live more than six weeks. To say I was thrilled is a vast understatement. I took a photograph of her with her blue ribbon and sent it to Dr. Joseph, the neurologist at the Animal Medical Center in New York, who was delighted.

The winter was wet and dreary. The ground was frozen, but it rained a lot. As a result there was a layer about four inches deep of a mixture of manure and mud that I will call slurry, to be delicate about it, on top of the frozen ground. One morning I awoke to the sounds of intermittent moaning. I looked out the window and saw that one of my ram lambs had become inextricably entangled in the electric netting which I use as fencing to separate the rams from the ewes. Apparently he had caught the irresistible fragrance of a ewe in heat and had tried to get through the fence to her.

I threw on my clothes as fast as possible. This was an emergency. While the shock from the fence won't kill an animal directly, the prolonged exposure to it can give them heart failure and he was completely wrapped up in the stuff.

I unplugged the fence and went through the little gate to the pasture, running as fast as I could to get to him. I went down so fast, flat on my face in the . . . um . . . slurry, I didn't even have time to put out my hands to stop myself. I had had time to turn my face, so only one side was covered. I struggled to my feet and kept on going, my immediate goal being paramount at that moment. Still, if anyone had been there they couldn't have helped but explode with laughter and it crossed my mind that it was lucky no one was. It's amazing how one's sense of humor can leave one at a moment like this.

I disentangled the lamb and got him back where he belonged, fixed the fence and plugged it in. I took a look at myself, covered from the top of my head to my boots with a thick layer of slurry. I considered going indoors and changing all my clothes, bathing and starting all over again, clean, to do the chores, but decided to get chores over with and then go in. Feeding the sheep and donkeys takes about an hour, so by the time I got indoors, the slurry on my face was caked hard and dry. The right side of my face, under the cake, had pulled the left side way over. It looked as though I'd had a stroke, but after it was all washed off that side of my face looked as smooth as a baby's.

My friends noticed this and said I should go out and fall on the other side of my face. I won't say here what I suggested they do. Phyllis Stevens even wrote a little poem:

> If you want a younger-looking face, then hurry—
> Go out and buy some of Anne Priest's slurry!

I went up to Nova Scotia in late June, determined to get the rest of the sheep off the island. My family made a surprise visit in July, which was heaven. Jonathan and Marnie had two sons by then, Stuart, aged four and Matthew, eleven months. The two older children, Clay and Liz, both teenagers, loved the place. I had enough notice from Jonathan and his family to alert Nat, who was able to get away from his business in New York. They all came during the one week of pretty good weather in the whole summer. We went out to the island for a picnic and I said to Jonathan, "I want my grandchildren to fall in love with Blue Island."

"I already have," asserted Liz. My plot was working.

Dirk Randeraad was still interested in buying the rest of my flock. I called him to find out what the minimum number would be to make it worth his while to come such a distance. He said fifteen ewes, but I couldn't promise that I would catch that many. Also, both Nell and I seemed to have less stamina than the summer before, so I decided to sell them to Leroy d'Entremont, who runs sheep on several islands and had already expressed an interest in buying my sheep. I called him and he agreed to the purchase.

Since Leroy would do all the gathering, I knocked about one-third off the price. It was worth it to me to get it done. It was a painful decision, though. I had been doing this work, virtually alone, for twenty-one years. Also, although I'm fond of Leroy—and have grown much more fond of him in recent years now that I know him better—it was galling to have to ask him to do the work, since he was very boastful and told everybody how good he was and how superior his dogs were. To his credit, though, he's very good-natured about the ribbing his friends give him about his boasting. In addition, since he married his wife, Mary, he has dropped most of his boastfulness. It's the best example I've ever known of what a loving relationship can do for a person.

Coincidentally, two new Scotch Highland cattle had arrived from Cape Breton a few days before Leroy came to gather the sheep. I had bought them because for years I had worried about what would happen if Gus or Charlie should die. Those two were so bonded to each other that I was sure the surviving steer would die of a broken heart. But with four cattle out there, I felt they would be safe. With the sheep gone, there would be plenty of food for all of them. Both of the new cattle were black (Gus and Charlie are reddish brown). One was a cow, the other a steer. They were adorable and seemed so small. It was hard to believe that Gus and Charlie, so huge by now, had ever been that small.

Leroy had brought a friend to help him load the sheep onto my barge once he had them gathered. I took advantage of their presence and asked them to load my new young cattle onto the *Baa-rge* so we could take them out to Blue Island. The *Baa-rge* was on my trailer already and I backed it up to the barn and lowered the transom (stern), which formed a ramp for the cattle. Leroy and his helper led them up the ramp and off we went to the Government Wharf.

The tide was high enough to launch the *Baa-rge* and we hauled it out to the island behind my boat. After being unloaded onto the island, the cattle disappeared into the interior. Later, Leroy told me that he had been present at Blackbeard's Cove when the new cattle sauntered out of the woods and came upon Gus and Charlie. All four cattle did a real doubletake when they saw each other, which Leroy found very amusing. Gus and Charlie had lived on the island for five years without seeing other cattle and were understandably surprised. They all got along well right from the start.

I left the *Baa-rge* anchored offshore and went ashore with Leroy to show him the gathering pen, the cabin where he and his friend would spend the night and to explain the layout of the island. Then he took off with his three dogs. He works one dog in English, one dog in Acadian French and the third dog in—? Who knows? There were several tasks I wanted to do on the island, such as weeding the drinking pond and cleaning out my cabin and I spent a couple of hours doing them. When I was ready to leave, I rowed out to the *Betsy* and was about to start the outboard when I heard a shout from the shore. Leroy's friend was pointing in the direction of the swamp, where Leroy was emerging with twenty-two sheep. Twenty-two sheep in less than three hours. How cheeky! When it took me a whole month, or more, to do as well!

I tied the *Baa-rge* up to the *Betsy* and brought her ashore. Leroy loaded fifteen of the sheep onto the *Baa-rge*, and I hauled them home, got some help floating the barge onto my trailer at the harbor and took them all to my farm to graze in my field.

Next morning, I went out to the island with the *Baa-rge* again. By this time Leroy had caught five more sheep. They were so far away from the front of the island that he had gotten his dogs to knock them down. He tied their feet to hold them while he led each one in separately, bringing them halfway around the island on the path, holding onto their horns. There was no way I could ever have done that, even at his age. I don't know many people, male or female, strong enough.

Of the twenty-seven sheep that he brought in, only sixteen were female. The chances of my having caught all those females for Dirk was highly unlikely, so I was glad I had made the decision to let Leroy buy them. Of the eleven males, seven were adults. I had one buyer for a breeding ram and I took the rest of the males to the butcher for my meat customers. Mrs. Mackay, one of my mutton customers, for whom I had one of the two-year old rams butchered, told me it was the best mutton she'd ever had.

One of the ewes was seven years old and I didn't feel right about charging Leroy the full price for her, so I gave her to him as a gift. She had a red ear tag, Number 67.

In the following few days I took friends out to the island for picnics. We saw . . . sheep! Only a few, but it enabled me to call Leroy and tease him about it. He laughed good-naturedly and said he would get them the following summer, which he did.

Also, the following summer, he asked if he might bring some sheep back to Blue Island to live. "Why not?" I thought. I missed seeing them and it would be good to have them to supplement the cattle in the ongoing clearing process, especially since I didn't have to catch them. Several of them had been born on the island, so they were coming home. One of these was red ear tag Number 67.

(In the spring of 2001, Leroy and I spoke on the phone. He told me that red ear tag Number 67, now twelve years old, had had twins that spring, as usual, and was doing fine. He had brought her off the island to live out her old age on the mainland. Now there's a gift that keeps on giving.)

Just as the sheep, born on Blue Island, were going back home, making a circle, so my shepherding life had been a series of circles. It had started on Blue Island with the Scottish Blackface sheep in 1975. Then I added the New York farm in 1985, where I brought my Scottish Blackface ewe lambs from the island, forming a circle. For the nine years that I trafficked in sheep between Nova Scotia and New York and back again, other concentric circles were added. Finally, when I concentrated on Leicester sheep in New York and stopped bringing sheep off Blue Island, the concentric circles were broken and a new pattern was begun. My life is full of theater, sheep, wool, spinning, weaving and new friends; a different life, but a good one.

⟡ *Epilogue* ⟡

In the summer of 2000, I wanted to start training Pie, my new Border Collie, and, not owning sheep in Nova Scotia anymore, I had to borrow some. I called Leroy from New York and asked him if he would put some sheep in my mainland pasture for the summer. He said that he would, that he had some good dog-broke sheep that would be fine to start Pie on.

By the time I got to Nova Scotia, the grass was so high that I couldn't see the sheep anywhere. There were only four of them and they had made no impact whatever on the eight acres of grass. If I couldn't see them, neither could Pie, which would make training her difficult, to say the least. I haven't been able to get anyone to hay the field for years now, so I had to hire a young man to mow a large square space to train her in. He also mowed the paddock behind the barn so I could start the process in a controlled area.

While I was waiting for the young mower to be free to come around, I got a call.

"Do you have sheep?" the woman asked. I wondered why she wanted to know. Did she want to buy some, or what?

"Who is this?"

She muttered a name that I couldn't understand. My ear hadn't gotten used to the strong local accent yet—it takes a while every year. I asked again. She repeated it. I still didn't understand, but I thought she said Cora Williams. She went on to say that there were four sheep in her yard and were they mine?

I looked out into the field and couldn't see any sheep, but then I couldn't anyway because of the grass. No one else in West Green Harbour has sheep, so they had to be mine. I told her I'd be right up to get them.

Since the woman's name was unfamiliar, I had to guess where to look. I wrongly assumed the sheep had gone westward and were somewhere on the Jordan Bay side of the point, where there are a good many houses. I drove around. It's about half a mile through the swamp, but a good three miles by road. I got to the other shore and started looking up and down the coast for the sheep. I asked several people if they had seen sheep. No one had. I went to see Mrs. Hallett.

"Do you know a Cora Williams, Mrs. Hallett?"

"No, dear, there's no one by that name around here. There's only Clare and Elaine Williams and Stan."

"Well, it was a woman. Maybe she mentioned Clare and I thought she said Cora." I was beginning to feel stupider by the minute.

"Yes, dear, it must have been Elaine. I know Clare has been swordfishing and I don't know if he's home yet, so Elaine must be alone."

I left and drove back around to Clare and Elaine's house on the Green Harbour shore where they were waiting for me. Clare was indeed back from swordfishing.

"Where are the sheep?"

"Well, they're down by the shore," he said. "I'll take you down."

I followed Clare down the path and there they were. "I think it would be best if you took them down the main road back to your place. You can't follow the shore from here and the old road that used to go down to it is so overgrown I don't think you could find it."

I agreed that the main road was the best course and sent Nell quietly around the sheep. The sheep weren't as dog-broke as Leroy had said. In fact, they were wild. They went up to Clare's house and, like it or not, they bolted down the old road. We had no choice but to follow them.

The old road, which started out open and clear, became totally overgrown after a while, as Clare had predicted. After tracking sheep on Blue Island for over twenty years, I've gotten pretty good at discerning bent grasses to see where they might have gone, and I followed the bent grasses for a long, long way before finding the sheep in a field in the middle of nowhere. They bolted again and took off down another path. We were getting closer and closer to the shore. This was clearly the way they had come. Nell and I came out onto the rocky beach where we could see the sheep far away. We stumbled along the loose, round rocks. We had come about half the distance through the woods, but there was still a good half mile of shoreline before we would get back to my place. The sheep stopped occasionally to watch us and then turned and ran on when we got too near.

"Boy," I thought, as the rocks rolled under my feet, "I'm glad I'm not doing this on Blue Island any more."

At last we got to where we could see my farm. I watched the sheep climb the bank on their way to the electric fence and assumed they would pop back into the field. Then I came to a curve in the shore and couldn't see them any more. I kept on going.

I had noticed several days earlier that the top wire on the fence was broken and kept putting off fixing it. Now would be a good time to do it. What's that cliché about closing the barn door after the horses have run away? I went into my boathouse and got a length of wire and pliers, unplugged the electric fence in the barn and walked out to fix the fence. I didn't want to spook the sheep again, so I left Nell in the house. I walked all the way down to the end of the field. No sheep. I looked down the shore to the west. No sheep. I looked back the way we had come. No sheep. Thinking maybe they were in the tall grass somewhere, I repaired the fence and walked back a different way, standing on some rocks along the way to see if I could see them. Still no sheep. I was so tired I decided to let them sleep wherever the hell they were and I'd look for them in the morning. Besides, I had to walk a mile back to Clare and Elaine's to pick up my truck!

Next morning, I went down to the end of the pasture with Nell. I had loosened the fence to give them a way to get over it and pushed it down into the grass as far as it would go. I still couldn't see them anywhere, but there was a boat just off the point with a man gathering Irish moss.

"Have you seen my sheep?" I shouted.

"Well, there are four white sheep right down there under the bank where you're standing."

I peeked over the bank and there they were, huddled in the shade. I was hoping to be able to send Nell around them and force them up the bank and back into the field. They had other ideas. They got up and started pelting down the shore towards Jordan Bay to the west. It took Nell and me several minutes to work our way through the wild roses on the bank before we could reach the rocks and I sent Nell out to fetch them. Nearly blind by now, she couldn't see them. She looked back at me. I sent her on with a "get back, Nell." Gallantly, she went on down the beach, stumbling over the round rocks until I noticed that she lifted her head as she saw them. They were a good hundred feet in front of her.

That beach, like so many in the area, is made up of round rocks that the ocean piles in during the winter storms, forming a crescent ridge about 20 feet high and about 250 yards long. With each pulling back and breaking of the waves, the rocks roll and roll some more, making them round and smooth. I watched the sheep disappear over the end of the ridge and later Nell disappeared after them. I waited and waited, knowing that I would either see Nell come back, alone, her tongue hanging out, or the sheep.

The sheep came first. Nell had managed to get around them to drive them back to me. My plan was to control them when they got to me by banging my crook on the rocks and extending it to the left as far as I could reach in the hopes that they would go up the bank. Then I would bring Nell around and she would get them to pop back into the field.

Again, the sheep had other plans. They went right past me without so much as a tiny pause and raced around the point back in the direction of yesterday's escapade up the Green Harbour shore.

I let Nell go into the ocean to cool off and we went back through the field. I didn't want to speed them up by going after them on the shore. Besides, we could make better time going through the field. We walked the length of the field and I gave Nell some water to drink. And then I started down the driveway on foot. Nell looked aghast.

"C'mon, love, we're not through yet."

Nell walked from cool shady spot to cool shady spot until we got to Rodney and Phemie's old house, where I knew there was a path through the woods to the shore. It felt good to be in the woods. We got out to the water and looked both ways. No sheep were in sight, but soon they appeared to our right. We had gotten there in time to cut them off. They seemed surprised to see us and turned around and slowly went down the shore. At long last, they were tired. We followed, slowly, and saw them go up the bank towards the fence again. Again, I didn't pursue them, not wanting to spook them, but went into the house and up the stairs. This is what I saw through the binoculars: The lead sheep went up to the electric fence and looked at it. I'm quite sure I read her lips as she said "Oh, the hell with this" and jumped over the loosened fence into the field, followed by the others. Heartily agreeing with her, I rushed to tighten the electric fence and plugged it in.

❧

I have often wondered what my life would have been like if I had never left Lincoln, Massachusetts. Would I have been able to continue my acting career when, a few years after I moved to New York City, two professional theaters opened up in

Cambridge and Boston? Similarly, I have asked myself questions about my life in Nova Scotia. What if I had purchased a piece of land in another part of the province? I never would have bought the island, never bought sheep, never heard of Brian Nettleton. It was an immense crossroads, one that never in my wildest dreams I could have foreseen. I don't regret one bit choosing the road I did. It has brought a richness and beauty to my life that I love and embrace, as well as many friends. And so what if the people in Greenville as well as West Green Harbour think I'm off my rocker?

They could think worse. And probably have.